Stories We Don't Tell

Copyright © 2019 by Stories We Don't Tell

All rights reserved. No part of this publication may be reproduced, distributed, or transmitted in any form or by any means, including photocopying, recording, or other electronic or mechanical methods, without the prior written permission of the authors, except in the case of brief quotations embodied in critical reviews and certain other noncommercial uses permitted by copyright law.

This book is a work of nonfiction. Certain names, situations, and identifying characteristics have been changed to protect the privacy of individuals and maintain anonymity in some instances. Events, locales and conversations are from the memories of the authors.

Published by Paul Dore Creative Services. 1 Shaw Street, Suite 316, Toronto, Ontario, Canada, M6K 0A1, storieswedonttell.org.
Cover Design: Tyler Blacquiere.
Book Layout: Paul Dore.
Editor: Steve Hostetter.

Library and Archives Canada Cataloguing in Publication

Benness, Brianne (1986-), Dore, Paul (1978-), Hostetter, Stefan (1989-).
Stories We Don't Tell

ISBN 978-1-9994067-8-3 (epub)
ISBN 978-1-9994067-6-9 (kindle)
ISBN 978-1-9994067-7-6 (pdf)
ISBN 978-1-9994067-5-2 (paperback)

Dedicated to the storytellers, hosts, and audiences.

CONTENTS

Welcome	1
Chapter 1: Brianne Benness	5
Chapter 2: Tyler Blacquiere	11
Chapter 3: Wafa Ktaech	17
Chapter 4: Jeanette Stock	21
Chapter 5: Sarah Flanagan	25
Chapter 6: Alena Cawthorne	31
Chapter 7: Sima Sahar Zerehi	37
Chapter 8: Erin Kang	43
Chapter 9: Tara Marina Pearson	47
Chapter 10: Jake Cohen	51
Chapter 11: Maya Fromstein	59
Chapter 12: Stefan Hostetter	65
Chapter 13: Rob Shirkey	71
Chapter 14: Marcus Hinds	77
Chapter 15: Tyler Blacquiere	83
Chapter 16: Dave Keystone	93
Chapter 17: Wafa Ktaech	97
Chapter 18: Shona Fulcher	101
Chapter 19: Paul Dore	107
Chapter 20: Tanya M. Cothran	111
Chapter 21: Barbora Grochalova	117
Chapter 22: Stefan Hostetter	123
Chapter 23: Monica Hamburg	127
Chapter 24: Maya Fromstein	133
Chapter 25: Michelle German	139
Chapter 26: L.K. Brighton	145
Chapter 27: Brianne Benness	151
Chapter 28: Maximilian Suillerot	157
Chapter 29: Jonathan Finn	163

Chapter 30: Luke Anderson	169
Chapter 31: David Hostetter	175
Chapter 32: Nicholas Dawkins	181
Chapter 33: Rhys Morgan	187
Chapter 34: Vivek Jain	195
Chapter 35: Elisa D'Arcangelo	201
Chapter 36: Paul Dore	207
Chapter 37: Monica Hamburg	213
Chapter 38: Elisa Watson-Smith	219
Chapter 39: Pepper Strauss Dorper	225
Chapter 40: Jennifer McKinley	231
Chapter 41: Erin Kang	235
Chapter 42: Andrew Cheung	239
Chapter 43: Joey Brooke Jakob	245
Chapter 44: Jesse David	253
Chapter 45: Mello Ayo	257
Chapter 46: Stefan Hostetter	265
Chapter 47: Alice Walker	271
Chapter 48: Joshua Stribbell	275
Chapter 49: Adrianna Prosser	281
Chapter 50: Adam Zawalich	285
Chapter 51: Nicole Borthwick	289
Chapter 52: Jessica Singh	295
Chapter 53: Brianne Benness	299
Chapter 54: Jon Aaron Sandler	303
Chapter 55: Mathura Mahendren	311
Chapter 56: Kale Ridsdale	317
Chapter 57: Rob Shirkey	323
Chapter 58: Jette Stubbs	331
Chapter 59: Veronica Antipolo	339
Chapter 60: Paul Dore	343
Chapter 61: Katarite san	347
Acknowledgements	353

Welcome

206 ... 208 ... 210.

You double-check your phone to ensure you have the address right before continuing up the stairs. The steps groan as you climb onto the porch. On the mailbox is a hand-written sign that reads: *Stories We Don't Tell, Bikes around back.*

The door opens three-quarters of the way into the entrance. Shoes, first well ordered then flowing into the hall, lead to the open doorway and you turn into the living room. You lean against the oak door frame, fifty or so folks sit on the floor facing the front of the house. The show's already begun, the host stands framed by windows and basking in a warm red light.

"... and on that note, we pivot to tonight's show, the Stories We Don't Tell: Book It."

"There are some stories that we get good at telling. We tell them to our friends, our coworkers, and even strangers at parties. We tell them because they are a part of us, and in doing so, they build up our sense of self. But there are also stories we don't tell, maybe because they're sad, or weird, or just a little too intimate. These truths are as much a part of who we are, despite being erased from our day-to-day conversation.

"For the past five years, we've been a monthly live event, held in living rooms across Toronto, that gives you a window into experiences that are so often left unseen. What we have for you tonight, however, is even more special.

"A retrospective. Sixty-one stories, all told to rooms just like this one. The tellers, all people like you, who came to an event and found themselves inspired to share a part of their

Stories We Don't Tell

life. It's been a unique pleasure, and a true blessing, for us to share in these stories and so it's an honour to present them to you here."

You see an opportunity in the break of speech to carefully make your way through the seated crowd. Finding yourself a spot on a large circular pillow that sits in the middle of the space, you relax into the cushion.

"Before we begin, we do have two and a half rules. The first is no talking. As you can tell, we're in a small space, and so during the stories everyone will be able to hear you, so please avoid that as much as possible. The second is that at the end of some of these stories you may not know what to do. Many cover tough topics, but I'm telling you right now that the right answer is clap. Even if it feels like you're cheering on something terrible that happened to them, we're all agreeing now that clapping is okay and encouraged.

"Finally, because these stories cover tough topics, we want to ensure that you take care of yourselves. If a story is triggering, please feel empowered to protect yourself by popping out of the room or skipping a few pages to the next story."

Another late-comer sneaks into the room.

"It is our tradition to introduce each storyteller with their answer to an absurd question. Do you prefer April or May? Do you believe in ghosts? On a scale of zero to three, zero being 'not in the game' and three being 'exceeds expectations' please rate your last date on its cheesiness. Etc. Tonight, however, we'll introduce them all at once and let them take it away."

You shift in your seat finding the most comfortable position. Your seat neighbour offers you some popcorn, you take a handful and pass it along.

"The storytellers you will hear tonight have little in

Stories We Don't Tell

common beyond the courage to stand up before you to speak their truth. They are your friends and colleagues, they are that person who caught your eye in the passing streetcar, they are the person with whom you Bunzed a house plant last week. These stories are all around us. They are carried deep in our hearts and loosely on our sleeves. Five years, over a hundred storytellers, and nearly three hundred stories have left us breathless. Breathless because of all that these storytellers hold. Breathless because of their ability to bring us into their lives. Breathless as we see ourselves reflected in their words as if they'd borrowed our voice.

For five years, we've been building a community in living rooms, asking anyone and everyone to join us, and these tellers have breathed life - their lives - into the space.

Tonight they're back.

So sit back, take a deep breath, and enjoy."

Chapter 1: Brianne Benness

"It would be easier," my sister hesitates, "if she just didn't exist." Although I know that this is where she was heading — it had to be — I'm still glad that she's the one who said it. It just sounds so flippant, so convenient. As if we are two petulant children wishing away our mother, instead of what we really are: a married 39-year-old woman with two children and a newly single 26-year-old girl, half-sisters who have both lost our fathers, who do not take the loss or dissolution of a parent lightly. My sister's father died on my 21st birthday. She found out an hour before we were supposed to leave her home for a day of wine tasting in the Sonoma Valley. My father died a week after her first child was born. I didn't meet my nephew until he was 10 months old because our accumulating grief prevented my sister and me from seeing what we might be for one another.

We are trying to decide how to talk to, live with, move past our mother. Neither of us has spoken to her in a year, but we still occasionally communicate with her by email. Communicate is an inaccurate term, really, since what happens is that we are lambasted, accused, excoriated. We are thrown off balance for days. This woman whom we are supposed to love — who is supposed to love us — is sad and lonely and raging and we have run out of salve.

It starts small. I don't send her the money for my car insurance on time, and she gets frustrated, angry. She feels unloved. She tells my sister how irresponsible and thoughtless I am. She tells me how snobby and irreverent my sister has become. I slowly lose track of my transgressions, but the conclusion still seems inevitable: I am mean, I am manipulative, I am selfish. I am inadequate; incapable of generating the love and caring that my mother needs from me.

***

    I am eight years old, sitting on a bench with a friend at recess. My mother has just realized that she was sexually abused by my grandfather. I have some sense that she confronted him, that this is why we won't be seeing her family for a while. I know better than to say this out loud, but it begins to punctuate my conversations. At eight, I don't understand what sexual abuse might mean, but I carry a blurry vision of shame and hurt. My friend asks me a question, and I answer without consideration, because I know that if I let my thoughts bleed into my speech then the secret and the shame and the hurt are going to come out. But it isn't my secret or my shame or my hurt, so I charge part of myself with guarding them and part of myself with making sure that nobody knows what I am guarding.

    I am 11 years old, trying to climb in through a ground-floor window of our old Victorian house. My mother and I have locked ourselves out somehow, and my stepdad is not around to let us in. He left earlier when my mother accused him of having an affair with one of her best friends, although she assures me that he'll be back. My mother's healing journey has brought her to a form of spirituality that I can only describe as new age. Her pendulum is her constant companion, a tool guided by spirits to answer any yes or no questions that she may pose. The pendulum has confirmed my stepdad's affair as well as her darkest repressed memories of growing up in a cult. In some people, she sees her secrets and shame and hurt reflected back, so she knows that they must have been abused too. She tells me who among my friends have been abused, whose parents are in cults. I try to be as understanding as possible about the shame and hurt that my friends must be experiencing. I know not to mention it to them directly, but I charge part of myself with guarding their secrets and their shame and their hurt and part of myself with making sure that they don't know that I am sharing their burden.

She becomes obsessed with exorcising our home, our lives. Once when we move, she throws out many of my stepdad's clothes because of their malevolent energy. The by-the-minute psychic that she calls when nobody is home tells her that she is going to win the lottery, so she takes the opportunity to replace the evil furniture in my bedroom and her office and the living room on credit. I have this sense that she is spoiling me with money that she doesn't have yet, but am not sure how to ask if it's ok. She tells me that we deserve nice things.

We start to see her family again. We form tentative relationships when my grandmother and then my uncle dies. I'm not sure which part of myself to give to these people. My mother and my sister are able to draw on their established relationships to feign some kind of normalcy, but at 11 and then 13 and then 16, I can barely feign normalcy to begin with. This family knows about the secrets and the hurt and the shame, but I'm still pretty sure that I shouldn't talk about it, so I just don't talk about anything at all. My mother accuses me of not loving her family as much as I love my father's family, of not trying hard enough. She is hurt and then angry when I say that I barely know them, that they don't feel like family to me at all.

When she drives me to college my sophomore year, we don't make it out of our own town before I call my stepdad because she and I are fighting so much that she almost hit me with her open palm and then almost hit a pedestrian with the van. He talks me down, and somehow she and I make the two-day trip to school. A month later she calls to tell me that her biopsy results have come back and she has cancer. Soon she begins chemo and radiation, and it is as horrible as the movies have led me to believe. I drink away most of the semester, and more secrets start to punctuate my conversations. When I walk past anyone on campus I want to stop them, ask them how their lives are proceeding so normally, yell at them that my mother was abused and her parents were in a cult and my stepdad had an affair and her brother died from cancer and now she has cancer.

Shortly after she goes into remission, my father is diagnosed with Alzheimer's disease. It feels to me like there are only so many memories and so many stories that we all must share. I'm not sure that I will ever get to know my mother because she changes with each memory that she uncovers. Her reality and her history have been evolving since I was eight years old, maybe longer. I'm not sure that I will ever get to know my father either, because he was already losing his memories years before I understood how precious they were.

When he dies, I can no longer contain my grief. I don't have any more parts of myself to charge with this pain. I forget how to interact with my peers. I'm not sure how to have a real conversation, because I don't have the means to cull the secrets and the shame and the hurt from the thoughts, feelings and ideas that I'm allowed to share. When I tell my mother that I can't spend Christmas with her because I can barely get out of bed, she tells me that I am manipulative, that I am lying, that I am using this loss to my advantage. She tells my sister that I am possessed.

Stories We Don't Tell

***

My sister and I have begun to catalogue our scars. For the first time, we are able to talk openly about the secrets and the shame and the hurt that we've been harbouring for our mother. About the anxiety we feel about inadequately maintaining relationships. About how just seeing her number on call display can leave us reeling for days. Does everybody feel like this? There are days when I am sure that nobody calls their mother as often as she would like, that we are mining our childhoods for Freudian trauma to justify our callous behaviour. But there are also days when I'm sure that I have never been possessed, that my friends did not grow up in cults, and that I am slowly building and testing the new foundations of the reality where I will spend the rest of my life.

Chapter 2: Tyler Blacquiere

Sometimes, life throws you curveballs.

Sometimes, it's 4:45 am on a Saturday morning, and you're crying in your room after having just finished watching the 2011 film, *Warrior*.

Now, not to take anything away from the film — which is great — or from the performances of Tom Hardy and Joel Edgerton — which are greater — but I don't think that the heartfelt MMA action-drama is what has caused the faucets of my eyeballs to leak onto my face.

In early October, I wrapped up my first "real job" after university. Two years. The end of an era ... or something. It's now December, and the joke of #funemployment has lost its humour. Anything remotely resembling motivation is long since gone. Between the entry-level jobs looking for five years' experience, the unpaid internships, the rejection emails, and the self-doubt and criticism — each one like a wave pounding the shore of my resolve — there are days when pulling myself out of bed before 1 pm seems impossible but for a small act of god. Or Cinnamon Toast Crunch.

Sometimes, it's hard to see a reason to wake up in the morning, and sometimes, it's 4:45 am on a Saturday morning, and you're crying in your room after having just finished watching the 2011 film, Warrior.

But I don't think the heartfelt MMA action-drama is what has caused the faucets of my eyeballs to leak onto my face.

It's early January 2012, and I'm walking home along Bloor Street in Toronto, coming back from a grocery trip at No Frills.

The thing about coming back from a grocery trip at No Frills, is that I don't live anywhere near a No Frills. But I'm a student, and I'm poor, and I have this stubborn belief that I should do the things I'm capable of doing. It's why I carried a mini-fridge from Canadian Tire to my dorm room in first-year university. It's why I moved the contents of my apartment — from desks, to shelves, to bed — by longboard, twice. And it's why I'm walking home along Bloor Street, six or seven grocery bags at my sides and a backpack filled with cans on my back. Because I can.

So I'm walking along Bloor Street, and my hands are crying out — the weight of the bags and their thin, shitty plastic handles are digging into my fingers, punishing my stubbornness, when suddenly, I feel the phone vibrating in my pocket.

I'm not in the most ideal position to be taking a call, but when you don't have caller ID, and you don't have voice mail and your first thought is "Who the hell could that be?", and your second thought is "Shit...what's wrong?!" — you answer the call.

So I awkwardly fumble for the phone in my pocket and, still holding the three or four grocery bags, lift it to my ear and say, "Hello?"

For then-me, it's early January 2012, and I'm about to experience the coolest thing that will probably ever happen to me, but for now-me, it's 7 pm on a Friday evening and instead of rock climbing with my friends, the crushing weight of my anxiety and my maybe-depression leave me anchored to my bed. In some miracle of alchemy, my blankets have transmuted and weave tight round my limbs, further shackling me in place. Cinnamon Toast Crunch has no power here, and as the rock-wall calls, now-me can't bring himself to answer.

Then-me, however, lifts the phone to his ear and says, "Hello?" I don't recognize the woman's voice on the other

Stories We Don't Tell

end, but she identifies herself as a staff member with the Canadian HIV/AIDS Legal Network, and she asks if I have a minute. I lie and tell her that I do, trying to play it cool so that she can't hear the strain in my voice from the three or four grocery bags that I'm still, for some reason, holding up to my ear along with the phone.

Mystery woman tells me that they want my help with something, but that it's "sort of top-secret," and before she says any more she asks, "Are you in?"

Yes. This is probably the coolest thing that will ever happen to me.

I have no idea what to expect or what they could possibly want that I could offer, but I say, "Yes. Of course I'm in." Mainly because I love their organization and have an intellectual crush on their executive director, but partially because this might be my one opportunity ... to become a super spy.

When she proceeds to explain the situation, I don't get my dream of being a super spy, but what I do end up with is a pretty close second.

I'm told that one of their staff members managed to record some footage with popular artist K'NAAN (of "Waving Flag" fame) backstage at a recent show, and the Legal Network wants to use the footage to kick off a massive petition campaign.

The only problem, she tells me, is that the footage is in a few different takes, and it isn't that great, and they need it in a finalized and shareable format, by tomorrow, and through all the chaos, they thought of ... me.

I know. This is probably the coolest thing that will ever happen to me.

I'm told to await an email with the footage, and so I hurry home with my six or seven grocery bags and backpack full of cans, to wait.

Then-me waits for footage so he can contribute to a huge civil-society movement six years in the making, but now-me has — in Houdini-esque fashion — found a way to loose himself from the bed-prison, and I sit, vacant eyes reflecting the harsh glow of the computer screen, the only light in a darkened room, waiting for Facebook to refresh, for probably the hundredth time this past hour. It's 11:32 pm on a Friday evening, and instead of feeling wiped from climbing I'm in the brain-dead state that comes from trolling social media sites for updates that either don't come or don't matter, all brain activity replaced by that smattering of test colours that graces the broken televisions of yesterday. Just when I think I'll be locked in this state forever, a single brain synapse manages to fire — I should look for pocket knives on eBay.

Now-me begins comparing blade lengths and handle styles, as then-me rounds the last corner to home. And now I'm at my shitty basement apartment and the groceries are put away and I'm at my desk in my cramped, windowless bedroom and I'm hitting the refresh button on my Gmail.

And I'm waiting.

A couple hours go by with no email and no word, and I begin to worry, but then the phone rings, and the footage is almost uploaded. When I finally receive it, I'm met with a grainy, poorly framed, 7-minute clip comprised of a few different shots in which K'NAAN (bless his heart) repeatedly makes mistakes regarding the more intricate technicalities of the issue he's speaking to. All the right facts are there, they're just in different places, and so I set out on the task of stitching together something useful.

Then-me tries to channel my inner seamstress, as now-me wades knee-deep in the murky quagmire that is internet

Stories We Don't Tell

shopping. It's 1:47 am on a Saturday morning, and I'm still looking for pocket knives. It takes a migration from eBay to Etsy, and hundreds more listings, for me to realize: I don't need or want, or even know what one would do with, a pocket knife. So I finally close my browser and start the 2011 film, Warrior.

Now-me dives into a heartfelt MMA action-drama, and then-me dives into a grainy, poorly framed 7-minute clip of popular artist K'NAAN. It takes most of the night to edit and the rest of it to get the video uploaded, but come morning I send it off to the folks at the Legal Network, who in turn send it off to K'NAAN's people for approval (I know). It takes a couple more hours, but it comes back with the a-ok, barring one minor change: K'NAAN's name is to be written in all-capitals, at all times. It's 3:19 am on a Saturday morning, and Tom Hardy's character is Fucking. People. Up.

Then-me sleeps soundly that night, having completed a video that will go on to get 21,000 views and help kick off a massive petition campaign that will get 51,000 signatures.

Now-me does not sleep, because it's 4:45 am on a Saturday morning, and I'm crying in my room after having just finished watching the 2011 film, *Warrior*. But I don't think it's the heartfelt MMA action-drama that has the faucets of my eyeballs leaking onto my face.

Chapter 3: Wafa Ktaech

This was supposed to be the best trip of my life. It wasn't the first time I went to Lebanon, but it would be the first time I went without my parents. I hated going to Lebanon with my parents — between having to hide the fact that I smoke to being forced to sleepover at cousins' houses that I didn't like, going to Lebanon was way more of a chore than a vacation. But this time would be different. I was going by myself, and I was going to have the best time ever.

I was NOT going to stay in the Dah-yeh. The dahyeh was where 70% of my family lived — it was a crammed neighbourhood that never had water or electricity. I was going to stay in B'shammoon, which was a little higher in the mountains, cooler, had more frequent electricity and water. My namesake, Amto Wafa, lives there and she's definitely the cool aunt in the family. I could smoke and drink, and she wouldn't care. This trip was going to be the best.

A few days into my trip, my cousin, Sophie, visited us in B'shammoon. She's maybe 8 or 9. I asked her to boil me some water, which you always have to do in Lebanon because the tap water is not safe to drink. A couple hours passed and I forgot that I had water waiting for me. By now the water had cooled down, and it's 40 degrees outside, so I drink what must've been a litre in five seconds.

It took only a couple of hours to happen. I started throwing up and had diarrhea. I thought it just must be the heat. But it didn't stop. I continued to throw up, multiple times in that one day. I ask Sophie, "Habibti, are you sure you boiled that water?" Her eyes go really big, and frantically she says, "Uh....". Sophie had not boiled the water.

In Lebanon, when you are sick you don't go to the doctors,

you go to the pharmacist. The pharmacist was a 40-year-old woman who was smoking a cigarette. She asked what we needed, so I explained to her my symptoms.

"Oh, you didn't boil the water? Oh, you're throwing up? Oh, you have diarrhea? Yeah, you definitely have E. coli poisoning. Here, take these pills. You're going to be sick for a very long time."

She was so right. For the next two weeks, I threw up ten times a day and could not eat a single thing. I had zero control over my bowel movements because my body was so tired from vomiting. I was pretty much glued to the washroom, just in case a fart was actually diarrhea. While B'shammoon did have better water and electricity than other parts of Lebanon, there was still about six hours a day with no electricity. And I don't know if you know this, but Lebanon is so fucking hot all the time. All I did was lay on the washroom floor, just to get some relief from the heat by trying to absorb the cold dampness from the tiles.

I was two weeks into my trip, and I had barely left my aunt's apartment. At this point in my illness, I was feeling a little better, and I was only throwing up two to five times a day. Noticing my improvement, my aunt suggested we go to the beach, early in the morning, stay for a couple hours and then come home so I could rest. This seemed like the best idea because I was getting really sick of being in the apartment. We went to the beach and it's everything I wanted out of my trip. The ocean breeze was heavenly, and it wasn't too hot because it was only 9 am. There were not that many people at the beach that early so I felt anonymous. I finally got to relax under the sun by the ocean and forget everything happening to me back in Toronto. I was so incredibly happy that I told my aunt we should stay all day. She smiled warmly and was also happy that I was having a good time.

Stories We Don't Tell

My aunt went for a walk on the beach and I stayed lying down, reading a book. All-day my stomach was rumbling, but that wasn't unusual in my state. Chapter 12, my stomach rumbled harder. Chapter 14, I felt intense cramps in my abdomen. Chapter 17, I could actually see my stomach rippling from the cramps. But I just swallowed a big gulp of fresh salt-water air and told myself that it's gas and once it passes, I'll feel so much better. There were some people sitting around me, so I stood up and walked a bit away from them to save them from smelling my fart. Walking hurt, but I felt like I was safely away from other people. I looked towards the ocean, inhaled the ocean breeze and exhaled to let out the fart.

That's when it happened. With about ten people lying down around me and me, standing facing away from them, I realized that I didn't fart. I shat myself. I am a grown woman, with shit the consistency of diarrhea streaming down my legs. I was beyond horrified, my heart sank to my feet, and I felt my eyes watering up from embarrassment. I quickly turned around so my shit filled bikini bottom was facing away from everyone, but everyone saw. Two kids were dying of laughter. An older woman was shaking her head, obviously extremely embarrassed for me. I beelined to the ocean and took off my bikini bottom and tried cleaning the shit off my legs and bathing suit. Luckily, it was very watery, so it came off pretty easily.

I walked out of the ocean with my head down, trying to make no eye contact with anyone around me. I laid back down, and my aunt was already back from her walk. She said, "Oh so nice! You went and swam a bit!" I grumbled something and said that I wanted to go home.

That night I called my parents and told them I was cutting my trip short to come home and see a doctor. My mom went on a rant about how I should've never gone to Lebanon by myself. I just quietly agreed.

Chapter 4: Jeanette Stock

When he learned he was diagnosed with lung cancer, my grandfather wrote down a Gaelic prayer on a piece of scrap paper for my oldest cousin, and asked him to read it at his funeral. He even scrawled the introduction at the top of the page: "Please bow your heads to pray."

He chose all his readings, actually, including Omar Khayyam's Rubaiyat. The only things he loved more than sharing a MaCallan scotch with a friend were my grandmother and vanilla ice-cream, so it only seemed fitting:

Drink! For you know not whence you came, nor why:
Drink! For you know not where you go, nor why.

I drank more this December than I have since I turned 19, but I don't really think that's what Omar Khayyam was going for. I booked my flight down to Florida to say goodbye an hour after my mother called to tell me my Sunday ticket would be too late.

I missed my plane and broke down in tears at the Delta Air counter. "I need to get to Sarasota." I somehow managed to choke it out.

In a display of empathy unseen before in the airline industry, the woman sprang into action, barking at everyone at nearby counters. "Let this woman through — she needs to get to Sarasota!"

I was on a plane within 45 minutes.

I was six hours too late to say goodbye.

Despite my protests that I could take a cab, my grandmother picked me up from the airport in her robin's egg blue convertible. It was a Christmas gift from my grandfather — a throwback to the first car she ever owned, a boxy station wagon that appeared outside the house on her birthday. The dealership drove it up that morning — and spelled his name wrong on the hand-painted sign attached.

Both my mother and my grandmother looked like they hadn't slept in days, but I knew it was more like weeks. I hugged them both, handed them coffees, and asked what I could do.

***

This December I learned I have an uncanny knack for obituaries. I learned this because at 11pm the night before my grandfather's obituary was due, my aunts and uncles were still fighting over the first line.

I confiscated their pens and papers, armed them all with wine and whisky, and gathered their best Umpa stories:

"Robert! That time you got pulled over driving the car as a kid! When the cops in town called Dad to ask what to do with him, he replied, *'Well ... throw him in Jail!'*"

"No, The paintball gun! He bought a plastic wolf to chase away those Canada geese, but they just perched right on top of it! He bought that toy gun. I'll never forget waking up to see him sitting on the deck in his bathrobe, shooting blue paintballs to scare off those damned birds."

I managed to keep any stories that could be misconstrued as illegal activity or animal cruelty out of the obituary.

My cousin Jillian and I took the three pages of notes we'd collected and worked to condense 86 years into something that fit in a newspaper.

We stayed up until 4 am, agonizing over each word choice. Like a good English student, I cut all the adjectives.

Even with this, it was still the only death notice in the *Globe and Mail* that ran the full page. In the Sarasota paper, it took up *two* columns.

***

This December, I realized I am not sure there is a God. This revelation came on December 23rd, as I was reading at my grandfather's funeral. I was stuck with the most challenging one to make it through without crying — "Death Is Nothing At All," by H. Scott Holland.

I used an old family trick to hold back tears: hold a golf tee in your fist. Each time I thought there was a risk I might cry, I drove the point into my palm.

Everyone else lost it at the first line, but I held on until the last stanza:

*One brief moment and all will be as it was before
only better, infinitely happier
and forever we will all be one together with Christ.*

For my mother and grandmother, this line is relief. He is waiting for them in heaven, playing cards and drinking scotch with his best friends.

For me, this is the final blow. All *will* not be as it was before.

I believe his atoms are already beginning to scatter. He is becoming grass and trees, just as he became a man from the atoms of the buffalo and the dodo bird and the dinosaurs.

Only one of us can be right.

Drink! For you know not whence you came, nor why:
Drink! For you know not where you go, nor why.

***

In my mind, his obituary reads a little differently than the one we published:

Denis Robert Evans of Toronto passed away peacefully in his blue chair, surrounded by family. His son held one hand, his daughter held the other, and his wife, Janet, held both. They sang his favourite Frank Sinatra songs at the top of their lungs and toasted him with Famous Grouse, his (second) favourite drink.

The party in his honour was two weeks and a $2000 bar tab long.

He was a larger-than-life character who believed in the indomitable power of the human spirit. He never said goodbye at the end of a visit — only, "you work hard now."

This summer, his granddaughter and wife will fly a floatplane over Lake of Bays, scattering his ashes over the golf course he worked at as a boy, the roads he built as a young man, and the cottage he grew old in.

As he would often joke, "most of my friends are sleeping outside."

He has now joined them.

Chapter 5: Sarah Flanagan

He looks so different now, but I would never tell him that. It would hurt his feelings. The chemo was a year and a half ago, but he's never looked the same as he did before it happened. They say that things change after chemo. Physical things that seem permanent but in reality, aren't, like hair going from curly to straight. My dad's hair is completely white now and has mostly grown back. I haven't touched it, but it looks downy-soft and like each individual hair has a tenuous grip on his scalp, like dandelion fluff before you blow on it and make a wish. His eyebrows never got the invitation to the party, though. They just never came back. Maybe there's still time for that. Maybe it happens in stages. For a long time, he claimed that his eyelashes hadn't grown back. He was strangely proud of this fact, like a soldier showing the neighbourhood kids where his thumb used to be. I finally had to tell him that, in fact, he did have eyelashes. I started to wonder what he saw when he looked in the mirror.

Hair aside, the most startling change is his colouring. His face has taken on a permanent ashen complexion. With the white hair and no eyebrows he's started to look like a marble statue. Or a ghost. I wish I could escape this image. At dinner, when he asks me to pass the water (usually just as I'm taking my first bite), unbidden, my brain lobs a synaptic softball at the part of itself that deals in facial recognition, telling me: *this is not your father.*

But it is, another area of my brain fires back.

Cancer is not how it appears in the movies. Here's the plot of *Cancer: The Movie*. The main character, usually played by Susan Sarandon, Julia Roberts or Dame Judy Dench, is told they have cancer. They then get chemotherapy and either a) recover, or, b) die. Both options don't take very long even in the compressed time-span of a movie.

Here's what happens in Cancer: My Real Life. My dad is told the pain he's been experiencing in his hip the past few months is actually advanced prostate cancer. That it has spread to his bones and that he has a tumour on his spine. He is treated right away with intense drugs and radiation therapy. We then enter the wild and woolly world of Cancer Management. Cancer Management involves the monitoring and treatment of the cancer as needed until there are no treatments left that work. This can be months, or it can be years, but eventually the cancer will outsmart any treatment it faces, even chemotherapy which is akin to having poison slowly dripped into your bloodstream. My dad will never be in remission, as I've wearily had to explain to so many friends after I told them the news (*He's lucky it's prostate cancer — it has a 90% survival rate,* so many of my friends told me. *Not when it's already at stage 4,* I respond, ignoring the word, *lucky*). My dad will always have cancer and, if a bus doesn't hit him first, it will kill him.

The thing they don't show you in movies is that most people live with cancer. Most people *live with* cancer.

My dad is a poet. His writing is compact and abstract. I don't usually understand his poems, but when I've heard him at a reading his words have moved me in ways that I can't put into words. Sometimes they make me feel like I'm falling down the stairs, or sliding down a really tall slide, or eating the best meal of my life while watching old episodes of *SCTV*. Because he's a writer, and more specifically because he's a poet, he very much inhabits his inner world. He thinks and feels and expresses constantly. This happens in his writing, which he does near-daily, mostly in the middle of the night or as the morning birds chirp. Or it happens when

Stories We Don't Tell

I phone him and open with the banal question, *How are you?* Warranting a 15-minute detailed analysis of how much sleep he got, if he's achy, what he ate for breakfast, if he has to take the recycling out, where my mother is, if he has an upcoming doctor's appointment, if he's worried about it, and do I think he looks okay, and he's feeling pretty good, so he's hoping for the best. For him it's all interconnected, the inner and the outer, the ache in his shoulder and the recycling bins are both part of the bigger picture: who is winning right now, the cancer or him? I know it's good that he talks about his fears, but sometimes I don't want to hear them. I want to pretend, just some of the time, that he isn't sick. These thoughts lead me into a guilt spiral that I know so well I can trace its shape with my eyes closed. So I listen and I always ask again the next time I call, *How are you?*

In the movies the emotional arc of family members fits cleanly, like a kids' toy where the cube goes in the cube-shaped hole. There is shock at the diagnosis, followed by coming together to support the cancer-ridden family member, despite complicated and awkward family dynamics. Then there is grief when the loved one passes away — after, of course, reconciling all their family issues. They learn about themselves in between. They make amends. They laugh. They cry. The circle of life, dear Simba.

But how do you manage your own life while your father's cancer is being managed? Life keeps happening. Living in the space of ambiguity, of not knowing when things will change, when a cold is just a cold or when a cold is a reason to worry, is hard. I feel the sharp undercurrent of inevitability flow through everything. Nothing is the same, but everything continues to be mundane.

The summer my dad was doing chemo we hatched a plan to go to Paris, all of us — my parents, my brother and me

— the following spring. My dad had visions of showing my brother and me the city that he loved. And believe it or not, we actually did it. We went the following spring, minus my brother for scheduling reasons. But it turned out not to be the vision my father had of strolling in the early spring Paris blooms, showing me his favourite neighbourhoods, cafes, and bookstores. He was deeply unhappy there. Paris was too loud, and he had already seen all the tourist attractions I wanted to see. He would stay in the apartment alone while my mother and I went to the Louvre because he was too afraid to venture out by himself. When we convinced him to come with us to the Musée de Cluny to see the Lady and the Unicorn tapestries, he walked a few feet behind my mother and me the entire time and sighed loudly like a petulant child not getting his usual level of attention. Eventually, I angrily turned to him and told him he was ruining my experience and if he was having such a terrible time he should just wait outside, which is what he did. There were too many tourists and too many motorcycles. He felt worn out. And I felt angry. Angry with him that he was ruining the few short days we had in Paris. Frustration and annoyance coursed through my blood like a pathogen, infecting every system in my body until I became sick. Sick of it, sick of his behaviour, sick of him.

Yes, I was an *enfant terrible* to my father on his make-a-wish cancer trip.

About two years into my father's cancer management, I became fixated on the need to have a baby. Or, rather, to give my dad a grandchild. I hadn't really experienced the ticking of my biological clock up until that moment, and some may argue that it wasn't really my biological clock ticking, it was something else. I knew that a grandchild would bring my father so much joy that I would start crying just visualizing it. In a very deep way, babies give us a reason to live. Obviously, had I had a baby (with whom exactly? My imaginary boyfriend, Bradbert?) it wouldn't have solved anything. I had to remind myself that babies don't cure cancer.

In the movies, when Susan Sarandon or Dame Judy Dench dies, I watch as their families go through the grieving process. I see the funeral, the tears, the drinking, the casseroles piling up in the fridge (or egg salad, if they're Jewish). As the viewer, the grieving process is a ritual I'm familiar with. I may not know how long it will take, but I do know that eventually there will be a point where the pain lessens, a point of forgetting, a point of moving on. But with this, this Cancer Management, there is no real moving on. I want it to stop, but at the same time I don't, because I know how my movie ends. But I guess that's true for all of us. Meanwhile, the third act unfolds as my father's cancer is managed and I attempt to play the best version of myself that I can. I try to be grateful for every moment I have with him, while managing the fear I feel all the time. I'm still learning how to be this person. I'm managing.

Chapter 6: Alena Cawthorne

I never thought it would be at a Starbucks, in the middle of suburbia, sipping on my black coffee while a cute hipster was drinking his latte, soya, vanilla something or other telling me stories of his family where I would realize I had finally accepted my origin story.

It's the middle of May 1991. My parents are in the midst of washing the dishes one evening when the phone rings, my mom answers, it's the call they have been waiting for.

"We have a baby, but you would have to leave tomorrow to pick her up. Are you still interested?"

Frantically my parents drive around to the store to pick up baby supplies, and to my aunt's to pick up hand-me-downs. The next day my mom is on a plane heading to Bucharest. From Bucharest to Corni on a small army plane, equipped with overly armed military personnel due to recent political tensions and the downfall of Romania's former leader, Nicolae Ceaușescu.

In a tiny apartment, in a small northern town, my mom meets my birth mother, my birth sister, and me for the first time. My brother by birth is away at their grandmother's for the day.

My match to my parents was purely random, my mom was closest to the van door at this house stop, she was simply next in line, and whoever was inside was to become her daughter.

***

Growing up, I never thought about my adoption. It was a small minor detail that didn't really matter. At times it was something special. My best friend Lisa, who was also adopted with me, found it to be a great story. A reason that showed how our friendship was more special than any other. "Did you know that as babies we slept in a suitcase together?" "We could actually be related." And for a long time, my friendship with Lisa and having a second loving family, her family, was the only reminder of my adoption.

Being adopted is not something that you are constantly reminded of. There is no physical demarcation that leaves me standing out against everyone else. Quite often, I forget that I am. Quite often I forget that it is a thing, until I am reminded by others that it is apparently a thing.

If my memory serves me right, it was at my first job that I was faced with the thought that I might be different. Some of my colleagues, my boss included, had somehow got onto the conversation of adoption. I glanced up from my work. Did I hear correctly? Adoption? I felt my face get hot as I sat listening to them.

"I just feel so sorry for them, how could you grow up your whole life knowing you were not wanted?"

"Well that's why those adopted kids grow up being so fucked up, it's what happens when you're not loved."

***

Lying on the couch in the basement, wrapped in the arms of my ex, one of the only serious long-term partners I've ever had, somehow the conversation of adoption comes up. At the time, I brushed it off, unwilling to discuss it. Unable to hear what he was saying anymore as my eyes started raining, and I had to focus my attention on the fact that my stomach was attempting to drop out of my body.

"It is crucial to me that if I have a child, that it is my own.

Stories We Don't Tell

I mean a child with my own blood."

"Why?" I ask meekly, "What's the difference?"

"Well, it's just not the same, you know? You won't be as connected to the child. It's just not the same. You don't understand."

***

A few summers back Lisa's mom planned a lunch with the woman who set up our adoptions. We drove to Welland, Ontario and were all sitting in a Jack Astors that was in desperate need of renovations. There I met the "adoption lady" for the first time and learned the detailed version of my origin.

It was here that I realized my being was a repercussion of a controlling political regime that forced a country into poverty, but also a wonderful consequence of this woman's lifelong mission, the woman whose name I cannot remember.

She was born and grew up in Romania, under the brutal regime of Nicolae Ceaușescu. Under his control abortion was banned, women were given medals for the number of children they had, and there was childlessness tax.

As the birth rate increased, Ceaușescu had the idea that the state could raise children better than parents. Thousands of children were sent to state institutions. During this time, Romania's economy collapsed, there were huge amounts of foreign debt, and new policies were put into place that forced many people into poverty. There were now more children under state care and less money to care for the children. This is where the adoption lady comes in.

While biting into her club sandwich, she told us how the sounds of children crying from the orphanage are her

Stories We Don't Tell

strongest memories of her life in Romania. When she immigrated to Canada, the cries from the orphanages continued to haunt her dreams. So when the horrors of Romania's orphanages were revealed to the world, and international adoption became permitted, this woman dedicated her life to setting up adoptions. She would travel across Romania to find a pregnant woman. Those who wanted to attempt sketchy adoptions, she would keep safe. Those who knew the state would take away their children, she would find them new homes.

Page 168 of my developmental psychology of children textbook will explain to you the various detrimental effects of neglect during the first six months of development. It will describe how Romania's orphans are the perfect case study, due to the high number of children in these institutions and the extreme levels of neglect. A bottle tied to the crib to feed, a spray of the hose for a shower, toys pinned to the wall to look at but never touch, and of course the absolute absence of human contact.

I guess you could consider me a lucky one; I was only two weeks old when I was adopted. I never had to live in such places.

Later that evening when we returned home, my dad was sitting at the kitchen table, waiting for us. I sat down as he began to tell me his story of my adoption. He had stayed in Canada while my mom was in Romania. He told me that all he remembered was the phone call from my mom the night before she was supposed to come home.

"I don't think we are getting the baby," she told him. The lines in the courthouse were long, and she had been waiting five days. My birth mother was restless after missing five days of work she couldn't afford to miss. Everyone else's adoptions had gone through, we were the last.

I thought back to something the adoption lady had said, that I hadn't paid much attention to at Jack Astors. "I remember your group. Your group was the last group I took out of Romania before international adoption was banned in the early 90s."

Fast forward to a first date. We're sitting in Starbucks in the middle of suburbia. I'm sipping on my black coffee, while he has one of those fancy drinks I never know how to order. Things are going great, and just when I begin to think to myself that there are people out there that I connect with again, he decides to tell me the story of his cousin ... who isn't really his cousin.

"What do you mean he isn't really your cousin?"

"Well he's adopted, you know? He isn't blood, he isn't really part of the family."

This time my stomach doesn't drop.

I smile back at him, politely excuse myself from our date, and go back home to watch a movie with my family.

Chapter 7: Sima Sahar Zerehi

Ough!

His heavy combat boot kicks me in the stomach ...

And I double over in pain as all the air in my lungs rushes out —

I'm flattened — deflated — collapse.

I gasp out for air, but the small office is pumped full of tear gas, my lungs are burning, and my eyes tear up from the fumes.

Close your eyes — shallow breaths — limp body.

But, Let's rewind a few days.

***

We got the news together. He just hung his head. I asked, "Is there anything else we can do? Any applications we can file — any appeals to stop the deportation or buy us time?"

But we all knew the answer. There were no applications left to be filed. No more appeals ... no legal manoeuvre to stop his deportation to Pakistan.

The others who were deported had ended up in jail — there were reports of torture, beatings, and some we never heard from again.

That's what Faheem was being sent to.

He said, "I don't want to go out quietly ... I want to fight!"

"You sure?" I asked, "If you make this hard for them — they could take it out on you."

"I want to fight," he repeated.

***

We called an emergency meeting at the Kensington house. We were a motley crew of scruffy activists and student organizers — we wore Kaffiyeh's and political t-shirts and lived in cramped communal houses that doubled as organizing hubs.

We sat in a circle on the floor — stone-faced and decided on an occupation of the minister of immigration's office.

After all, the minister could stop this with the stroke of a pen. She could save his life ... But she wasn't going to and we wanted people to know that.

We were all business that night — no one wanted to let things get emotional — Faheem was there too, adding a sense of urgency to it all.

We talked time, meeting spots, legal support and bail money.

We also decided that only those of us who identified as people of colour would take part in the occupation ... those of us who looked like Faheem.

It was supposed to be simple. We'd get into the front office, walk to the minister's private room, close the door and declare that we were occupying the space. We were going to explain that this was in protest of Faheem's deportation.

There wasn't much time to plan ... it was all going to happen in two days ... on the day of Faheem's removal.

***

That morning we met at the Tim Hortons across from the plaza where the minister's office was.

Everyone was tense — I was mostly sad and angry, preoccupied with thoughts of Faheem at the airport.

In my mind, the occupation was going to be a relatively clear cut action. A symbolic piece of political theatre — just something so Faheem didn't get deported quietly.

We had a plan — get inside the office and occupy the room for a few hours until the police removed us.

I thought that they'd get a key, open the door and pick us up one by one off the floor, maybe as we chanted something like "stop the deportations" That was the norm. That's how it was done.

I thought — tops one night in holding — a court appearance to set bail the next day, and we'd be out to deal with the charges over a few months. It was going to be inconvenient — but that was all. A small price to pay for Faheem.

I had prepared a media release. It was going to be sent out as soon as I made the call from inside the minister's office. The plan was to take media calls during the occupation on my cell.

We wanted to get press so news of Faheem's deportation to Pakistan would spread.

We told ourselves that the goal was to get media attention. To send a signal to the Pakistani government that he was being watched. That they couldn't get away with disappearing him or torturing him without making headlines.

What we didn't say was that we were just angry and wanted to FUCK SHIT UP!

Our friends from OCAP and other allies were going to rally outside to give us more visibility. That was the PLAN. But that's not EXACTLY what happened.

***

Marika was our decoy. She buzzed in — her excuse — to get a letter from the minister celebrating her grandma's 90th birthday.

The rest of us — seven in total — were hiding around the corner waiting for her signal.

Recently, they had put up new security measures at the minister's office. The front door was now locked and you had to buzz in. A security guard was also posted at the door. They used these retired guys — old men who were deputized as commissionaires.

Marika walked up to the office — I couldn't hear her voice, but could see her speaking through the intercom. Then she signalled, and I started running — the others behind me.

We rushed to the door as the ageing security guard scrambled to close it. He was no match for the eight of us — we pushed it open and poured in.

The old guard stood there feet apart — arms out and said, "Do you wanna rumble?"

We had no time to appreciate the comedy of the scene. We just ran past him going from the main reception into the back.

I checked the photos on the desk to make sure we had the right office — the minister was in one of the frames sitting with her whole family on a lawn in front of a big house. "This is it," I said.

The others all ran in, and as we closed the door, I heard a THUMP from the front room.

The security guard was down — none of us had touched him — but the excitement was too much for the man. He had fainted.

Our friends in OCAP were dealing with the situation — an ambulance was called, and medics from the rally were checking on him.

Looking back, that was the first sign that this occupation was not going down like the others.

But we were too wrapped up in our sense of justice,

Stories We Don't Tell

too angry to see Faheem get deported to uncertainty, too self-righteous in our struggle to think twice about the repercussions.

Within a few minutes, I was in a corner taking media calls, spouting the message box to anyone who would listen.

"It's outrageous that the Canadian government would deport anyone to a place where they can be imprisoned and tortured ... to a place with a deplorable human rights record ... to kangaroo courts."

I was giving a CBC reporter the play by play. "Yes, a group of riot police have arrived at the door. They'll probably ask the office staff for a key and remove us ... no we won't leave ... we're holding our ground."

"No ... the police are not unlocking the door, they brought tools ... yah a toolbox ... they're removing the air vent from the bottom of the door."

"Honestly I'm not sure why ..."

"Yes we are still all here ... there's maybe a dozen cops in riot gear ... wait ... they're putting on their gas masks ... why are they putting on their gas masks?"

"NO the officers have not communicated with us."

"OH NO! Gas ... gas ... they have gassed the room."

"Choking ... axe ... they're breaking down the door."

"Yes, axe ... breaking down the door!"

"They're coming ... kicking ... beating ... punched ... dragging us out."

That's when it came. Heavy combat boot, right into my stomach, hard, sharp pain ... collapse.

The only way I can describe it to someone who hasn't been beaten ... really beaten I mean ... is to say it feels like heartache, rejection and self-loathing all rolled into a single excruciating blow.

I blacked out for maybe a minute, and when I came to,

41

blue uniforms and heavy boots were dragging me out of the office and then shoving me unceremoniously into the back of a police van.

The others were already there, the girls on one side and the guys on the other. Everyone in a panic ... this was their first arrest. I had orchestrated this. This ONE was on me.

And as the metal door slammed shut, I thought, I wonder if Faheem's flight has taken off.

Chapter 8: Erin Kang

"I love Asian girls."

He doesn't say the words, but his eyes tell me; I can tell by the way they don't fully meet mine how he's into me. Others have been and will be bolder and just tell me up-front, like a compliment. I haven't yet told any of them that it'd be cool just to say they like me, not all the peoples of a continent, but some people really like to go big.

He towers over me in a puffy jacket and toque, his breath forming flash-frozen clouds in the night air. An hour earlier he'd checked my ID to let us into the bar, and now his coworker is goading me on, spitting reasons why I should give Tall Man my number, as the two of them fake-don't-let-me-back-in-the-bar. I let them run their act, fake-trying-to-get-past-them, coatless in mid-November on Queen Street after running outside to answer my phone.

I was born in Niagara Falls and grew up in Niagara-on-the-Lake, a small heritage town known for its wineries, theatre scene, and flower-lined streets. It's the kind of hometown that's too expensive for me to go back to visit now — home sweet home is only sweet if you can afford it, honey. Korean was my first language, though once English began to influence my tongue, Korean felt foreign to me for years.

It wasn't such a small town that I never saw other people of colour, and my family would often stuff our car with pillows and blankets and take trips to Toronto which I understood to be larger, busier, more diverse. We'd get our kimchi and Hello Kitty dolls and Mom would get VHS tapes of Korean dramas. But it doesn't take long or much for the idea that you're not as cool as other people to form, especially in a small school. I didn't own clothes from Old Navy. My parents weren't lawyers or dentists. I didn't have golden hair. When I did get blonde streaks in my hair, they were weird, not cool.

I look back at Tall Man and give him a once-over, evaluating whether I should give him my number. I decide not and head inside. I'm in university and exams are coming up — I can't waste this precious time away from staring at income polarization maps. When I step back out with my friends later, he asks for my number again. It's late, and we just want poutine. I start dismissing him again until I notice the Harry Potter font on his phone. I give him my number.

When I first moved to Toronto, I'd only stepped on a subway train once before. My old town was too small for public transit, and "downtown" was only three blocks long. The only source of Korean food that I could see was from my own kitchen. But here, I began to see Korean things every day — restaurants, grocery stores, cafes, people. In middle school, I hit a milestone moment, falling hard for a boy who shared my broadly Asian heritage. He never liked me back, eventually going on to date a white girl.

"You're different than other Asian girls."

Tall Man and I start dating, casually. He's not the first to say that, and he won't be the last, though the reasons will always change.

"You're not ... quiet like most Asian girls. I don't usually see Asian girls with tattoos. You must be wild. But you're not really Canadian. You're not really Korean."

I feverishly collect information about what I'm not and stockpile it with information about the good things I am. I'm hardworking, like my people. I can hold liquor, unlike my people. I'm so kind, like my people. I'm so cool, unlike my people. It will be years before I can look at any of it with even minimal honesty.

I tell my best friend confidently that Tall Man and I aren't seeing each other seriously. I make sure to tell him, make sure to tell my friends, make sure to tell myself this isn't serious in case it turns out that he really does only like Asian girls, not me.

I meet his friends, a crowd of somewhat-older, clubbing-type-looking people who meet my gaze the same way as he did. They're friendly but look through me. I tell distasteful jokes to get laughs, laugh along to theirs. Twenty of us sit on the kinds of faux-luxurious tall stools that you find in faux-luxurious restaurant chains. Now and then someone catches my eye, throwing me a knowing smile.

"I already know you, girl," their smiles say. "Our buddy, he loves girls like you."

In high school, I used to wear this shirt with hearts on the front that said "Asian girls like to have fun" in cursive. This was despite the fact that you could often hear me say things like "guys, but I'm the whitest Asian ever." "I'd never date an Asian guy." I'd hate when people asked me where I'm really from or what my Asian name is or if I'd give them an Asian massage.

Years after dating Tall Man, I will run into a classmate from my hometown in a room full of plaid shirts and beanies. When he reminisces about the good ol' days, I will smirk and remind him we had two very different experiences growing up there. His eyes will meet mine with genuine confusion which — let's face it — I'm used to. I will point out how my family were pretty much the only Asians in the school and he will rebut, What about that one girl from a couple grades below us? My sister. But no, there were more, even younger than that! Ohhh, my cousins ... We stopped talking pretty quickly.

Stories We Don't Tell

"I'm only physically attracted to you."

Tall Man doesn't say the words, but his body tells me; I can tell by the way it doesn't listen to mine. He's not the first to say that, and he won't be the last. Around Christmas, I bring him a Life Brand chocolate advent calendar, and he gets me the Complete Set of Harry Potter Movies on DVD. I never see him again.

Chapter 9: Tara Marina Pearson

It hadn't rained there in three years. I was living in a desert, just east of the red mountains. I was getting used to how hot it was. I was getting used to starting work at 5 am and going for runs long after dark so as not to overheat. And I was even getting used to the chronic dehydration that seemed to mean I'd never have to pee again. But I never got used to the impossibility that the sky could break with rain, and I never got used to how far away he was.

In just a few hours I am to get on a bus, another eight and I will be there, after months of occasional weekends and the privilege of five-minute phone calls, we are spending an entire week together. "I know how hard it's been." I say, "I'll be there soon." But the voice on the phone is strange. Devoid of the excitement it could barely contain an hour earlier.

"I don't love you, anymore."

My face is burning. I hang up the phone and stare at the mountains. For the first time since coming to the desert, I have nowhere to go.

In the darkness, I walk to my room and find my bed where it sits on the dust-covered floor. I lay there trying to understand these new words, a language I do not speak.

I. Don't. Love. You. The darkness remains, the only thing preventing my body from splitting apart.

I wake to light streaming in through a crack in the shutter. "It's a dream," I tell myself. But the body knows better. I push the shutter tight and crawl back onto the blankets. 1, 2, 3 … 4 hours, paralyzed. 'Fear-napping' is a technique I learned from a dear friend. When life is too much, too hard, when your brain is screaming, and your body is ready to rip apart: go to a room, preferably cooler than the air outside.

Make it as close to pitch as you possibly can, and just, be. Sleep if you can. Escape in the darkness. The world will be there when you wake up. For now, your only task is to be there in the dark, until the fear passes.

Of course, the fear doesn't always pass — but food, water — these small necessities pull us from our hiding places and force us to squint in the light of the sun. I call Anat. She knows him. A year or so earlier, she was our reluctant matchmaker. "He doesn't love me," I say, the words scratching at my throat for the first time. "Fucking Shtuyot. Come to me," she says, "Get on the bus."

I walk the desert path to the highway. A mirage of green sits between me and the concrete bus shelter; the exact place I last left him, dressed to go back to his training base. I shake him out of my vision as best I can and sit on the hot metal seat. Blue buttoned-down shirts, podcasts on Saturdays, head scratches, and all the love I remember — fill me.

The bus arrives. I climb up the steps, pay the driver, and make my way back to find a seat. Mostly full, I find one empty by a window and crawl in over a sleeping soldier, M-16 rested casually between his spread legs. He bristles. "Slicha," I say (Excuse me). I feel the cold tip of his gun brush against my skin. He doesn't look at me or say anything. I slip in against the dusty window. The sky is clear. I don't love you, anymore. I take a hot drink from my metal canteen and wonder: Why couldn't he look me in the eye? I feel his body beside me, the same green uniform I never quite got used to sitting beside. His eyes are closed. His tanned neck peaks out from under his collar, sleeves — rolled up as they all do, expose his forearms; cold metal still resting between his red boots.

I close my eyes. I feel his right leg press into mine. The rough cotton of his uniform — is familiar. The pressure on my thigh is slight, but constant. Am I imagining this? He shifts his weight. Maybe he's just getting comfortable? But the pressure returns and is building. His leg is pressing hard against mine now and again I'm paralyzed. I don't love you, anymore. With his eyes closed, and mine now straight ahead, he reaches his hand across his body and begins to stroke the inside of my left arm. Who is this? Why is he touching me? This isn't my soldier. Mine is still eight hours north — I know that. But maybe ... maybe his hands, entitled in their misplaced claim on my body, will disarm this grenade in my chest. Maybe if I squint ... maybe I won't know the difference.

I don't know how long I let him touch me: One minute ... two ... thirty seconds? But soon, his hand stretches further and lands just under my left breast. And I know this isn't Jon. I know these aren't his hands. This uniform is not enough. "Ma ata ose?" I manage (What are you doing?). He looks at me finally, for the first and only time, and in English replies, "I thought you wanted."

I don't know how he knew.

Chapter 10: Jake Cohen

I'm 28 and I wear a tie to work, which means I'm supposed to like the movie *Fight Club*. And since I work with books, I'm supposed to like the novel even more. But I don't.

Fight Club has never made a lot of sense to me because its defining mantra is, "You are not your job." And I am totally my job.

It doesn't matter what that job is at any given point — whatever it is, that's what I am. If you ask me what's new, I'll tell you what happened at the office that day. If you want to know what kind of mood I'm in, I'll tell you about our latest sales report. Any plans for the summer? Why yes, I'm reorganizing our filing system from chronological to alphabetical. And if you want to see me have a serious identity crisis, just tell me that I am not my job.

So the summer I'm 21 I have a problem, because I do not have a job. Which means I am nobody. Immediately prior to this I have been Jake the temp, I've been Jake the intern, Jake the intern again, Jake the consultant, Jake the freelancer, and Jake the jobless, all of which are fairly shaky foundations upon which to build yourself. And maybe that's why I get just a little too excited when I'm combing a job board and see a posting from a sightseeing company asking if I'd like to be Jake the Tour Boat Driver. Also known as, Captain Jake. All respect to Tyler Durden, but I'll take Captain Jake over Not Your Job Jake any day of the week.

So I apply. It's a small tourism company, running one-hour cruises around the Harbour, and they're looking for students to pick up summer work. Do I know anything about boats? Nope. Can't even drive a car. But they say that doesn't matter — they'll train me. But for this job I'll need to learn engine maintenance, firefighting protocols, emergency first aid. Do I have any experience with any of those things? No, but I once almost refilled the photocopier toner all by myself. Apparently that's all I need.

The two-month training program is one of the more challenging things I've ever done — and it's a little hard to be just Trainee Jake — but my fellow Captains-in-waiting and I tough it out, and soon enough we're writing our exams with Transport Canada. And then I have a card saying I'm a ship's master, and my boss is pinning four gold stripes to the epaulets of my uniform. When you go to work each day dressed like Val Kilmer in Top Gun, you are absolutely your job.

And things start to change pretty fast for me — and in a very good way. Two months before, I couldn't fix a broken shoelace, and now I'm putting out engine fires. Old guys wearing Navy hats are regularly saluting and calling me Skipper. I start saying things like "goose the throttle" and "hard over port" and "abaft the beam." I buy boat shoes, and I wear them unironically.

It feels great.

I have a few screw-ups along the way — I bump the dock, I drop a line, I scratch the paint — and I take it pretty hard, because when you are your job, you are your mistakes. But on the whole, things go well, and I start picking up extra shifts, as many as I can get. Because when you are your job, you want to work as often as possible.

There's one rule: we don't drive when it rains. And it's not for safety reasons. As much as I like to act like this is a thrilling nautical adventure, the truth is we're boating in the safest conditions in the world. We're driving giant steel canal boats, boats that feel like a tank on water, and we're always inside a sheltered harbour. Very little wind, no

Stories We Don't Tell

waves, traffic at a minimum. At no point is anyone's life ever in jeopardy. But still, we don't drive when it rains ... because it's a sightseeing tour, and there's not much to see when the windows are covered in water.

Usually this is straightforward: You wake up, you look out your window — if it's raining, you stay home. But sometimes it gets tricky. The weather can act differently on the Harbour. There can be a biblical storm downtown, and bright and sunny on the water. And the effect is doubled right around September, just as the seasons start to change ...

So August is winding down, and I'm about to leave the boats for the year and head back to school — which is a bit of a problem for me, because I am definitely not my studies, and I don't have another job lined up. So I'm cherishing every last minute I have behind the wheel.

It's a Thursday and I'm scheduled to work with Tyler, who's become my hero over the summer. Tyler looks like me — which is to say, short and maybe a little nerdy — but he drives a boat better than anyone on the Harbour, and he gets respect for that. I've seen him work magic with a diesel engine. He's performed miracles with a twin-screw, and he's been deified for his abilities with an outboard. He's trained me, taught me everything I know. I want to be Tyler.

It's a slow day — the summer is over and there are fewer and fewer tourists in the city — and it's getting late. We've been expecting rain all afternoon, but it hasn't come yet. In between shifts we keep checking the radar, and each time it says there's a storm heading our way. But it's only now that the sky's starting to get a little dark.

So Ty says, "Maybe we should shut down for the day."

But I don't want to do that. Because it's my turn to drive. So I say, "I think we're good."

Ty turns to the two families who are in line for the ride

and says, "It's probably gonna rain."

And the parents say, "It's our last day in the city, we want to go now."

So we load up the boat, pull out of the dock, and start driving west along the skyline as Tyler begins the tour.

Immediately the trouble hits.

First, the sky goes black — completely, black — like a bad special effect in a Bible movie. I turn on our running lights and hold the course. Just as I'm coming up to the island airport, lightning hits the CN Tower. I turn around to watch, and my shoulders bunch up, and when I turn back, the island airport is gone.

It's disappeared behind a solid wall of rain and mist blowing off the lake. Visibility on the Harbour has instantly gone down to nothing. And then the wind starts slamming in over the islands and kicking up waves, so big that the boat starts rocking up and down, but more like a ski that's detached from its owner and is going down the mountain unguided.

Tyler pulls the microphone away from his face and says, "I think we should probably turn around."

And I say, "That's a good idea."

But then three things happen all at once:

- A sailboat that's trying to get back to dock capsizes right in front of us.
- My windshield wiper snaps off.
- And our gigantic foam and fibreglass life rafts that are sitting on our roof get caught in the wind, blow away, and take the sliding roof with them.

So now we're not driving a steel tank so much a big canoe with no oars, and everyone's blindfolded.

Stories We Don't Tell

My breath gets caught in my chest, and Tyler runs down the aisle, jumps onto a bench and grabs the roof before it can fall into the Harbour. As he's standing on the seats, holding the roof shut, I push open the now wiperless front window with one hand, getting drenched by the storm, and with my other shaking hand try to safely navigate around the upside-down sailboat. But I can barely see, and the boat's having trouble turning in the waves.

Tyler shouts up to the wheel to ask if I'd like him to take over.

Now Tyler's a senior captain, and he has years of sailing experience from before he even started this job, and no matter what happens, he can get us back safely. I, on the other hand, am a rookie in the middle of my first storm and there's a really good chance I'm going to have a panic attack before we get home. But I say, "I got this." Because if he lets go of the roof, it's gone, and if I let go of the wheel, I don't know what's going to happen.

At this point, we start spinning around in the waves, looking blindly for our dock, and the parents on board are freaking out, but the kids are loving it. And I think that's a good sign.

Eventually, we manage to get back to our slip, and I'm feeling a little like a hero, but just as we're pulling in, I see something confusing coming through the rain. Our neighbour, a sleek, manoeuvrable twin-propeller boat is turning around and heading back out into the Harbour. This doesn't make sense, because the Harbour is not where you want to be right now. Where you want to be is in the safe, warm dock.

But I don't have a choice. Our neighbour is heading right for us, so I have to get out of the way. I shout an apology to our passengers and start cranking the wheel. As we head back into the Harbour, I can hear the blood beating in my temples. My arms hurt and my eyes are burning. And all the fun is gone. The boat is rocking and shaking and it really does feel like something bad is going to happen. And now the parents are calm, but the kids are freaking out, and that's a bad sign.

As I try to get out of the way of the oncoming boat, Tyler, who is still holding our roof closed, asks again if I want him to take over. I say, "No, I think I got this." But by now it's very clear to everyone on board that I do not got this.

My entire uniform is soaked through from holding open the front window, and my glasses are covered in water. And the way the boat is rocking ... someone else should probably take over.

But I power through, and after a horrible ten minutes, we get back to our slip. This time our path is clear — I've got a straight shot at our dock. I am Luke Skywalker lining up for my attack on the Death Star. We are about to blow this thing and go home.

But just as I start slowing down to make it into port, I begin to understand why our neighbour had to pull out and head back into the Harbour: the wind is too strong in our slip.

Our spot is sandwiched between two condo towers, and the angle of the storm is kicking up a wind tunnel right where we need to park. As soon as I start to slow down, I lose all control and the boat blows right towards the centre of the dock. If I continue, I am not going to make it. I'm going to drive us directly into the wooden planks and steel girders of Pier 6.

But if you give up that wheel, you are not your job.

And now I'm starting to get that it's a problem that I am not my friendships, I'm not my family, I'm not my hobbies,

Stories We Don't Tell

I'm not my t-shirt collection, I'm not my love of coffee — I'm my job.

This time Tyler doesn't ask if I want him to take over. He just watches. So I have to shout, "Ty, I need a hand."

I run to grab the roof before it can fall off, and Ty takes the wheel.

Instantly I feel like crap, and everything else gets better. Ty gets us in safely, the clouds blow away, the sun comes out, and our very terrified passengers get off and go home.

And I, in that minute, am not my job. I'm not really anything.

So five years later, I'm on a boat, again, heading into another storm, and my trainee turns to me and says, "I don't think I got this." And I, Senior Captain Jake, Bachelor of Arts Jake, Publishing Apprentice Jake, Dungeons & Dragons level 5 elf mage Jake, boyfriend Jake, aspiring amateur pastry chef Jake, but still God-damn Captain Jake — I take the wheel, flip on the running lights, and take us back to dock.

Chapter 11: Maya Fromstein

Dear third-year geography students. I have just spent many hours submerged in the world that lives inside your heads that you have unleashed and submitted for these assignments and I am coming out for a breather. I was not able to give you all personal feedback because despite the wild amounts of racism and white superiority pouring out of your papers that I have so neatly alphabetized, it was not the assignment's intention for you to really see how you were doing anyway. That is not your fault, third-years. I sit down to read this latest assignment, a quick in-class 'watch this movie and make any sort of connection' sort of assignment. I let it blast through my computer speakers. I sit alone in my office, and when I am not distraught from your responses, I dance away in my chair.

Welcome to my Saturday night. You do not make for good company. I know your lives are more than just this document I have marked up in blue pen. I read your assignments, and I imagine what your lives are like outside these narrow margins. You obviously didn't do the readings, and in their stead, I imagine you living the life I never had. Choosing not to do school to spend time with real friends, making real relationships, maybe just catching up on sleep or your favourite show. It's not your fault that I didn't live a life outside of school. That I wasn't more than my grades, my assignments, my weight. It is not your fault that I envy you and that it makes it hard to see straight. It is not your fault that with every wrong answer I picture another distant, perfect moment that I am forced to come to terms with the fact that I have lost those moments. That I don't know what coming to terms with that even means. That with every wrong answer I mourn the life I never had. And on most days, especially the sleepless nights, I imagine I never will.

The mental illness is no one's fault, it doesn't matter. My undergrad was different from how I picture yours. In between your 'could not be more wrong' responses and imaginings of a life I do not live, I'm drawn back to my own third-year, fall semester, finals. Although my family and I never really discussed my anxiety, we hadn't put that all-encompassing label on it yet. I must've recognized something was going on because for the first time, I was taking fewer courses than normal. This, for the girl who didn't take a spare in high school, might have been an indicator. It is not unusual for me to call my parents in tears, more and more frequently of late but tonight, today, something is different. I have never heard of a true panic attack before. I have never yet recognized that inability to breathe, the racing heart, the uncontrollable sobbing. My parents are in different places and not knowing what to do, they maneuver a conference call between all three of us.

The two of them are confused as they try to decipher what is going on from the unintelligible sounds and sobs I am powerless to restrain. I am the good student, I am well-behaved, I do what I am told. I follow instructions. It is alarming for all of us that I cannot follow the instructions most critical now. Stop crying. Take a deep breath. Go write your exam. Once or twice I think I can manage, I think I can choose to be okay and we all hang up. Only I can't, and my body paralyzes anew. My legs give up on me, and I fall in the cramped bathroom stall I've shoved myself in. Careful not to take up too much space. Careful not to let anyone see how I feel. Eventually, I admit defeat and this fight, me against my body, me against my anxiety, I lose. I couldn't follow the instructions.

Stories We Don't Tell

I leave the washroom stall, but I cannot escape this. I move gingerly, wounded towards the doctor's office. The doctor gives me an unconvincing note for an unconvincing story that I make up. Something about all the puke. I don't dare tell her that for once this is a lie. I don't dare tell her that she is the first clinician to whom I've ever mentioned puking and problem together. I fear that if I tell her the truth she will tell me to suck it up, that this is not a valid excuse. I fear it is not a valid excuse and that I should have sucked it up. I say none of this, and instead, I feebly lie about all the puke.

The room still spins, and my heart still races. Nobody buys my story. The doctor doesn't ask me if I'm okay, and I don't tell her that I'm not. It is months before my very first therapist tells me that what I had was a panic attack. It is still more months before I realize that I have had many before. Moments where I've told myself I should've sucked it up. It is not as if I'm new to stress, I am not, but I have a way of coping. I have a release valve for when things get to be too much, for when these pesky emotions threaten to boil over, but it didn't work this time.

My eating disorder is supposed to work. My eating disorder therapist three years later will tell me my anxiety and unstable mood, these panic attacks, that they will improve with treatment. The therapist calls my coping mechanism symptoms and says they actually make it harder for me to think straight, to regain my calm after the storm. We find out together that my depression and anxiety are not because of the eating disorder. Eating disorders often have friends. The therapist, the books, the help groups all tell me that. It seems both myself and the eating disorder are lousy at choosing company.

It is not your fault, third-year geography students, that I spent my third year in such anxiety and with such a familiar and dangerous means of coping. It is not your fault that I didn't have a choice to do the fun things I see you do instead of school. It is not your fault I see your poor grades as a reflection of your perfect life and not the possibility that you had the same third-year I had. It only makes sense for a library seating hundreds of caffeinated and nervous students to have two washroom stalls on every other floor. This meant that my third-year was spent strategizing on how to have one with privacy. The handicapped washroom on the fourth floor, the abandoned washrooms on the second, careful not to let anyone see how I feel. Careful not to let anyone see how I cope. Even countless other decisions, choices made that I didn't know I was making, that I didn't get to make.

Looking back as I do with each of your assignments, with every wrong answer, I am too often filled with the sadness that comes from realizing how much I gave up. A sadness that comes reliving those moments and seeing over and over again how differently my life could have been if I had real friends that I could talk to. If the ones I had told had cared enough to listen. If I had known that I couldn't just suck it up, that I needed and deserved help. If I hadn't changed the topic and all those uncomfortable jokes made about my body by strangers, teachers, friends.

It is not your fault that the way you frame choice stings me. That every time you say that if them poor Africans would maybe just get jobs, maybe they wouldn't be so goddamned poor. Maybe if they knew how precious you think the environment is they wouldn't cut down trees to build their homes or fuel their stoves. That if they would only choose to be happier, choose to be less poor, if they would just choose to fix their problems, then all of this would go away. It is not your fault that I share that voice. That every time you frame choice that way, I have to fight harder and harder against the voice in my head that tells me that if I had just chosen to try harder, chosen to not be sick, then I wouldn't have to be where I am.

The playlist I listen to while I repeatedly transport between your present responses and my past missed opportunities is one that I made for my housemates in my last semester of undergrad. I had finally made the friends that I had wanted to make all the years prior. I had finally found someone, just one, that I could talk to about both of our struggles with eating disorders. I look back on that semester, by far some of the happiest four months of my life and I think, if only I had done something different. If I had made different choices, maybe I could have had this the whole time.

Chapter 12: Stefan Hostetter

"You have five minutes, I'm sorry, I cannot give you any more time." I nod, turn down the steep steps and onto the Brooklyn sidewalk.

Fuck. Fuck, fuck, fuck. Redial, I hear the giggle at the beginning of his custom message, hang-up. Fuck.

The already sizable ball of anxiety that sits in my chest begins to expand further, pushing the air out of my lungs. Without thinking, my feet begin to move, away from the bus, away from everyone else, I have five minutes.

Left, left, left my wife and 45 kids in a starving condition with nothing but gingerbread, think I did, right? Right, right from the country Hayford Strawford shift by jingle left, left.

My parents separated when I was 4. My sister was 9, and my brother 3. Throughout our childhood our weird split level family was held together by the incredible work of my parents, who remained remarkably amicable. I can close my eyes and see myself in the back seat of my dad's van, brother in front of me, sister riding shotgun, as the street lights of the Danforth flashed through our car windows. Dad lived in walking distance to our school so on the nights we were at our mom's he'd drive the half-hour to pick us up and bring us home to sleep. Being in transit became something like a third home. A home that, often, only Dave and I shared.

Left, left ... I reached the cross street, the mouth of the steps up from the subway gaped at me. Mocking me in its emptiness. I'd just left a bus and 45 activists in a dubious position with nothing but a promise I'd be right back with him. But I didn't know where he was and really didn't even know where I was beyond the name of the one street where the buses were parked. When I'd volunteered to lead one of the five buses to New York never once did it occur to me that I might not be able to be on the bus back, but here, now, I was four minutes away from that reality. I frantically glance up and down the street and still don't see him. I call again, voicemail. Fuck.

I look back and see the four remaining buses, all ready to make a convoy back to Toronto. All waiting for one last person. My seatmate, my brother, Dave. I'd learned a lot about the regulations that long-distance bus drivers face during this trip, and the most important one was that they legally were not allowed to be working for longer than 12 consecutive hours. The bus ride to Toronto was ten hours long, and they'd been waiting for us to board for the last two. My anxiety had now transcended beyond anything I'd felt before. I couldn't hold together a thought for longer than a single brain synapse. My breath was shallow, eyes darted everywhere and then back to my phone. Where are you!

Three minutes.

My phone buzzes. A picture I took months before in Portugal pops up. Dave's standing, his back turned to me looking out into the Atlantic ocean.

"Where are you?!" I half yell into the phone.

"I'm just outside the station." His voice is indignant. "Where are you? The bus is on Clinton, right?"

"What? FUCK, NO! Where are you?!" My voice is shaking, I've officially lost control.

"I'm on Clinton, where are you?"

"Have you walked away from a main street?"

"Yes."

"Go towards it."

And I take off. My back to the setting sun that has just begun to peak around an old red brick walk-up. I have to trust that he got off at the right stop. I have to trust that he's close. I have to trust that I'm heading in the right direction. I have to trust we'll find each other.

Each stride pulls me further apart, I'm stretched out, my body ready to snap back to all of the responsibilities the bus represents at the second I can no longer withstand the tension. I had chosen to guess that he was east of me because the through street was more obvious, and if we were going to make it, he couldn't be far.

Two minutes.

As I run, I shout into my phone.

"Do you see someone who is running like a fucking maniac?"

"What?"

"Do you see me?!"

I stop abruptly at the corner of the next street, glance up to the street sign and discover I had guessed correctly and yet, he is still nowhere to be seen.

"Where are you!?"

A woman, sitting on a pink folding chair at the side of a convenience store, glances at me and gestures across the street. I follow her arm and see him. His bag slung over his shoulder, walking south towards me and the intersection.

"Dave," I pant into the phone. My voice trembles with a cocktail of panic only vaguely controlled by the adrenaline coursing through my veins, "I need you to run."

Left, left ... My mom taught us this marching song she'd picked up as a child, and when we went for especially long walks we'd sing it. Dave and I travelled everywhere together. To school in the morning, home, whichever one it was that day, every night.

In grade 6, my class went on a trip for three days up north, which at the time, by my recollection was the longest consecutive streak of separation we would have experienced since he came into this world. My body revolted, the first night after being kept up in part to due homesickness I vomited from the top bunk all over my friend's bags. A life on the road can only be seen in segments by those of fixed address, a childhood spent in transit can only be seen and understood in full by those on the train with you.

One minute.

I hang up, slip my phone into my pocket, and take off back in the direction I'd just come, refusing to look back to see if he was following. Foot underneath foot, tired legs pounding into the solid sidewalk cement. The sun still peaks around the red brick, now half blinding me as I try to dodge the confused pedestrians. Everything I'd brought with me was left on the bus so there was nothing to weigh me down. Halfway back up the block, out of the corner of my eye, I catch movement from the other side of the street. Someone is matching my pace, another few strides and Dave's distinctive curly hair comes into view. His olive green backpack sagging and pulled backwards by the wind. I steal a glance across the street and see him sprinting. Running with the vigour to match every ounce of anxiety that my now expanded lungs were forcing out of my chest. Stride for stride he matched me. Two neurons from the same synapse.

Left, left, left my wife and 45 kids in a starving condition with nothing but gingerbread, think I did, right? Right, right from the country Hayford Strawford shift by jingle left.

I round the corner as he darts through traffic to get onto our street. In front of us, only one bus remains. I beat Dave to the door, but stand to the side so he can board first, as he does I turn to follow him. Nodding to the bus driver, stealing a glance to the woman who's kept my bus distracted, trying to convey my thanks without words, and slump into my seat, Dave's adjusting his bag beside me. The bus pulls away and into New York traffic. We don't speak of what just happened, of what just almost happened. We don't need to.

Chapter 13: Rob Shirkey

"Dad, I think I made a mistake, I don't think I want to be in law school."

I was two weeks in. I hated it.

I had just spent four years of my life in undergrad studying for tests and writing papers that no one would ever see. I was sick of highlighting textbooks. I was all schooled out and eager to get out into the real world to start making a difference.

But law school was always the plan. I thought: If I were a lawyer, people would take my ideas a little more seriously. Sure, it's credentialism, it's not fair, but that's just how things work. I'd play the game, become a lawyer, and get better access to decision-makers so I could start to change things.

But, when I moved out West to start school at the University of Victoria, I found myself wondering, "How did I get here?" I had a great job doing environmental work with a prestigious organization and I left. For what? Three more years of highlighting textbooks and writing papers that no one would ever see? It weighed me down. I didn't want to do it. I couldn't do it. I was done with school. I wanted to get out there and start having an impact.

So, two weeks after moving to B.C. to start law school, I phoned home.

"Dad, I think I made a mistake, I don't think I want to be in law school."

"Rob, there is no fucking way you're quitting law school."

It's not how I hoped the conversation would go.

Eventually, we landed on this: It made sense for me to stay for at least the first semester, to get a better sample

Stories We Don't Tell

period and make a more informed decision. Plus, I was already paid up for the four months so why not just stick it out? I'd then come back home for Christmas, and we would talk about whether or not to continue.

Of course, we both knew that he wasn't even supposed to be around that Christmas.

You see, not too long before I left for law school, Dad was diagnosed with a rare and aggressive type of cancer. By aggressive, I mean that everyone who gets it dies. The five-year survival rate for people in his condition is actually 0%. In Dad's case, doctors said that he wasn't likely to make it to the end of that year. So, that September, when I hopped on a plane from Toronto to Victoria, I thought I was saying my final goodbye.

It was a tough semester, but I made it. And, for some reason, Dad did too.

That Christmas, he made me an offer.

"Rob, law school is important, you may not see it right now, but I think one day you will. I tell you what: We both know my prognosis. We both know that I'm not even supposed to be here right now. So how about this: You stay in school for three years and finish the degree, and I'll hang around long enough to witness you do it."

I looked at him. I considered it. He had lost weight since I left for school. His skin was jaundiced. He wasn't even supposed to be here right now. The survival rate is zero.

The offer ... part of me felt coerced, resentful. But part of me ... I said yes.

We shook hands. The bargain was made. I would finish law school, and he would live long enough to witness it.

Several months went by. The patients with the same type of cancer in his study group who were being treated by an experimental medication had all died. Dad was the only one alive. Doctors were puzzled.

Another test group. Vary the treatment. Several months later: all dead, but one. Dad.

This is how three years of law school went. He had ups and downs with his health, but he had a promise to keep.

We had a lot of phone conversations during that period.

"Dad, it's so beautiful out here. I just walked along the shoreline to get to school and saw two massive eagles."

"Dad, I've been hanging out with a really cool girl. Last night we made a blanket fort and read stories to each other. I think it's getting serious."

I'd also call him when I was down and needed support. Sometimes, with the three hour time difference, I'd ask him if he could call me early in the morning to wake me up. He would, and I'd get a nice "Good morning, Rob" to start my day. While I was definitely sick of highlighting textbooks and definitely still wanted to quit, hearing his voice reminded me that I had a promise to keep.

During the last few weeks of my final semester of school, Dad's voice started to sound different, weaker. I remember calling my mom to get her perspective. She happens to be a physician who works with cancer patients. She confirmed that it would be his last down. He didn't have much longer.

I had completed all my exams. All my courses were done. I just had to hand in one final assignment, and I would complete the requirements of the degree.

I had a really hard time finishing that assignment. Completing it would mean that I would fulfill my end of the bargain. Dad would be free to let go. For the first time in seven years of school, I actually asked my prof for an extension.

Eventually though, I did finish it.

I phoned home. "Dad, I just handed in my last assignment.

I finished law school."

I didn't have an articling job lined up. In fact, I didn't have any work lined up at all. I just wanted to spend a bit of time with him. I just wanted to come home.

My dad loved newspapers. It was his thing.

My routine that summer in Toronto was the same every morning. I would wake up early, put on a t-shirt and shorts, and load my pockets with quarters. I would quietly walk by my dad's room, see that he was still asleep, and leave home to walk to the corner of York Mills and Leslie. There, I would reach into my pockets and plug my quarters into four newspaper boxes: the Toronto Star, the Toronto Sun, The Globe and Mail, and the National Post.

When I got back home, I'd head to my dad's room, sit on his bed, and wait for him to get up so we could spend the day reading the news together.

It was how we spent that last month.

Eventually, I ended up finding work for an environmental NGO. It helped me get back on my feet. Later, I decided to article and practise law. Two years ago, I launched a small non-profit that's doing some really unique climate change advocacy. It's getting legislative traction in several communities across North America and actually getting media attention around the world.

Every now and again, I still feel this urge to call him.

"Dad, check out the Toronto Star. I'm in it!"

"Dad, the project is in the Sun, the Globe, the Post."

"Dad, it's getting passed into law!"

"Dad, I've been feeling tired lately. Can you call me in the morning to help me get out of bed again?"

Last year, I wrote a 40-page legal report for municipal staff to help advance my climate change project. A law prof in Australia came across it and contacted me to do an

Stories We Don't Tell

interview over Skype.

"What? You actually read it? You mean, all 40 pages?"

People are reading what I wrote.

The project is now featured in his textbook. It's also in a textbook in France, a textbook in Canada, a design publication in Sweden. It's spreading. Last year, I found myself in B.C. giving a lecture to a packed room in the very same law school that I had once wanted to quit. It felt surreal.

None of this would be happening if I didn't have the legal background to move this project forward. None of this would be happening if I wasn't able to have conversations with politicians that begin, "Hi, I'm a lawyer who's running this climate change organization... ." It buys cred.

Sometimes I want to call him up and say, "Dad. You were right. Thanks."

Chapter 14: Marcus Hinds

"This is gorgeous" she said. To which I responded, "Yeah isn't it just great?"

She walked all around it inspecting the trim, the details, the paint job, everything!

I said "here, look" while opening the hood I explained to her how it worked. "It's got a 3-litre direct injection naturally aspirated engine with double overhead camshafts and Valve Over technology with tiptronic shifting". She looked at me with a side glance and a dead stare right in the eyes and paused. With a serious look on her face she quipped "Boy, you better not get any ideas with my car".

"Mom, come on, you know better don't you?" "Fine!" she rebutted, and with that she walked away to the back of the house leaving me to admire her brand new Opel Vectra, imported directly from Europe. The dealerships on the island had a way of taking your money and manipulating you for both time and extra money whenever something went wrong with your car. It was for this reason that my Dad and I decided to do everything ourselves, and by everything, I mean the purchasing and importation, servicing and maintenance, licensing and insurance applications.

I felt very excited about this new vehicle, almost like a big kid with a new toy. Exactly like a big kid with a new toy. I felt very excited about change and having something new in my life after the way college was going. I had decided to continue living at home during college to save some money and to be honest, ease of access to food and other amenities très useful for a college student. I found college to be easy and a breeze to begin with, I didn't see what all the hype and studying long hours was about. Maybe I was doing something I was passionate about and it came naturally, or maybe I was just simply approaching it wrong. Either way I wasn't sure, but somewhere in between the two, I had picked up street racing. It happened subliminally I guess, from hearing all the budding engineers in my class talk about cars day in and day out. My peers. It didn't help that my lecture theatres were next to a main thoroughfare, so I'd be seeing, and hearing tuners and racers pass by the college every day. That didn't help the situation one bit.

You see, there, our buildings are made of concrete and really large louvers are built in in order to let natural fresh air circulate. The wind blows constantly. With construction like this, you will certainly hear the outdoors and anything that is happening therein. You will certainly hear car horns, you will certainly hear burn outs from tuner cars, you will certainly hear thumping stereos so powerful they sound amplified times and times again. Outside my college was a noisy hustling bustling place and being stationed on the fifth and highest floor of the building didn't help anything. It just meant that we had a bird's eye view of the street and parking lot below, almost like the booth at a race track! The sounds of the surrounding streets traveled to us directly, clearly and loudly as if amplified like those same car stereos. I often stared through these windows day dreaming of working on progressive projects through the company that I founded and discussing the work behind it with National Geographic on shows like Modern Marvels, Megastructures and Megacities. I thought engineering at college would be more hands on than this, more in depth and gory, more of a challenge. I didn't want to sit there and listen to how and why Plato came up with his theories and ethics. I didn't want to learn how to speak and write English, and least of all did I want to sit there and listen to what engineers do

Stories We Don't Tell

for society. I wanted to get out there and build, destroy, construct, deploy, shape, employ and ply my craft. The fact that what I envisioned had not come to light seemed to be a common thread here.

After cleaning and inspecting this new specimen of a vehicle I decided to take it out for a spin. And little did I know the spin we would go. As I roared through the countryside streets, well paved and sidelines covered with bush on either side, I got a thrill from seeing the shrubbery ruffle as I passed. Of course I was hanging out the window to see this while driving, all the while inspecting the wheels as they turned and listening to that new European goddess of an engine purr under the command of my foot at the pedals. My phone rang and it was my best friend Enrico inviting me to come race on an underused stretch of road nearby. Excitement getting the better of me again. Excitement always got the better of me.

Lamberts was a stretch of country road with a 500-metre straight, a series of visible S chicane corners just before going into another 300-metre straight, a blind U with 60-foot cliff on either side and ending at a blind but busy intersection. Treacherous to say the least but I knew the lamberts stretch was an avoided piece of road and hardly anyone ever used it so I knew I was fine. I pulled up to the line and smiled. "Your time to beat is 3 minutes," Enrico said. I revved my engine to let him and spectators know I was ready. That European Goddess under the hood was ready and I could tell.

I pulled off the line hard and powerful and in no time I got to the first corner and I realized this thing was fast and powerful. I braked and turned and flew through he first corner, smiling to myself that I had gotten familiar with the steering and braking in such a short period of time. I could feel that I was way ahead of the allotted time and I began laughing at those Japanese and American opponents that I had. I got to the last corner before I was ready to let her rip for the second straight stretch and what I saw directly in front me invoked sheer terror, horror and pandemonium inside me. A truck! Crawling at 20 km per hour in the middle of the road in a corner, waiting for god knows what. I was coming fast and I had to think equally as fast. I swerved left and everything thing around me became intensely still as the car angled towards a neighbouring field. It's as if it had a mind of its own and the thought that I was out of control hit me and it hit me hard. Or maybe that was an object in the car. The vehicle had left the road and I was now field borne. I swerved right to try to break the slide and regain some control. I thought maybe I was doing something I was passionate about and it came naturally, or maybe I was just simply doing it wrong.

 As that second swerve made me start to spin, everything was still and slow around me. I sat holding my breath and observing every millisecond in sheer terror, horror and disbelief. My phone was airborne, inches away from my face. My house keys were also in mid drift. My shoes that I'd taken off to drive in were magically in mid air as well. Every spin that the car took reminded more and more of my life. Like maybe how I had decided to continue living at home to save some money and to be honest, ease of access to food and other amenities très useful for a college student. Or maybe like how I didn't quite grasp the basic concepts of Engineering like I should, much like I didn't know the responsibility of having a car.

 The fact that what I envisioned had not come to light seemed to be common.

 The spinning went on for what seemed like an eternity, and I helpless at the helm, desperate to regain control.

Stories We Don't Tell

It took me a few seconds to get out of the spin, oddly contrasted to my college experience. Easy to get into, not understanding completely how you got there and not sure if you're enjoying the ride. The spin stopped and I sat there in my driver's seat deep in the field and far from the road. My feeling of bewilderment and sabotage, and basic confusion by what had just taken place was only evident through the fact that the contents of the car were wildly shifted. That and the fact that I wasn't where I was supposed to be. I was dizzy and in mental delusion. How could this happen, so quickly, so easily. But yet, why wasn't it worse? It could have been worse. It should have been worse. I was shaken and clearly in shock and disbelief.

I hopped out to look for any damage to the Goddess. My mother would kill me. No damage thankfully, None!

Chapter 15: Tyler Blacquiere

In the journey of your life there are certain moments that change the way you perceive, understand and interact with the world around you. Certain moments that, for better or worse, irreparably shape your reality. On a cold day in late February 2014, sitting in a room with 20 or so strangers brought together by shared experience, I encountered one such moment. Spurred on by an unexpected but not altogether surprising realization, tiny atoms of struggle and challenge, strength and perseverance, began to swirl together in a dense mass.

Over the course of the succeeding two-hour support session, a rare cosmic event would fuse these particles together in a ball of superheated energy. The result would be a new sun at the centre of my, and her, solar system, around which the planets of our lives would revolve, for the months and years to come.

She and I had met a few months shy of a year earlier, and it had started like any textbook romance: I, weary from a lengthy video editing trance, stumbled out of my room and ... found her in my apartment.

Odd, I know, but her presence had a simple explanation. She was, as I'd learn, the lifelong best friend of a friend. That friend also happened to be dating my current roommate. She (the apartment stranger), having spent a semester in Panama, was back in Toronto for the first time in months. And so, all of them (her, friend, roommate) were in the apartment.

As I appeared from around the corner toward our living room, what should have been a simple greeting morphed into a social train wreck, as I (still only halfway in the room) awkwardly tried to reach over the top of the couch and over the head of my roommate, to shake her hand.

After a technically brief but conceptually eternal series of puzzled glances and stuttered movements, I completed my entry into the living room, and we greeted with a hug.

The rest of the night passed by in a flurry of laughter, weird YouTube videos and terrible drink combinations (as they do). For the record, past-tenant sink top cupboard blue curacao and raspberry sourpuss do not a delicious cocktail make.

Now, I can't tell you that it was the fabled love at first sight, but whatever it was, I was pretty smitten. And it sort of just grew from there.

I'd find out about her eating disorder sometime around late August or early September.

Now when I say that I "found out" about her eating disorder, it was really the most minimal of conditions that lead to the truth of that phrase.

"I have an eating disorder." Full stop. Or, as a former English professor would always say, "Period, end of paragraph."

Wanting to let her tell me things on her own terms and time, I didn't press for more. And so, was left sitting in the somewhat vague position of knowing that eating disorders were a thing that existed, and not much more beyond that.

So I kept waiting — ready to be there when she needed me, but otherwise, feeling pretty useless. It would be a few months — late November or early December — until either: the eating disorder began to take a stronger hold, or she became more comfortable telling me about it.

Slowly at first, and then with greater frequency, the number of conversations we'd have about the difficulties it was causing her would grow. By January, it was becoming increasingly clear that the eating disorder was a force that she couldn't tackle on her own.

With the growing impact it was having on both of our lives, I would start attending the family and friends support session at Sheena's Place — a community centre offering group support for individuals struggling with eating disorders — where she had been taking some sessions.

And so that was how I ended up, one cold day in late January 2014, sitting in a room with twenty or so strangers brought together by shared experience, watching an unexpected but not altogether surprising realization kick-start the formation of a new sun at the centre of my, and her, solar system.

Walking into that first session — my first real steps into the more clinical world of eating disorders — I knew (at least in theory) that this was a long road. I knew that this wasn't the sort of thing where you pop a Fisherman's Friend and then everything is a-ok.

But it wasn't until I was in that room, surrounded by twenty or so strangers ...

It wasn't until the story from one parent, of their daughter's sudden and harsh slide back into relapse ...

It wasn't until the sixty-something year old man, there for his wife who for thirty years of their marriage had been dealing with her eating disorder ...

... that the length and inclination of the road we were setting out on, and just how completely our lives would come to revolve around this, really sunk in.

They say that when faced with situations of hyperarousal or acute stress, we have a physiological reaction known as fight-or-flight. In that moment, in that room, faced with the enormity of this faceless thing that had forced its way into her, and now, my life — I knew I wasn't going anywhere.

There was no question.

Common wisdom is that there are plenty of fish in the sea, or, in keeping with the space metaphor, plenty of galaxies in the sky. And though I didn't know what to expect or how I would handle it, this mysterious and unknown it, I knew that this particular solar system, with her, and I — and now, this new sun — felt like home. And I wasn't about to be uprooted.

But that didn't make it any easier.

By late February of last year, it was becoming clear that the group sessions that she was attending through Sheena's Place weren't enough to combat the punches her eating disorder was throwing.

"I need you to understand. This thing, if left unchecked, could kill you. You're standing on a train track, and you need to make the decision about whether you're going to step out of the way."

She, her parents, and I are sitting in a family-based treatment session, and the therapist finishes this statement and takes a long look around the room.

I find a sudden fascination in the floor, and so can't tell what everyone else is thinking. I just keep replaying the therapist's words over and over in my mind.

This thing could kill her. This thing, that I can't see or touch or interact with. This thing that I try desperately to identify and understand and help her combat on a daily basis, feeling of failure often not far behind. This thing, this mystery, could kill her. Her, this very real, very present person that, in contrast, I can understand, and hold, and love.

And it's terrifying.

There's no handbook on caring for someone with an eating disorder. Every person's unique reality and experience

Stories We Don't Tell

with the illness guarantees the truth of this statement, and though, ultimately, it is up to her to best this thing, I can't help but feel the need to do more. Even if I don't know how.

This family-based treatment session is the answer to the "what next?" that came when it was clear that Sheena's Place wasn't enough.

The treatment is one normally used with young children who are struggling with eating disorders and involves the parents taking complete control of all things food-related — from purchasing, to preparation, to portioning, and meal supervision. The goal is to restore the patient back to a healthy, target weight. The logic is that maintaining this healthy weight is a crucial first step toward long term recovery, and the treatment of the eating disorder's other, more internal challenges.

Though very successful with young patients, the amount of control necessitated by the treatment method becomes harder as the patient matures and develops more autonomy. The study we're in now, though, is an attempt to adapt these methods to an older audience.

What this means, in practice, is that she decides who she brings in (her parents, and myself) and then we take responsibility for buying, preparing, cooking and portioning all of her meals, and for doing everything we can to ensure that she eats them. Ultimately, we take consensual responsibility for guiding her journey back to a healthy, target weight, and together, we all decide on the strategies to make this happen. It also means weekly, hour-long group sessions with the therapist, to take stock of progress and talk through any challenges.

Even if we had been doing nothing else at all — if we lived in an eating disorder vacuum where we could pause time and deal with this, and this alone, it would still be overwhelming. But that was, of course, not our reality.

As the days went by, I began to feel like I was trying to separate myself into two people, coming apart at the seams to be in two places at once, stretching from my downtown Adelaide and Spadina office, to our Bathurst and Eglinton-ish apartment, or wherever she happened to be that day.

The challenge was equally physical and mental. Physical in that I was waking up earlier to ensure there was food prepared for both breakfast and lunch, and snacks, and coming home to do all of the dinner prep and cooking, regardless of the day I'd had. There was no more, "fuck it, I'm having cereal."

Mental, in that while trying to focus on the hectic nonsense that is a full-time job at a small and overly ambitious Canadian charity, I'd try to ensure, from afar, that she was eating two meals and two snacks. Sometimes this meant text message reminders. Sometimes this meant phone calls or in-progress Snapchats of meals. Sometimes, on days when things were very difficult, it meant Skyping her from a meeting room during lunch, to help her through it.

Adding to all of this was the fact that, in the beginning, I had no idea what to give her to eat in order to restore her weight. I didn't even eat properly — whatever that even meant — how was I supposed to be in charge of someone else's restorative nutrition? In those early days, my answer to everything seemed to be: "put some nuts on it!"

Some days were easier than others. Some days I was in a better mood, and so cooking was easier. Some days she was in a better mood, and so eating came easier. I didn't always know what to say, and I didn't always know what to do. And I never did get comfortable controlling someone else's life in such an extreme way. I never did get comfortable giving her portions that I myself would have struggled to finish.

And I constantly worried about the potential impact that all of this was having on our relationship. As I absorbed what felt like an impossible amount of responsibility over her life, it felt hard to stop us sliding away from a relationship of partners and toward a relationship of caregiver and receiver. I didn't know if anything was really changing, I just had this fear of waking up one day and discovering that something had. I just wanted to do what was best for her.

I just wanted to see her recover.

But things only got harder before they got easier. At our next FBT session, we'd learn that she had lost more weight.

I knew this wasn't my fault. In theory. But in practice, I couldn't help but feel a crushing sense of guilt. After learning the news, I sat in a state of shock, as if a mortar had just gone off near our trench — in this battle with the eating disorder — and all I could hear was the ringing sound of having failed her, all other conversation fading into the background.

I couldn't stop my mind from racing through the scenarios of the preceding few days, trying desperately to discover what I could or should have done differently. The times when I could have added another spoonful or a bigger snack. Maybe I should I have put some nuts on it?!

I knew that it wasn't my fault and I knew that she would tell me the same. It was — as the therapist had said — her job to step off the train tracks. But there's a difference between understanding and accepting.

As the weeks wore on, it would get harder still. Less so because of the eating disorder itself, and more so because of my own struggles and unhappiness at work. More and more I found myself coming home without the energy to do all of the cooking for that night's dinner, or for tomorrow's lunch. But like a soldier with PTSD flashbacks, I couldn't re-live that feeling of having failed her.

Throughout all of this, she kept telling me that she was there to listen to my struggles, too. That it was a two-way street. And I knew that she meant it. That she wanted me to share.

But there's a difference between understanding and accepting.

It becomes all too easy in situations like these, I had learned, to convince yourself to just bury it.

I got better and better at doing what she would often excitedly tell me about trees. "Do you know what happens to trees when they get hurt?!" She'd ask, maybe forgetting that we'd had this exact conversation at least a few times already, maybe just really stoked on trees. "They compartmentalize!"

And so I did, too. I threw myself wholly into being a good eating disorder recovery partner and packed all of my stresses, anxieties and fears into boxes, simply sprouting my limbs in new directions when emotions got in the way.

And there was a lot to compartmentalize. The fear of not doing enough. The guilt that came on days when I forgot to check in with her to see if she'd eaten. The self-criticism that came any time I felt like complaining about everything I was trying to hold together. The worry that all of this — our new rotation around the eating disorder at the centre of our solar system — was irreparably changing the dynamic of our relationship.

It was during these harder weeks when speaking with a close friend who found herself in a comparable situation, that I learned an important truth. After pouring out many of my compartments for the first time, piling them up on the café floor, she passed on words that a friend had recently given her: "Sometimes you just need someone to tell you — man, that sucks, I'm sorry. That's so hard."

And she was right. It sounds so simple, and so surface level, and so banal, but when you're locked in the Gollum/Sméagol guilt spiral of "this is so exhausting | But she's your partner! | I'm struggling a lot, too, though | She's the one with the eating disorder — how can you complain?" Sometimes, you just need tacit acknowledgement that it's okay to feel like that. It is hard. And it is exhausting. And there are days when you want to give up. But admitting as much doesn't lessen your devotion or commitment — it just means you're human.

As time went on we began to find a rhythm. Though I still didn't really feel like I knew what I was doing, I began to learn strategies and pick up on visual cues that alerted me to how she was feeling. Like how eating somewhere other than the kitchen often made difficult meals easier. Or how to manage the situation when she just didn't want to eat — taking a break or knowing how to talk her through it. Occasionally, it just meant playing the role of obstinate hardass, and not giving her eating disorder any room to budge.

Whatever it was, it was working, and her weight began to climb, and then stabilize. Within a few months she had reached and was maintaining, her target weight.

We're now done with FBT, and her weight is still above the level it needs to be. But it's still not easy. There are days when the eating disorder rears its head, and eating is hard. There are days when the depression — the other end of the eating disorder teeter-totter — rises, blocking out much of the light.

There are also all of the other and more internal battles that she must fight. Her negative associations with certain foods or activities. Her difficulty with exercise. Her concerns about the new and different body she finds herself in.

And so our journey is ongoing. And, if clinical averages

are to be taken into account, likely will continue, in some shape or form, for at least a few more years to come. As long as she'll have me, I'll be there every step of the way, working through challenges, and silently hoping that I'm doing enough.

I don't expect it to be easy. But I've come to understand that that's partially what love is. The movies so often tell us the opposite — that love is easy and carefree. That love is something you stumble into, like rounding the corner to your living room and seeing her there, sitting on your couch.

And it's not that this isn't necessarily the case. It's just that there's this whole other kind of love, that is hard; the kind you must believe in and choose to cultivate. The kind that is filled with struggle and challenge, perseverance and strength. Like sitting in a room, surrounded by twenty or so strangers brought together by shared experience, watching a new sun form at the centre of your solar system, and buckling down to adjust to this new orbital trajectory.

Chapter 16: Dave Keystone

A few years ago, I went to Costa Rica on a surf trip. I was with a buddy whose motto was "the party's over bro". He had a girl he wanted to marry and so he just wanted to surf, get massages and go back to the room. I, on the other hand, was there to strictly party. And so I did.

One night I was at the bar, and a few girls came up to talk to me, and one of them ended up hanging out a little longer. She was very attractive, blonde, curvaceous, gorgeous big green eyes, and perfect teeth. We were hitting it off. She was from Costa Rica and when she asked where I was from, and I told her Toronto, she said, "no way! I'm moving there on Wednesday to study holistic nutrition for a year!"

The night after we met, we were on the beach by the bar, and we were standing in the sand with the water through our toes, and she said, "Dave, do you want to make love on the beach?", and I said, "Ummm ... Yes".

We proceeded to "make love" on the beach, by the bar, people walking by, under the moon, my pants around my ankles, scrunched up condom on a half limp pecker because I was also drunk and sand in my butt, and I'm on top of her, and she looks up at me as I struggle to try to make this all work and she says, "Dave, your eyes are empty". The most instant turn-off thing a person could possibly say. As if trying to have sex under those conditions weren't difficult enough. And of course, I'm like "No, no, they're full! They're full!" Needless to say it wasn't the best sex anyone's ever had.

She moves to Toronto. I help her find her way. I help her move in. I become friends with her. We talk on the phone. We become friends. We hook up. We get closer. We become lovers. My foot always remains out the door because I'm scared she's eventually going to have to leave. I KNOW eventually she is going to have to leave. She has to go back to Costa Rica. But between you and me, it's not because of that that I kept a foot out the door, it's because I had never experienced anything like that and I was scared.

Scared of what it might mean to give myself entirely to someone. Scared of being in a relationship. Scared of what? The truth is, I don't know, but I never let myself, or should I say "us" get into a serious relationship. We never called each other boyfriend or girlfriend, but the truth is, we were in a serious relationship. I loved her, and she loved me.

She would say what I was thinking all the time. She was so powerful. She believed in me. She encouraged me. I believed in her. I encouraged her. I once asked her what she would do if I were broke my whole life (I was asking just looking for any reason to think we couldn't be a couple) and she said, "Dave if I want money, I will make it myself!" It was the perfect answer I was hoping she wouldn't give.

I used to swear, and she would say, "Dave nooooo!"

She used to give me a hard time about the fact that I never just stopped her on the street for a big French kiss. She always wanted a big French kiss at times that I thought it was more appropriate to peck on the lips, like when you come home from work, she wanted a big French kiss. That Latin flavour.

She always had an excitable tone in her voice. When I'd pick up the phone, she'd say, "Dave! How are you!?" I still hear that in my head sometimes.

She always made me turn off wasted running water.

She would scrub fruits with soap and water before eating them — even peelable fruits.

She extended her visa twice. Sometimes we disguised it

as her wanting to learn more about Canadian culture and practice nutrition here, but we both knew a big part of it was to stay longer with me. We called each other friends, but it was more. We hooked up, we dated, we loved each other, we were, essentially, best friends.

Occasionally we dated other people, but we kept coming back to each other. We tried to end the relationship a few times because it was taking such an emotional toll on her, but I would say, "What's the point of some other guy that you just met driving you to the airport when you leave? Let's just ride this out until then". She always agreed.

Before she left we went to my cottage in Algonquin Park. There's a cabin by the lake with a clearing and a deck. I asked if she wanted to make love on a blanket outside, she said yes. I was on top of her, and we looked into each other's eyes. I, of course, thought back to three years earlier when she said my eyes were empty. This time they were full. When we finished, I told her I had that thought about the empty eyes comment, and she said, "Dave! I thought the same thing!" We never spoke more about it but I think we both knew what it all meant.

We hugged at the airport when she left, like two people mourning a death. Puffy cabbage patch doll faces. Intense tears like nothing I'd ever experienced. She walked away holding her face. It was the saddest thing I had ever seen.

About ten months later, she started dating someone in Costa Rica and messaged me because she felt guilty. We spoke on the phone and to deal with my emotions, while on the phone, I opened a word document and typed every word of the conversation to distract myself from getting too sad while speaking to her.

I messaged her on her birthday, and she wrote back: "Hello, thank you for your message, I hope you're doing well too." It felt cold. For the first time, it felt like it was over.

It's hard now not to compare every new girl to her. It's amazing that I think back to the first day she was here walking out of the hotel. I didn't know her. But organically it developed into what it was. I need to open my mind to the possibility of that happening with someone new. But it's hard for me.

She became my friend. She was one of my best friends. I still think about her as that even though I know she probably doesn't think that of me. She said, "Dave, I've realized and learned, you're not my guy, and I'm not your girl. What happened here in Canada is what it needs to remain. It was beautiful and important, but now it's over". She was always so damn rational.

Before she left, we went on a trip to drive the Banff Jasper highway that we called our honeymoon to end our relationship. It was a deeply powerful trip full of good times and at times, tears. I brought a ukulele on the trip because my guitar was too big. She and I both learned to play it.

When we got home, I bought us matching ukuleles and sent her home with one. Here we cottage — in Costa Rica they go to the beach. Secretly, I was hoping that by sending her home with the ukulele, she would think of me, when she plays, on the beach, looking into the sunset.

The one that got away? The one I let get away? The one who's helped send me on my way ...

Chapter 17: Wafa Ktaech

"Has anyone ever told you that you look exactly like your mom?"

"Yeah, I get it all the time."

Short, big thighs, tiny feet, same nose, same hands, same skin, same smile. Fuck, my mom and I really do look alike.

There is one thing, one fundamental thing, that we don't share in our appearance. Her curly hair is tucked neatly behind her hijab. My mom didn't always wear a hijab though. She started wearing it back in 2002 after my brother got sick. There was this lump on the side of his neck that slowly got bigger and bigger. As this lump grew my parents' fears that something horrible was happening to their son grew along with it. Not knowing what else to do, my parents prayed their little hearts out that he was going to be okay. The lump kept growing though. Like sailors stuck out at sea with no hope, they decided their last resort was to promise God that they would be better Muslims if my brother made it through this.

The lump was not cancerous, my brother was fine, and my parents kept their promises.

I came home from school one day and found my mom at the door of our house with a hijab on. I thought she had just finished prayer and paid no attention to this. She asked me if I noticed anything different.

"No, what is it?"

"I'm wearing a hijab."

"Like, forever?"

It was forever. From that day forward, the hopeless, lost sailors found their refuge in God. *In their God*, the God that was homophobic, racist and judgmental. My siblings and I did not find refuge in this God.

My dad used to tell me that the happiest day of his life would be when I decided to wear a hijab. I didn't have the heart to tell him that would never happen. I was scared to tell them that I was queer, drank alcohol, smoked weed and ate pork. Like, petrified. If I ever told them, they wouldn't love me anymore.

I spent my whole life lying to them about who I was. Like the lump on my brother's neck, my hatred for them grew slowly. It grew until the day I told them that God didn't exist and that my sister wasn't going to hell for being with a black Christian man and that I was queer. They told me to leave and never come back. So I did.

I found refuge in my brother, sister, sister-in-law and nephews. My new family loved me no matter what, and it was everything I ever wanted. I rid myself of the chains my parents put on me and started developing myself as a person. I moved in with my first roommate ever, and I was finally me. Not this person my parents wanted me to be.

In March 2014, I decided to go on a trip to Costa Rica with mostly strangers. I had never, ever, travelled alone because my parents forbade it. Young women needed to be supervised at all times. On this trip, I met Brianne, a strong, smart woman who taught me about how to love myself, the real me. That's why when Brianne suggested I move in with her in the summer of 2014, I quickly said yes.

My mom used to tell me I wasn't enough of a woman. She said I dressed too much like a boy, I was too fat, I needed to wear makeup to hide my acne and told me that I needed to walk lighter because I clunked around too much. She also taught me about the importance of keeping a clean, controlled household. *Sit il Beit* — woman of the house — is what she used to say I had to be. It was my duty as a woman.

Stories We Don't Tell

The day I moved in, Brianne was away on vacation. This day was also the first time since I moved out of my parents' home that I felt like I had inherited features from my mother that were not biological.

This house wasn't clean enough. It wasn't clean enough to my standards. It needed to be in order.

I spent the whole week Brianne was gone passive-aggressively cleaning this dingy basement. Even after it was clean, I felt that it wasn't clean enough. And these feelings continued for the two months that I lived in that basement. Every day I woke up, I just saw dirt everywhere. It consumed me.

When Brianne and I moved into our new apartment, I felt that this was an opportunity to start new. It was above ground and generally very clean. I made a conscious effort to think about my relationship with cleanliness, and I understood that it stemmed from my mother beating these ideas into my head about what women were supposed to do. It was not a healthy attribute and even worse, it's another thing I shared with my mom. I hated it even more than the fact that I looked like my mom because I should be able to control this aspect.

I moved in one week before Brianne did, which was great for me because I could clean the apartment on my own. In the hallway right outside my room was this black spot on the floor. I thought I had scuffed it up so I got a bowl of hot water and a scouring pad and got on my knees and went to work on it. I scrubbed and scrubbed and scrubbed but it wouldn't go away. I got all the cleaning products I had and tried so hard scrubbing this black spot off the floor but it wouldn't go away. I just wanted it to go away, I just wanted my mom to die, I just wanted never to talk to or see them again.

I sat outside my room for an hour, sobbing uncontrollably because I couldn't get rid of this black spot on my floor. It's still there outside my room to this day. But just like the black spot on the floor, my parents would forever be a part of me.

It's never going to go away. I will always look like my mom and I will always have to deal with this problem I have with cleanliness. But I have this incredible roommate who loves me and my siblings who love me and friends who love me. I am loved, even though I can't get rid of this black spot on my floor.

Chapter 18: Shona Fulcher

When I was 27, I was ... Well. I was 27 .... I had just finished university, I was waiting tables for a living, dancing a lot, drinking a lot, having deep, real conversations into the wee hours of the morning and sleeping almost not at all.

I was deep in the thrall of extended youth and comfortable in my totally unconscious but ironclad belief in my own immortality.

And so, when one morning I woke up to find that my baby toes on both feet were numb.

I didn't think much of it. I mean, I was a waiter; I was on my feet for hours on end. It was likely nothing.

And then a month later it had spread. Now three toes on each foot were numb. I still wasn't worried. But thought I should tell my family doctor anyway.

I went to see her, gave her a laundry list of small complaints, and added at the end; Ps: my lower back hurts ... and by the way, my toes are numb.

Well, my family doctor is flighty and forgetful, and a little bit silly. She giggles, she is always late, and can NEVER find her pen. But she listens. She took me seriously and decided to send me for some tests.

Fast forward three months, my toes are still numb, in fact now they are ALL numb, and the numbness has started to crawl up my legs. I keep expecting it to get better. But so far, it's not.

I find myself back at the doctor's office. "Yes, my cold is better, I'm feeling fine ... but my toes ..."

For four months, my doctor keeps sending me for tests, more tests, new tests, different tests. Specialists ran current through my body, they poked me, they prodded me, they told me everything seems to be fine. My nerves were healthy, my muscles were strong, I was fine.

Ok.

But my toes?

Some of you will understand what that is like. I was frustrated. I was alienated. My mysterious malady was like a transparent curtain dividing me from all the normal people.

What is wrong with me?

Why can't someone just TELL me what is going on?

My doctor decides it's time that I see a neurologist.

On February 24th, I went to see the top neurologist in Toronto. By the time I went to him, the numbness had spread up to the middle of my chest. And I wasn't so steady on my feet anymore.

But I wasn't afraid. I was kind of excited actually. You see, I still thought that I had a pinched nerve in my back somewhere.

I was 27.

I was immortal.

I was wrong.

It was a tuning fork. After all the high tech poking and prodding, it was a tuning fork that changed my life. If you've never seen one, a tuning fork is a particularly humble instrument. It looks like an overgrown two-pronged fork, and when you strike it on a hard surface, it begins to vibrate and emits a single pure note. You can tune an orchestra with it, but for me, it was the vibration that mattered.

He took the instrument, hit it against his desk to set it to vibrate, and gently set it against my knee.

"Tell me when it stops vibrating," he said.

He repeated this in several other spots on my body. The whole test took only moments.

I was admitted through the emergency room that

afternoon.

I remember calling my mum from the emergency room telephone.

"Hi mum, it's me. I'm at St. Mike's hospital ...

"Yes, I'm fine.

"They're admitting me through emerg right now.

"No, no, it's ok, you don't have to come up ... I'm fine."

I was calm, so very calm. I was fine, right?

My mum came up anyway.

They got me a bed on the neurology floor and scheduled an MRI for me the following day.

Now, St. Mikes is a teaching hospital, so I had a second-year neurology resident as my doctor that first night. He looked in on me as I was getting ready for bed, struggling to make myself comfortable in the sterile chill of a hospital room. He came in and said, "Your MRI is tomorrow, it might be cancer, it might be multiple sclerosis, ok ... Goodnight."

Yeah ... I didn't sleep much that night.

Less than 24 hours later, I had a prognosis. I was special (Well, yeah, my mum always told me I was special).

I had a very common kind of tumour in a really rare location.

Have you've ever seen anyone with a port wine birthmark, a dark red blotch on their skin somewhere? Well, that's technically a hemangioma, and that is what I had, but mine was in my spinal column. A tangle of overgrown blood vessels that was slowly pressing up against my spinal cord, and gradually, like a growing glacier, trying to shut down the lower half of my body.

The doctor came in with a herd of interns in tow and told me my body was betraying me.

In the most clinical of voices, he told me that as the tumour continued to grow, it would crush my spinal cord, and I wouldn't walk anymore.

Jesus Christ!

My options were limited — radiation treatment, which might still damage my spinal cord and lead to the same outcome, or surgery.

I chose surgery.

Exactly a week after I was admitted into the hospital, I spent 10 hours on the operating table. They removed most of one of my vertebrae and replaced it with a bone graft and a metal plate. My aunt, who used to be an OR nurse likes to refer to it as the "family-sized" plate as it covers six vertebrae in my thoracic spine, fusing them all together.

I spent three days in intensive care and four more in the regular neurosurgery ward.

Two weeks. It had been two weeks since I sat there in that neurologist's office, feeling the gentle buzz of the tuning fork fade to nothing against my leg. That fucking tuning fork! I get one lousy test wrong, and now I'm not going to walk?

Two weeks from immortality to immobility.

I wore a back brace for four months after the surgery, and it took me two years to stop flinching any time someone put a hand on my back.

I'm not sure if I'll ever get back the sense of my body as an inviolable dependable whole.

I've got a scar on my chin from falling off my bike when I was 4, and one on my toe from stepping on a razor clam when I was 8. I have one on my knee from hitting a crack in the ice when I was 12.

And now I have two scars on my back that between them are over a foot and half long.

The surgery might have ended my dreams to be a pro golfer, and I'm not allowed to bungee jump.

But guess what, I still have deep meaningful conversations

into the wee hours of the morning, I still sleep less than I should .... And I can still dance!

Chapter 19: Paul Dore

When I was a child, our basement had nothing really down there, it was just storage. I always remember there was a painting hanging on the wall. It was like a leftover from some previous owner because it just didn't fit with anything else we had. I remember this painting because it was the face of a young woman, and it was one of those creepy paintings that looked like the eyes were following you.

I was reminded of this painting last winter, I had been 'sort of' seeing Lucy for a few weeks. She was an artist, we were at her place, and we were looking through some of her work. Flipping through the pages, I stopped when I came across one that was this painting of a woman's face. It was coloured yellow except for drops of blood dripping down her cheek like a tear. It wasn't the same painting as the one from my childhood basement, but it had the same creepy eyes. Lucy noticed my reaction and said, "If you want it, you can have it."

I met Lucy on the internet. You never knew what would happen with her. On our first date, we were driving at night in a snowstorm by Casa Loma, and she insisted we scale the gates. Every time we went out to eat, she always stole something. Ketchup bottles, cutlery, pint glasses. I had about five different types of hot sauce in my fridge. These were definitely some red flags.

But there was something exciting about her.

I had a frame that fit the painting and hung it in the hallway by my front door. Although the eyes kind of freaked me out, they also kind of reminded me of my childhood.

Since meeting Lucy, I started noticing that little things were different around my apartment. When she stayed over, she'd usually be gone by the time I woke up in the morning. I kept finding little things happening. The towels on the towel rack in the washroom were switched around. A cabinet door was slightly ajar. I work as a freelancer in the television industry, and the past few weeks were stressful. I had a bunch of projects all at once and was working long hours, and there was a lot of pressure. But I refused to believe that this was the reason for these little things happening. I went to leave for the day and walked past the painting with its eyes. The front door was unlocked. I never forget to lock the door. These little things kept happening over the next couple of weeks. One of the blinds left open. The computer on when I'm sure I turned it off the night before.

Lucy and I were going out for dinner one night. After work, I stopped and bought two bottles of wine: one red, one white. Before heading out to dinner, we opened the red, had a few glasses. We were going to one of those fancy restaurants in a back alley with no sign. Lost, we cut through a parking lot. A parking lot attendant was backing a car into a space, and he was just taking far too long. Frustrated, I started shouting at him, he shouted back, gave me the finger. I almost got into a fight. Lucy pulled me away, and we finally found the restaurant.

We went inside, and she quickly went to the washroom. She came back, sat down, looked around and said, "Where's your friend?"

"Your friend. The one that was walking along with us and came in with us."

"There was no one with us." She shrugged and picked up the menu.

In the middle of the meal, Lucy got up from the table and returned with a man. He was introduced as Lucy's 'friend'. He sat down with us. She ordered him a drink. He

spooned some of our Spanish tapas on to his plate. It was explained to me that she invited him to join us and she had told me this earlier in the day. This is something I would have remembered. I looked across the table at this guy, this 'friend' who had his hand on Lucy's thigh, and I thought.
"I've really got to make some changes in my life."
Obviously, I was uncomfortable, so they ended up leaving together and leaving me the bill. When I got home, all I wanted was to open that bottle of white wine and have a glass or maybe three. I looked everywhere for that bottle, but it had disappeared.
I guess I wasn't ready to change yet.
A few days later, Lucy called me. She was at her parents' house, and there was some trouble. She asked me to come and pick her up. I had never met her parents, and from what I understood, this wouldn't be a good time. She assured me they weren't at home. She let me in, and I waited in the front foyer as she was getting her stuff together. Through the window, I saw a car pull up behind mine. I thought to myself that I really should have parked on the street because in case something goes down, I'm now blocked in. A woman, who I assumed was Lucy's mother approached the front door. The foyer was small, and as she opened the door, I got caught behind it. I did what anyone would do, I put my hands up like I was being arrested. Her mother closed the door, turned around and didn't even flinch. "Who are you and what are you doing in my house?" Before I could speak, Lucy came in the room, and they started arguing. They went up the stairs, and her mother looked down at me, "Go outside and give us a few minutes, I need to talk with my daughter." I looked to Lucy but didn't make a move.
That night, I couldn't sleep. Finally drifted into that space between being half awake and being half asleep. I felt Lucy

get out of bed, I assumed to go to the washroom or get a glass of water. She didn't return for a while. I heard the sound of floorboards like someone was walking around. I opened my eyes, rolled over to face the doorway and I saw Lucy in the hallway. She was naked except for a blanket covering her chest. She stared at me. She stared for a very long time.

    Until suddenly, she dropped the blanket, rushed at me, slapped me on the side of the head and ran back out of the room. I didn't move for the rest of the night. The next morning she was gone.

    Maybe it was time to make an actual change. We took some time away from each other, but I did try and contact her again a few weeks later. Her phone was disconnected, her Facebook profile was gone, and my emails to her bounced back. She completely disappeared. The only thing that remains of her is the painting.

Chapter 20: Tanya M. Cothran

"Why are you going to Malawi?" the lady on the plane next to me asked as our jumbo-jet descended into the dusty Lilongwe airport. We had travelled more than 18 hours together — from San Francisco to Washington D.C., through Addis Ababa, to Lilongwe. My mouth was dry and icky after sleeping and then deciding not to brush my teeth in the cramped airplane bathroom — the flavour only adding to my nausea, a result of not being able to eat more than a few bites of food catered by Ethiopian Airlines.

Her eyes showed her excitement and interest, "So, what group are you with?" It was clear, looking around the airplane, seeing groups of youths wearing matching t-shirts with peppy Bible quotes, that they were coming here for that life-changing trip, which would both open their eyes to the suffering of the world and allow them to provide hope to the masses. A week later they'd be on the same plane, flying home; their cameras filled with photos of barefooted children in school uniforms. Their heads filled with stories of personal transformation that they'd share in university admission essays and share with their churches to raise money for their next trip.

But I wasn't wearing a matching shirt, just a slightly worn-out blue shirt that I got from Target the summer before. "I'm here to visit the projects that my organization, Spirit in Action, has sponsored. We've given grants to a community in northern Malawi for eight years. Now I finally get to meet face-to-face all those people I've been emailing with!" We chatted a bit more, comparing the list of vaccines we had to get, lamenting over my partner's mild case of yellow fever after his shot, wishing each other a good trip. Enjoy — no matter what, it's going to be amazing.

I left unsaid that even though I wasn't wearing a matching shirt, I too was hoping for a transformation.

I walked up to the meeting house of the village savings and loans group enveloped in a sea of voices. A thrill swept over me as they loudly clapped and sang their welcome. I listened to hours of testimony of lives changed, of businesses that are now making enough money so that the family could buy a proper bed and send children to school. There were more songs, hugs, invitations to tea. Photos of that day capture the bliss on my face. "This is IT!"

Years before, right after university, I had applied to jobs at dozens of non-profits. I wrote cover letters enthusiastically describing my passion to serve. I wanted a job that fit with my beliefs, and that would contribute to a better world.

And then I got hired to do data entry at an insurance company. Looking at life expectancy reports, calculating the probability that the person would die before their policy expired. My friend's job was to call to see if they had died. I learned how easy it is to shut down a conversation by saying, "I work in insurance."

When I got the job with Spirit in Action, I was just so happy to not be working for a soulless corporation. Here was the opportunity to use my skills for something other than growing hedge funds. With each grant update I got in the mail, plastered with stamps from Kenya, Malawi, Zambia, or Uganda, I revelled in the thought that these stories of change were part of my work. Finally, I had a job I could be proud of. When I told people what I did, they'd respond, "oh, you're one of the good ones." And I felt that I was.

But in the very next moment, I'd think that even though I worked for good, it didn't always seem good. Most days it was just a job, and a lonely one. An email ding would

Stories We Don't Tell

bring a dread that it'd be another story of hungry children and money needed for education and medicine. At some point, I stopped believing most of the stories. I wondered, "Is rejecting someone's grant request because their budget seems unrealistic so different from rejecting their life insurance because they will live too long?"

If I really was one of the good ones, I reasoned, I needed a story of a strong calling or some deeper connection to Africa to get that stamp of authenticity on my work, and to slow my growing cynicism.

This need felt even more urgent after our founder died, and I became the only person running the organization. I could easily talk about our grant-making process but still felt that people were expecting some heartfelt story about my connection to rural Malawi. "Have you read that book about the nurse woman in Rwanda?" I hadn't, and I scoffed at the description of how she experienced "a love affair with a country and a people that spanned half a century." I was gifted several copies of the "The Blue Sweater," another memoir set in east Africa. In this one, a woman gives away her beloved blue sweater to a Goodwill in the U.S. and then finds a child wearing her exact sweater when she's travelling in Rwanda. Some part of me realized how contrived these narratives sounded: you go to a place where you don't know the culture or the language, and suddenly you discover yourself?? But another part of me felt that these stories perfectly described that purpose I longed for. They were stories of belonging, of "small world" connections, of passion and a calling. And I wanted one.

***

After that first inspiring day in Malawi, I went to sleep

tired, but so excited to see what would unfold over the next four weeks!

By Day 10 the bliss had thoroughly worn off. In Meru, Kenya, I had been sat down in front of 40 teenagers who had recently completed a "girls' empowerment workshop" sponsored by Spirit in Action. The leader of the training wanted us to communicate directly with the girls. Wonderful! Only my Swahili was non-existent and their English not much better. My husband was with me, which didn't foster a super great environment to talk about women's sexuality. It quickly devolved. They laughed at us for being so old (28) without any children. They told us that it's customary to remain silent when eating. I later learned that's actually not the custom, but it did create a welcome pause from our forced conversation.

The next day, waiting on an empty, dusty tarmac for the flight to Nairobi, Kenya, we took swigs of whisky straight from the bottle. The airport attendant refused to give us any information about when the plane might arrive or why it was already two hours late.

Day 15 I woke suddenly in the middle of the night, my brain unable to stop its frantic thinking. The day before I had received travel reimbursement requests from some of our partners. Something hadn't looked right, and it was bubbling up in my thoughts now, after midnight. I turned on my flashlight to look over the forms again. The numbers just didn't add up. People who had travelled together had different amounts for the same hotel room. Simple addition mistakes resulted in different totals. I collapsed back in bed, wanting to cry, and wondering where I would find the will to confront them in the morning. How had this trip drifted so far away from that sense of hope that I felt on the first day, surrounded by singing?

Stories We Don't Tell

On that trip, I did not fall in love with the entire continent of Africa, or even just Kenya or Malawi. Day 24 I returned to the U.S. so exhausted and disillusioned that for the first few weeks, I had to force myself to talk about my trip. I had heard and seen amazing evidence of lives changed for those who had used our grants, but I was seriously questioning if I was really "one of the good ones." My "love affair with a country and a people" is best described as a one-night stand. Turns out, a lot of the day-to-day work of a non-profit has more in common with insurance hedge funds than blue sweater dreams.

Post-script: Since this first trip to visit grassroots organizations in eastern Africa, I have returned three more times. Each time the places and people, cultures and customs, become more familiar and comfortable to me. Still, each day on a site visit trip has an equal chance of being exhausting and draining, or thrilling and inspiring. When submitting and updating this story, I am writing from rural Kenya. This week, I put my project evaluation in Malawi on hold, flying back to Kenya to care for an American friend who had emergency surgery. "I'll have so many stories to tell," she faintly whispers to me when I visit her in the Kenyan ICU unit.

Chapter 21: Barbora Grochalova

– We should find someone to take a photo of us.
I get impatient with my dad's impatience.
– Of course, but we're doing fine, I still have thirty ... seven minutes before I have to go through security.
36 minutes.
I've had to become good at airports.
I took my first transatlantic flight when I was 11. My family had packed up as much as we could, and boarded a plane for Toronto. At 12 years old, I made the trip back home to Slovakia on my own for the first time. During my six-hour stopover in Frankfurt, I did my best pre-teen impression of a responsible adult: I rode the light rail train between the terminals, and covertly covered myself with perfume in the duty-free. I had a favourite airline before I even started high school. And although I've mastered the liquids and gels rule, the lead-up to the security check is always the hardest.
I'm sure you can picture the scene: you've just had an Austrian businessman take another family photo: same place as last time, but the kids are a bit taller, and the adults maybe a bit shorter. Everyone hugs, again, as twenty other families are doing the same. You hand over your boarding pass and then crawl through that eternal line-up. The line meanders, back and forth, slowly. Someone is chugging back a can of pop they had forgotten about. You look back every few steps and struggle not to cry, so you just make funny faces instead, and wave.
But eventually, you need to make the choice to turn away, because those you are leaving behind won't. They'll wait there, and wave, and watch, until you've walked through the barriers, through the mirror sliding door, until they find

they're waving to themselves.

31 minutes.

– Hey dad, there's some empty spots by the window.

We sit on the hard plastic seats, attached in a row, facing the tarmac.

When I first left Slovakia, I didn't really lose a home so much as I gained another. A few months after moving to Canada, I was back in Europe again, in order to somewhat fulfill the custody agreement. I was already used to not seeing my dad every day, but this was a bit different. It's hard to go on bike rides every other weekend when I'm across the Atlantic.

But phone calls and skypes aren't the worst, and even my grandmother learned how to email. As I got older, my dad and I talked about anything from conspiracy theories to why I was feeling sad that day. I shared stories of my high school life, hoping to give him a glimpse of who I was becoming, yearning for his feedback.

But, inevitably, the gaps in our understanding of each other grew wider. When I was 17, home for the summer, walking out his door to go hitchhiking with a guy I had just met at camp, my dad tentatively yelled after me, "and that whole, you know, sex thing, that can totally wait, you know that, right?"

27 minutes.

We watch planes take off, and fumble over some formulaic summaries of what a great visit it's been.

The thing is, ten months earlier, as I watched the sunrise from a window in Toronto General Hospital, I wasn't sure I would make this trip again.

There really wasn't much I could do to get ready for open-heart surgery. Risky, unexpected — those words don't even come close. After making all the phone calls I could make, and saying everything I wanted those close to me to know, I just thought about coming back home again.

I thought about the view from the plane as it lands at the Schwechat Airport in Vienna, and the fields of wind turbines sown onto the countryside. I tried to picture every detail I could remember of the drive that would then take me to my home town, replaying especially the last part: when the road cuts a turn around a hill and the valley of the Hron river spreads open, and in the distance, for the first time, I can see the mountains standing guard over my town. The mountains, where even on the hottest summer day the air is so cool and refreshing, it smells like spruce — it smells so clean I can almost believe it's healing me with every breath.

But what healed me last summer were the gifted hands of Canadian doctors.

20 minutes.

I have to be efficient with my visits to Slovakia: if I don't really connect with someone in person, the phone calls might become rarer.

When my dad picked me up at this airport five weeks earlier, I could tell he was trying. I know he had to pull some strings to come greet me alone so that we could really catch up. I climb into his van.

Wait, he drives a van now?

– Oh yeah, it's so spacious, isn't it? See, I was thinking about the Toyota, but this one has better-shaped doors, and it was less pricey, although I think I could get better mileage with the Toyota ...

I catch a glimpse of those wind turbines as we drive on. We cross what used to be a dangerous border between the East and the West, now barely noticing that we've actually entered Slovakia, but still my dad has not stopped telling me about the benefits of this vehicle.

Stories We Don't Tell

And I know he's driving, but I just want to take him by the shoulders, shake him and say, "why can't you just ... ask me how I've been? Ask me to tell you what I've been through? Ask me how I feel about having the scar on my chest, ask me about my flight, my break-up, just ask me something, anything, instead of telling me about the fucking van!!"
– Do you think you'll ever move back?
5 minutes.
My mouth dries up. Airport hall announcements echo around us.
I've been here for five weeks, and now —
Five minutes left.
I stare out onto the tarmac.
Just three days earlier, my grandmother suddenly fell ill. Helpless, I raced to the hospital I remember from my childhood, weeds growing out of the courtyard, hoping to see her one more time, only to find that visiting hours are only between 2 and 3pm, excluding weekends. It was Saturday! I wouldn't even be in the country long enough. Nepotism finally got me in, but turns out it didn't get Grandma a room with ventilation, or an adjustable bed. The doctors apparently didn't bother to tell her what her prognosis was, or that they had put her on anti-depressants.
I always feel queasy in hospitals, especially in Slovakia. I leaned over the railing that was secured by gauze and caressed my grandmother's arm. I didn't know how bad the stroke was, and she didn't show whether she could feel it. I was just grateful I could be there.
I hadn't been there long before two thoughts completely overwhelmed me. I couldn't help but picture myself in that rickety bed that has been rusting since the Velvet Revolution.
And the vivid memory of the look of awe on the face of every cardiac specialist in Toronto when I told them the

name of my surgeon: "Wow, there's, maybe, half a dozen in the world who could do what he did," they would repeat.

I tried to hide my panic, so I walked over to the corner of the hospital room to wash my hands, but the sink was empty.

– No one remembered to bring me soap, Grandma explained.

– So do you think you'll come back? (My dad's voice is quiet in a way it didn't used to be.) At least I always thought you would. And when you started talking about a career in environmental law, I just thought you'd get a job in Geneva or something, though even that's too far, when ...

3 minutes.

When someone gets sick, he wanted to say. Even down the street is too far when someone gets sick.

But for the first time since I was 11, I'm no longer mulling over possible life paths. I'm no longer wondering who I would be if I had stayed. My scar gives an answer I can't ignore.

I finally take my eyes off the tarmac.

– If I lived in Slovakia when I got sick, I wouldn't stand a chance.

And now I have to go.

So we get the rest of the family together, and a stranger takes our photo.

This time there's no line-up. I just stick my boarding pass into a scanner, and with a "beep" the mirror doors slide open. I turn around at the last second and see my family waving back.

Chapter 22: Stefan Hostetter

I like to think I'm likeable ... actually, let me rephrase that, I need to know I am. I'll agonize for days over an awkward goodbye or the possibility of someone taking something I said wrong. I am the king of the follow-up text, lord of the check-in, sultan of the small talk. It's hard for me to place why I am this way, but from what I can remember, I always have been. Now some people might call it pathological, and I would agree because I want them to like me. From what I can tell, it's in my nature, and currently, it's a problem.

It's a problem because I'm in love with a man I'll never meet. It's an unrequited affair that may be based more on what he did and who he was to people I care about, but love has certainly been built on far less.

It's 4 am and I sleepily make my way out of the sixth-floor apartment and stumble towards the elevator. There is a peacefulness that comes with the middle of the morning, which somehow permeates the cement walls. I await the slowly rising elevator, one he must have known far better than I, and exit the building out into the small parking lot, cross the four lanes of dead road to await my ride.

Olive's grandfather, who was really more of a father to her than anyone else, resonates through the glass-encased bus shelter and settles into my bones. I saw him only once in passing, we never spoke, he never knew I existed and for good reason. Yet here I stand, the cool night wind making me happy I had thought to bring a sweatshirt, the effects of the night's wine mixing with the late hour leaving me in a semi-sleep state. I am a soldier at my post; I tell myself that he could have respected that.

The sighting occurred as I sat in her Starbucks, nearly

Stories We Don't Tell

two years before. It was early in our relationship, but, even then, if you'd asked me whether we were meant for each other, I'd have bet you a bottle of $20 wine that we'd last. In fact, I did.

Olive walked her grandparents past me towards the door and smiled in my direction as they passed. I knew even then that there was not going to be an introduction and that, likely, there never would be. I would see him in countless pictures after the fact and would learn much about him there. How he fought in the Second World War and how he defined himself by this time at war for the rest of his life. A decorated Canadian Jew who fought against the Nazis and won. A legacy anyone could be proud of. His civilian life centred around his wife, whom he still provides for even after his passing. He was a man of his times and all the things that came with it. Olive was his favourite.

I stand at attention. His death called me here. A young twenty-something trying to do his best and desperately hoping it was 'enough'. With death there simply seems no appropriate response. I spent a while researching the logistics of getting a game that she and her brother had loved on Windows '95 to work on her computer. Unfortunately, the setup proved beyond my ability. Years later I will realize that 'enough' simply doesn't exist in this context, but this dirt ridden glass bus shelter is my post, and I bat down my fears and allow myself to think that I am at least helping. I'm supposed to be good at this stuff, I pride myself in it, but here, I found myself floundering. I'm sorry, I don't know what to do.

Nothing about his exit from this world was terribly surprising, except perhaps the length at which he was able to stave it off. He had defeated cancer once, only to have it return years later. He sat in palliative care, and the man who

Stories We Don't Tell

I'd been told was basically immortal, slowly slipped away. I knew this day would come and I always wanted to be ready, while never really being sure what to expect.

I was not to go to the funeral, given that the fact that I was a gentile was enough to keep me from meeting him in life, to have me there could be seen as in bad taste. I was not to go to the Shiva either. Olive's mother felt like the weeklong mourning period in Jewish tradition was not the place for me to meet the family and who is anyone to argue with the woman who just lost her father?

And so, in the end, this bus shelter was my commitment. Each night, tell me when you are home, I'll be there until you're falling asleep. The text would usually come around 10pm, she was leaving the Shiva. I hop on the Bathurst 7 north and arrive no more than 45 minutes later. I take the slow elevator up to the 6th floor, make three lefts and walk to the end of the hall, door on the right. Her mother's already in her room, sleeping soundly. Olive pulls the door open slowly, making sure to pat down the clear plastic doormat that has a habit of bunching up. A quick embrace and perhaps unnecessarily whispered hellos precede my removing my shoes. I aim to tread as quietly on the thick-carpeted floors as possible as I follow her into the living room, which is adorned with massive cross-stitches of her mother's making and pictures of family on almost every surface.

I take a seat on the couch as Olive finds us dense glass cups to hold our boxed red wine. To my right is the balcony. It overlooked a cemetery and had served as a refuge for us before. She'd sat with me when I'd learned of a friend's unexpected death. I remember not really knowing how to react or respond or even move. She'd asked me questions about him, and I had answered them. She came with me to

Stories We Don't Tell

the funeral. Stood with me at my father's door as I spoke to his grieving father, who had amazingly remembered my childhood home. Held my hand when it needed to be held.

Tonight, we'll talk or watch something, or just sit in silence. The night will wear on, and we'll decide that starting a movie minutes before 2 am really just makes sense. Tell me when you are home, I'll be there until you're falling asleep.

This is what being a man of my times is. This is my sense of duty. And I would like to think that he would at least be able to respect that. I may never know the worst things he ever saw, but I would like to think I've seen a few of the best. I know what it means to want to help so badly that you'd do anything to be given the chance. I know what it's like to look at someone and see a better person than they themselves see when they look into a mirror. I may not know true grief, but I do know devotion.

Chapter 23: Monica Hamburg

It was so wonderful to hear you say, "I really hope you move here soon."

My plan of being in New York for 6 months wasn't specifically for you. I was dying to be back in the city I lived in in the 90s, the city I deeply loved, that I missed with an intensity like heartbreak.

I needed to feel and siphon its inspiration and vibrancy. Remember who I was, the potential I once felt I had. Immerse myself in comedy.

But it sure was lovely knowing I would hang out with you. I was thinking of you, and our connection, moments before the car hit me head-on.

I'm fine.

It makes a better story if I'm hurt, but it sure makes a better reality that I'm not.

It's odd and surreal to feel a vehicle make contact with your body. And if you're fine, it becomes a novelty story instead of a source of trauma and damage.

A moment like that could, literally, change your whole life. Derail your plans. Destroy your body. It didn't, in my case, and I am super grateful for that.

I was crossing the street at 2pm, in Times Square, not a busy street, though. My light. I was mid-way across, and suddenly, I heard — and then saw, a car swerve, coming around the corner. I turned quickly in its direction, there was no time to do anything, I put my hands up, an odd and instinctive defensive move — no protection against a vehicle, and I thought: "Oh, they're going to stop."

But that didn't happen.

You don't get taught what to do when you get hit by a car.

They tell you, since you're a kid, what to do if you're on fire: "Stop drop and roll."
You know what you do when you're hit by a car?
You take it.
You take it like a bitch.
The car crashed into me, into my chest.
And I went over the hood and then fell back and to the ground.
It felt like slow motion. I hate being trite, but that's what it was like. It was so quick and yet so slow, simultaneously. There's a part of me that wishes I could see a video of it. To understand what the timing of it actually was.
I am fascinated by the disconnect between what we feel and what is actually reality.
I hit the ground.
I'm a narcissistic performer (redundant, I know), and I've had infinite fantasies about people screaming about me.
They just never involved being hit by a car.
I heard the screaming around me.
And then, a moment passed, and I thought, "Well, I guess I just pick up my purse and move along now."
So, I picked my lip gloss, which had fallen out of my purse, off the pavement, and I got up. I picked up my bags. I stepped onto the sidewalk — which was sadly, really, fucking close.
And I looked into the car. Four girls in their twenties, all shaking and staring at me like I was some creature in a horror film that got up after being shot.
I looked at the driver, uncomprehendingly: "You hit me with your car. It was my light. What's wrong with you?"
It's weird how unfair it feels when you do things right, and shit happens anyway.
I wanted a good reason. SOME reason. But what answer

would have satisfied me there?
What could she have said: "Epilepsy."
"I just lost my job."
"Oh, OK. Well then, I'm less concerned about the possible internal bleeding."
But the driver didn't say much. Couldn't. She could barely catch her breath, and she kept repeating, "I didn't mean to, I didn't mean to."
Well, obviously, it wasn't intentional. She didn't know me. If she did, she might have ample motivation.
At least, that's my standard joke. Despite my true belief that I'm pretty easy to like.
A middle-aged man ran over. He picked up my glasses from the road: "Are you OK?"
"Yes, thank you. Thank you very much."
"You should get her licence," he said definitively. In that authoritative New York way.
And, I looked at her, in the car, shaking, barely able to speak.
And I thought: "Oh, What a fucking hassle."
I think that's the point you get to, either by 40, in general, or when you've lived in New York. Almost nothing registers as anything but a drain in possible energy.
And I said to him, "Look, I know I'm in shock, but I feel OK."
Which is ... super dumb.
That's like, "I know I'm idiot, but I have a strong opinion on the subject."
The two things automatically negate each other.
If I know I'm in shock, I should also be clear about the fact that that's why I don't feel any pain.
I thanked the guy for his concern.
The driver kept saying, "I'm sorry, I'm so sorry."

And I went, "I don't know what to tell you. You hit me with your fucking car. I mean, it's not OK. I don't know what to tell you. But whatever, take care, I guess."

And I walked down the street.

And about half a block in, I stopped.

And I started to sob.

God, this felt so lonely, all of a sudden.

I was just hit by a car.

And that was it.

There was no real room for drama. No real space for a reaction. No one emotionally close to me nearby to care about it all. Except me.

When I was walking down the street moments ago, I was thinking, "I could use a hug."

Then the car hit me, and I thought, "Now, I could really use a hug."

My hands shaking, I took out my phone, and I posted a joke on Facebook about the incident.

Because converting pain into humour makes anything I'm going through feel infinitely better.

I do react differently to vehicles than I did before. Before, I hadn't thought about how it would feel to have a car come into contact with my body. I didn't understand how it would bring about an awareness of my frailty, the sense that comes with knowing how close you came to real damage.

But: You just have to move on.

You can't half walk across the street. You have to be able to take a deep breath and do it and trust that most the time it's going to be OK.

But falling in love isn't like that. You know that, most of the time, it won't be OK.

You'll open yourself up and you'll be gutted.

You stopped speaking to me a few days after I arrived in

your city. You never saw me the whole 6 months I was there.

And every day, I think about you, and I feel an intense wash of hurt and fury.

The knowledge that I was so small to someone I saw as so big. It fills me with such loss and sadness.

I was hit by a car, and I sustained no damage.

I wish I could say the same for being involved with you.

You pressed at me to allow you to get closer. I remember the day you told me what friendship meant to you — and that no matter what, you wanted me in your life, that you would always be my friend. There was such a sincerity there. That's the moment I gave you my trust.

I meet people all the time. I'm told I'm magnetic, easy to like. Memorable.

But not to you.

When you pursued someone and started a relationship with her, although you'd told me you weren't ready for a relationship, I was profoundly hurt.

But you were that special to me, it was that important to have you remain in my life, that despite all the pain involved, I would have tried.

I would have done the work to get through the agony of the loss of potential.

I would have attempted to be happy for you, when you gushed about how unique she was and how special your connection was.

I was absolutely prepared to try.

But you couldn't? It was easier just to cut me out?

Which is the worst.

It conveys: "You meant nothing to me."

It tells me: "Your relevance in my life was so inconsequential that your being there or not doesn't even register. You don't register."

I temper every interaction with men lately with, "This is, honestly, how little I can do."

Didn't you know how little you'd ultimately be able to give me?

A car hit me. And it made little impact.

But my connection with you actually damaged me.

You can't half walk across the street. But you can half-date. You can put yourself out there and meet people and feel nothing and be elated that you feel nothing.

Because then you won't feel the crushing impact.

Chapter 24: Maya Fromstein

I've been here before, though this place looked, felt different then. I tried to get my bearings in my new, but familiar surroundings. Their familiarity is what haunts me. I force myself to keep looking, moving forward. I've been here before, but never arriving on the path I come from now.

The other road that leads here is so well-travelled, so well worn. I can feel myself making the grooves that now form it. The path I'm on now, I don't know where it goes. I try not to linger too much at this crossroads.

As you all should know, all people obsessed with health things drink kombucha, and the super obsessed brew their own.

Step 1: Learn what kombucha is.

It's November 2012, and I'm in my fourth year of undergrad. One of my three roommates has been accumulating jars with coffee filters for lids on our shared bookshelf turned food pantry. They've got an herbal tea-coloured liquid in them and a terrifying alien on top. The fruit flies can't get enough of this stuff. They don't actually get in, but hell, they will die trying.

It turns out this tea and alien baby are actually home-brewed kombucha, a fermented tea that is naturally carbonated and the alien on the top is called the SCOBY, the mama of all things, good bacteria and yeast. I find out kombucha brewers actually call it "The Mother" and I think that's pretty weird. My roommate is experimental and a little lucy goosey with food safety, and when she says it tastes like apple cider vinegar, I steer clear.

I have my supplies at the ready, almost, spread out amongst three different homes. At my parents' place, I've got my new beautiful glass bottles with the tops that swing. In my kitchen are big glass containers from Value Village still to be emptied of their resident lentils and pasta. And most importantly, my friend is still housing her baby SCOBY that awaits my return to Guelph from the break.

I can't believe I've committed this far into this project. This follow through is so unlike me lately. I'm so excited. I text my friend, The SCOBY Breeder, about the newly acquired bottles, the last checkbox on my list before I can begin: "Oh man, perfect. Smiley face emoji. Let's brew."

Step 2: Fall madly in love with the idea of it.

It's June 2013. I've graduated now. I've just started working at this cool new food co-op that's a 45-minute bike ride away from where I'm living. All of my friends, but for the three I have now in Toronto, have scattered about the world, and we are all fairly awful at keeping in touch.

One, who's moved in with her folks in Connecticut, messages me excited that she is brewing kombucha. I've still never tried it, but my friend sent me some links about how she's doing it and pictures of her very cute swing tops, just bottles, just waiting to be immensely enjoyed and I'm hooked on the idea.

I spend hours for weeks, months Googling different health properties, different recipes, how to buy swing top bottles on sale online, whether or not it's practical to spend $80 on a high-end kombucha brewing tank, but most of all I am fixated on the idea of how healthy this will be for me.

On days when I recognize and admit, only to myself, that I have an 11-year-old eating disorder, I'm convinced that I have outsmarted it by learning about nutrition and making sure I get enough of the individual nutrients themselves despite not getting nearly enough food. I'm obsessed with healthy things that I am sure will help me on this quest

Stories We Don't Tell

towards perfected health as well as anything that might help settle the gut I have so badly wrecked by now.

I still haven't tried it, don't even know where to buy it, and yet spend too many hours for days, for months looking into the ins and outs. The eating disorder won't actually allow me to commit to anything that might nourish me even as slightly as kombucha, but it will let me yearn.

I know that this path isn't the path I've travelled on so thoroughly in the past and yet that the two meet here throws me. A full year out of eating disorder treatment, I find myself looking forward to an activity so clearly outlined by my eating disorder skeleton.

Like an anticlimactic discovery, I find myself arriving at this place only to find it has already been claimed by my past. Reclaiming it for myself isn't quite so easy. I have put food in front of every step for so long now, it can be hard to distinguish if I or my eating disorder is propelling me to take the next one.

Step 3: Actually try kombucha enough times so that you've acquired the taste for it.

Step 4: Talk incessantly about your quest to make kombucha, so that your mom finally buys you the perfect swing top bottles for it at IKEA.

October 2015 and I am in the second year of my Masters now. We are at a Second Cup by my campus. My mom and I had been running errands all day, and so we stop to get a coffee, a latte. My mom has heard me talk about kombucha for months now and she asks if I think Second Cup will have any.

Because we are in Guelph, someone standing next to us in line takes it upon himself to educate us where we might find some kombucha in this fair city, and also informs us that he himself has started brewing recently. I ask him, like a jerk, what tea he uses for it. That's my latest obsession before I commit to brewing my own. "Do you use black tea, green tea, a combo? How do you make it not taste vile?" We talk for a few minutes about this.

After my mom and I have left the Cup, I make fun of him for being weird and so Guelph and my mom makes a face at me that I decline to interpret. A month later my mom lets me know that she's gotten me several litre bottles that I've been talking on end about.

Step 5: Make kombucha. I am braving the decision to ferment tea in my kitchen with the support of friends who want in. One curious housemate and a partner who, from 3000 miles away, is there for me.

I have just started a new medication for my bipolar depression that has been known to play rough with one's liver. It doesn't play particularly well with coffee either. All this translates into me finding creative ways to wake up in the morning. Granted, not being depressed is a good one, and to offset the medication's side effects that result from its abuse of the liver. Kombucha is on a list of things that my body wakes up from and my liver likes, so that's a go.

I am on this medication, something I've been avoiding for seven months from fear, from rigid rules my eating disorder set in place long ago about denying my body the support it needs, about waiting till I'm at the brink till I am allowed to pick myself up. Taking this medication alone is an act of defiance against what has held me back for so long, an act of self-love, and hope that life can and will be better.

My eating disorder is strongest when my mood and anxiety are unstable. It is the one coping mechanism I had developed over my 13 years with it. And despite having graduated from treatment a year ago this month, it is still the strongest coping mechanism I've got, so getting my depression and anxiety under control are the biggest steps I can take against my eating disorder right now.

But what muddy waters we enter when the medication to fix my depression, and essentially to help me curb my eating disorder, pushes me back to my old eating disorder behaviours. It is the eating disorder that brought me here originally. It is the reason I've studied food systems for coming on six years now. My symptoms and behaviours evolved into hobbies and activities. Things that once were forced upon me by my demons I now choose to do to bring me peace. I start brewing next week.

Chapter 25: Michelle German

"Fuck, holy shit!"

The pain shot up through my body. I looked down at my foot. I felt the poison go through my veins. I looked down and saw a very thin, long body of a very venomous snake.

I grew up going to summer camp in the Appalachian Mountains. For those of you who have not been to summer camp, it's this really magical, weird place. You spend four weeks sleeping in a room with 20 of your peers in bunk beds, and it's awesome.

You start to dress alike, you start to talk alike. You start to sing weird songs that you made up, you hold hands a lot. And when you get older, your periods sync up, 100%. My camp crew and I met when we were all about 11 years old, and we named ourselves the Friendies.

When the Friendies and I were campers, our camp was wildly underfunded and really poorly staffed. Our cabins were in the shape of geodesic domes because it used to be a space camp. We hid from a lot of activities by pretending to take showers. By the time we were counsellors though, there was a new director, who was brought in to revitalize the camp in the hopes of making money again.

Among other changes, this meant a zip line to the lake, air conditioning for the infirmary, a new theatre, a new arts and crafts shack, and a pool facility with three water slides. It was terrible. Along with the superficial changes, though, came some regulatory changes and rules. One night at the staff meeting, the new director told us all that we had to wear shoes. People were stubbing their toes, there were often long line-ups in the infirmary, and frankly it was costing the camp too much money.

Well, this was stupid. We had walked through these trails our whole lives, and we had never worn shoes. So that night, Emily and I, holding hands, singing a weird song, looking at the stars, walked up a new trail, up to the newly-shaped cabins.

"Fuck!" I looked down at my foot, and I saw the snake.

The rest of the night was a blur. They took me to a 20-bed hospital in rural Pennsylvania. They asked me to rate my pain between one and ten, and I just stared at them and said, "I think I'm at least 11, your chart makes no sense." When I came to next I looked down at my leg, and there was a black vein coming up it. The one surgeon on staff who got called in took one look at it, put me in an ambulance, and sent me to a much larger hospital where I spent the next 10 days in intensive care, and had two surgeries.

I was 16 years old at the time, and it was terrifying. I really should have worn shoes. The next few years were difficult. I had a lot of snake dreams. They were chasing me whenever I felt anxious. I thought I saw snakes everywhere, which made sense when I was in my backyard. Sometimes I thought I saw them in the 7/11 parking lot. I always made sure to wear shoes.

But I only skipped one summer at camp. My Friendies made a very good case. They said, "Let's go back, this is the last summer for us to be together before we do adult jobs and do adult things." What can I say, I really loved my Friendies, and I couldn't say no.

This time around, we were senior counsellors, which meant that we got to choose the kind of counsellor that we wanted to be. You could be a theatre counsellor, where you choose your favourite musical, and then you make awkward, Jewish kids sing it in front of their peers. Or you could be an archery counsellor, where you stand in a field and let kids shoot at a target until all of the arrows are lost in the woods, and then you're just standing in a field.

You could be a regular cabin counsellor, which was low stress. It meant that you just take your campers from activity to activity and hang out. I wanted to be the nature counsellor, which meant leading multi-day canoe and camping trips on the Potomac River in nearby West Virginia and on the Appalachian Trail. It meant that I was in charge. At the time, I was about 110 pounds, and I had never taken a first aid course.

But I knew that I had to deal with the snake issue. I had to take back nature and had to really toughen up. So that was the plan. The first trip started out really great. It was just with the other trippers, made up of myself and two burly men who really knew camping. They could start fires, and they had lots of stories, so I really trusted them.

Then we had two young Israelis who were about to go into the army, but first they came to rural Pennsylvania to go to camp. On the second night of this trip, we were all sitting around the fire, we're having a great time, we're bonding, getting to know each other, building some trust. I reach down to put another log on the fire, and there's a baby Copperhead that slithers right near me.

As I'm bending down, I freeze. Nate, one of the senior trippers, looks at me, looks at the snake, and he stomps it dead. It continued to be a little rough from there. Nate and I led two canoeing trips later in the summer. The first was with twenty 12-year-olds. We were going to sleep on an island for the night. We loaded up, we're just canoeing out, and immediately Nate gets stung by something. He started to swell up and said, "Hey, I got to go back. You'll be fine." I did not know how to start a fire.

The next trip started a little bit better. It was with a

similar number, about twenty 12-year-olds. The first night was fine, and as we're embarking on day two, because it had been raining so much, the water was rough, and there were rapids where there weren't usually rapids. We tipped one of the canoes with all of our food in it and the personal belongings of a couple of these pre-teens. It was just too dangerous to go on.

So the trippers, myself and one other, had to pull all of the canoes back upstream through the rapids, one by one. It took about two hours. When we got out our legs were bloodied from the rocks.

On the longest trip of the summer, I thought that it was going to be great. There were both senior trippers, myself and three additional counsellors to take our oldest, most mature, most comfortable group in the woods on a five-day four-night hike in the mountains. We made it to day two, and everything was going great. The Appalachian Mountains are really lovely to hike because in that area they're more like rounded hills than mountains. You just go up and you go down, you go up and you go down.

Occasionally, when you get to the peak, you let all of the men go and pee collectively off a cliff. It's very charming. It was about 40 degrees Celsius, so it was a little hot. By the time we got to our campsite, it took us a while to get everybody settled, and all of those grumpy, horny teenagers into their own sleeping bags. The rest of us, the staff, went over to the fire and debriefed over a beer.

When it's time for us to go to bed, we decide to give the campers some space. We put our sleeping bags just outside of the general camping area. As we slip into our sleeping bags, I start to hear a very faint buzzing. I learned later that although ground bees are not really a thing in Canada, they're definitely a thing in the states.

Stories We Don't Tell

We had put our sleeping bags on a ground beehive, and before we knew it, we were being completely swarmed. I couldn't even see from here to there. And just as we're figuring out what's going on, we start hearing screams from the kids who are just 10 feet away from us. Everyone is freaking out. I look at the two senior trippers, who have both developed weird bee allergies this summer, and they're just gobbling as much Benadryl as they can.

We quickly get everybody across the campsite, away from the bees, into a little wooden lean-to. All of the campers are bundled up together, most of them crying, very angry and uncomfortable because they've been stung. I ask the two additional counsellors to watch them, calm them, talk to them. I find the epee-pens in our first aid kit and hand them to the two burly men and leave them hovering over each other, waiting to strike if needed.

Then I look at the other counsellor, Matt. "Matt, what are we going to do?" And he's just crying, and the realization hits: Holy shit! We're in West Virginia, we have no cell phone service, and the only way to get help, looking at the map, is to run through very dense woods to an unknown road. And these woods are full of snakes.

So I take my flashlight, I grab his hand, and we start running. As we're running, I'm stomping as hard as I can, thinking I'm either going to step on a snake and kill it, or it's going to feel the vibrations of my step, and it's going to take off, because it's probably just as scared of me as I'm scared of it. Which has been a big thing that I've been working through these last few years. If someone stepped on me, I would bite it.

We finally got to a road, and I look at Matt, and I said, "Left or right, man?" He's still crying. So I say, "All right, left." We run until we see some lights of a house. We bang on the door, an elderly lady answers the door, and she is not pleased. I quickly tell her, as calmly as I can, that we have about fifty people in the woods, some of them might be dying, and we need to use her phone.

We call the police, the rescue squad and the camp. It doesn't take long for three really big ATVs to show up, an ambulance and a bus. Then it's back through the woods, through snake country to show them where everybody is, and then right back out with everybody else. That night six people went to the hospital.

I eventually got back to camp. I walked up that same road two years earlier I had encountered the snake. I woke Emily up and brought her out of the cabin. We were sitting on the bench as I started to tell her what had happened, and as I started to calm down I looked at my body, and I was completely covered in bee stings. It hurt a lot, but the fear was gone.

Chapter 26: L. K. Brighton

Mother, I was exhausted but restless. After 10 hours on Air Canada, there were still three more hours of my flight across the Pacific to Korea before I would lay eyes on my birth family. Five years — I'd known my birth family for only five years. Here I was on Christmas Day on another pilgrimage to my homeland to be with my family, my people — my history.

I was born in South Korea and grew up in an orphanage with the name Ah Kee Chung. Then at four and a half years old, I was shipped around the world to join my adoptive family. I arrived at the Seattle airport with nothing but a small backpack with a change of clothes and a passport the Korean government issued specifically for my first international trip. Stepping off the plane, never having seen white people, I WAS TERRIFIED. There before me were the equivalent of aliens, pale skin, brown and blond hair, and blue eyes.

What, you might ask, is the most logical reaction for any child? Why, it's to run, and I mean full-on sprint, and BOLT away from these aliens chasing after me in the Seattle Tacoma airport. After total exhaustion, I acquiesced to my adoptive parents' embrace. They captured me, and I began my life with my new German-Canadian heritage.

And now, during the remaining two hours of the flight back to Korea, I put the finishing touches on the photo album and edited the video footage of Parliament and Ottawa I'd taken to show my birth parents my life. The stewardess finally announced we were nearing the Seoul, Incheon airport. "Please stow away your carry-ons and prepare for landing." I didn't know then there was no way I could prepare for what awaited. We landed, and I completed the familiar routine of getting my luggage and buying my ticket for the four-hour bus ride to my hometown, Kwangju. I'd just missed the bus, and there was a 30-minute wait before the next one came. During my wait, I thought about my first flight and voyage to meet my birth family.

It was 2007, and I was a penniless grad student. How was I to pay for a $1,500 ticket for a voyage back across the Pacific? Well, I got dressed in my best $20 H&M blazer and 75% off Aldo shoes and marched down to the Korean Consulate in Vancouver. I introduced myself to the receptionist as the Ambassador for Korean-Canadian Adoptees. With such a title how could they not meet with me? I met with a series of old male Consuls and introduced myself accordingly and then made the pitch. Would they ever so mind paying for my flight to Korea? A couple of weeks later they called and asked who gave me my title. I replied, "Ahem ... I did." Stunned silence, but by then the gears had already started to turn, and they ended up paying for my ticket.

That August, I flew to Korea. I met my birth parents in the adoption agency at the age of 24. It was surreal. Opening the door and rounding a corner, there they were. There was my DNA alive, coursing through the veins of these two people; two people that I was made up of in equal parts. There wasn't crying, or shouting, or rejoicing. If there was one word, it was quiet. A quiet exchange, a searching in each other's faces, looking for hints of decades lost. During this visit, my Oma gave me my Korean name Hee Su Kim and birth certificate. It was official. I was born. I stayed with them for a couple of nights, and it was incredible. I saw my Oma in her very gender stratified role as a mother and wife. She cooked and the stove never seemed to turn off. It was as though she had 24 years of food to stuff into me in 48 hours, and she was quite determined to make that happen. I didn't learn much Korean outside of, "I'm sorry, I'm full!" And, of course, "I love you."

***

My bus finally arrived at the airport, and I boarded for the drive to Kwangju. It was stuffy, and there wasn't much to see other than the city lights in the night. The last time I'd seen my Oma was two years before in 2010. During those intervening years between 2007 and 2010, I'd founded my first non-profit for Asian adoptees who had a similar journey as myself growing up in transracial homes. My organization was the sole one representing Canada at a conference that year in Seoul for 500 adoptees from around the world. I was given a beautiful glass plaque as a thank you. I took the train from Seoul to Kwangju just to show my oma. As I unveiled it from the crushed velvet case, her face was total awe. Her pride and amazement needed no translation. She had seen photos of my life, my graduations, my job as a speech-language pathologist in Vancouver, but she'd never touched the tangible "proof" of my life. Her expression was beautiful, and I basked in the warm glow of a parent's love and pride.

Ding, the bus driver, announced we'd finally arrived in my hometown. I disembarked to see my oldest sister and my sixth sister waiting to greet me. Yes, that's right. I am the seventh daughter. By this time it was the dead of night, 1 am Boxing Day in Korea, still Christmas Day in Canada. Upon arrival, I insisted we go to the hospital. Two months earlier, I had diagnosed Oma's aspiration pneumonia during a Skype call. As a speech-language pathologist, I had heard this voice quality in patients' voices, and I knew it didn't bode well. We arrived at the hospital. For her ward, there were no set visiting hours.

We walked into her room, and I could barely recognize my Oma. She was sickness itself. She lay propped up, and our eyes connected. I sat on her bed, held her hand and couldn't help the tears from falling. I knew how much pain she must be in. I leaned in and kissed her forehead, and as I did, I could feel her entire body relax. She had waited over two months for me to come. We left that night with the intention of coming back the next morning so that I could give her my gifts.

The next morning came with a phone call as my alarm. Still jetlagged and disoriented, my fourth sister was calling to say that Oma wasn't doing well and that we needed to come to the hospital quickly. By the time we arrived, she'd passed away. I was soon to get a crash course on Korean culture and funerals. In case you're wondering, they're immediate, and they're also three days long. They consist of renting out a room and serving food and drink to all those in the deceased's network.

We went to the funeral home, and I sat with my family as they discussed the details of the food, the flowers, and the signage. There is a sign they place on the door of all the remaining family members. When they went through listing the names, my father, my oldest sister all the way down to my sixth sister. Then the room went silent, and they looked at me. I had been dead of these 29 years to most if not all of the family and friends. My physical presence and life was the family's biggest source of shame. It was quiet, but not the same quiet as when we first reunited. It was the quiet of secrecy. No, my name was not to appear on the list. It was my father and six daughters. No more. No less.

It didn't matter. In a sense, it was as though the entire funeral service was my oma's redemption — her way

Stories We Don't Tell

of shouting that she had found her lost daughter. I met EVERYONE: aunts, uncles, cousins, co-workers, neighbours, everyone in her life and it was incredible. Incredible to see a different slice of her life, to see how many people's lives she touched. I watched my sisters and nieces serve the food and clear the tables and I followed suit. Language was still a barrier, but I didn't need anyone to translate what was expected.

In all this, my father's shame prevailed. On more than one occasion, he tried to hide me — physically remove me, his living, breathing, pulse beating failure. It stung, but I understood. For the last five years, I was safely stowed away in Canada. Their story that I was a stillbirth survived as my contact with family and friends was minimal. Now, I was there, linguistically inept but with an undeniable familial resemblance to sisters four, five and six. Everyone knew.

On the third day, we buried my Oma in the family plot. It was a miserable day, rainy, cold, and far. We trekked up the mountain and, upon arrival, there before me were the graves of my grandparents, aunts and uncles. I stood with my legacy, meeting them for the first time. We lowered Oma to be with our family. I placed one shovel of dirt on her casket as did my six sisters.

I returned to Canada. Though time has softened the loss, it's still sad to speak about my Oma and her death. If there is one thing that pervades my thoughts, it is her love. A love that crosses linguistic and cultural barriers. And a love that even today remains after death. It's an odd feeling to yearn for and miss a mother that I never had the chance to know well. But there is beauty in the unconditional love that she communicated and gave, and for that I am forever thankful. *Sa-rung-hae-yo, Oma.* (I love you, mother).

Chapter 27: Brianne Benness

Before I decided to get married, I read a lot of books about commitment. I read memoirs from commitmentphobes and I read advice books written by therapists and I invited my future husband to spend a weekend in Montreal with me where I could tell him everything I'd learned about the institution of marriage. And because he is patient and also because he wasn't really worried about what it would mean to be married, he agreed. We did a lot of surveys. They were about how we would manage household chores and how we would raise any future kids and how we would handle it when our values and politics were at odds.

Because we were 28 and considering a life together, we talked about who would do the laundry and if we would have kids and who would stay home with them if they got sick. We talked about how often we wanted to have sex and what our love languages were and what we would do if I got unexpectedly pregnant. We talked about faith and monogamy and where we were going to live. We talked a lot about what we would do if either of us had a mental health crisis. About putting romantic expectations on hold and keeping each other accountable to manage any future grief, depression or anxiety.

We did not talk about what would happen if all of these questions became irrelevant.

***

Based on all the books I read about commitment and the fact that I'm a founding member of Stories We Don't Tell, you won't be surprised to hear that I love reading first-hand accounts of relationship crises. And one of my favourite places to find those is the dead bedrooms subreddit. In case you aren't familiar with it, Reddit is a website made up of millions of very specialized niche communities. There are feminists and there are men's rights activists and there are people who love to make grilled cheese. If somebody wants to talk about it, then there is a subreddit for it.

Dead bedrooms is a subreddit for people in long-term relationships whose sex lives have died. Many of the people there are now divorced, and many are trying to navigate decades-long marriages where they have not even hugged their spouse in five years. It is an incredibly vulnerable place.

***

Right around the time I got engaged, I started to get this mysterious skin pain. It occasionally felt like the skin on my thighs was bruised, except it wasn't. Sometimes it felt like a sort of buzzing beneath my skin and sometimes I didn't notice it until I was touched. Always, it made me flinch.

So weeks after we got engaged, I found myself shrinking away from my fiancé's touch. Sometimes. Because it was new and it was unpredictable, neither of us remembered that just a gentle hand on my lower back might cause me pain.

***

I read a story on dead bedrooms once from a devastated man who was trying to bring intimacy back into his marriage. I'm not even talking about sex here, he just wanted to cuddle with his wife, to spoon with her. But whenever he reached for her, she turned away. He described how worthless it made him feel. Lower than low.

I asked my fiancé if he was worried about our sex life. It was true that sometimes it hurt when he touched me, but I still wanted him to feel like he was important. He told me to stop reading the dead bedrooms subreddit.

***

Eventually, we got married. The skin pain had become an unpredictable but ongoing part of my life. I didn't have an explanation for it, but it was always worse when I didn't get enough sleep. And it wasn't just the skin pain anymore. When I didn't get enough sleep, I had this throbbing pain in my lymph nodes, and my thoughts got cloudy.

I started to really prioritize my sleep. I tried to get in bed by 9:30 every night, when I was so drowsy that I occasionally needed help keeping my balance on my walk to bed. My husband would tuck me in and turn out the lights and go back to the land of the living, because my 9:30 bedtime didn't really suit him.

I told him about a story I read on dead bedrooms from this heartbroken man who had sex with his wife about once a week, but she just lay there staring at the ceiling and asking him to hurry up. He wanted desperately to feel connected to his wife, to feel loved by her, and he didn't know how to do that when she was so shut down.

Since I was barely coherent in the evenings, I asked my husband if he thought we should try to get more into morning sex. He told me to stop reading dead bedrooms.

And actually, once I thought about it, I realized that mornings weren't that great either. Six months after we got married, I started waking up with swollen feet and swollen knuckles and I would sneeze non-stop for at least an hour.

***

About eight months after we got married, I decided to stop working before I got fired for missing major errors in my editing workload. And so each day, I would wake up, swollen and trembling and aching and foggy. My husband would make my coffee just the way I like it with protein powder and coconut milk and stevia. He would help me out of bed and walk me to the couch and cover me with a blanket while I settled into some Netflix. Then he would disappear to do whatever it was he had to do that day.

At lunch, he would bring me a smoothie with spinach and greens and berries and more coconut milk and more protein powder. Then I would watch more Netflix. Sometimes with my eyes closed. At dinner he would cook grass-fed meat and low-carb veggies and experiment with spice blends before joining me on the couch. Then, eventually, he would help me to bed.

On good days, sometimes I would go outside. On bad days, he would help me walk to the bathroom whenever I needed it. On most days, I wondered if this was my new normal. I began to reckon with the very real possibility that this was how my life would be from now on. That I wouldn't be able to earn my own money or prepare my own food or walk myself to the bathroom. That my husband of less than a year would become my caretaker for as long as he chose to stick around. I would be all of the burden with none of the benefits.

***

I read this story on dead bedrooms about a man who was

at his wit's end because his wife had chronic pain and so she almost never wanted to have sex with him. And when she did, she needed so many accommodations just for it to be tolerable. He wanted to know how to motivate her to really tackle her health problems so that she could have sex with him the way she used to when they were first dating.

At this point in time I had a tremor and miscellaneous nerve pain and my knee reflex had stopped working. And because of all that neural dysfunction my body had basically forgotten how to orgasm. Also, because of my skin thing, affectionate touch was more likely to cause pain than pleasure. Oh and also, I really needed to have my head supported at all times. It wasn't a recipe for great sex.

In fact, here's what we did during our first year of marriage when we should have been having sex on every flat surface in our house: we watched all 13 seasons of Supernatural. We learned to play the cooperative board games we'd received as wedding gifts. He gently scratched my head when I woke up in the middle of the night with painsomnia.

And when I asked him if he was worried about how my health was impacting our sex life, my husband told me to stop reading dead bedrooms.

***

Ten months into our marriage, we finally found a doctor who could help me. My husband came with me to the appointment for physical and moral support. I got a Fitbit to track my heart rate and was not surprised to learn that most days I barely broke 500 steps.

***

A year after we got married, I was walking on my own

again. I still slept a lot and I watched a lot of Netflix, but I also took myself on one-hour walks in the woods some afternoons. I occasionally hit 10,000 steps on my Fitbit.

***

And one day we kissed and I realized that I wasn't just thinking about how much longer I could stand to have my head unsupported. And the painful hotspots on my skin were retreating, so I didn't cringe when he touched me. In fact, I kind of liked it. My whole body flooded with possibility. This thing, this moment, where my body felt good and his body felt good and we were in tune with each other, it was familiar. I had forgotten that it used to feel like this.

And he felt the possibility too. He stopped kissing me and he buried his face in my neck and he held me. Crushed me, really. Because while I was obsessing about our dead bedroom and worrying about what it would mean if I wasn't the exact wife I'd promised to be that weekend in Montreal when we planned our life together, he'd been terrified of losing me entirely.

Chapter 28: Maximilian Suillerot

I bought my first pack of cigarettes when I moved to Paris. I was 18 years old. Marlboro reds. The ones my dad used to smoke when I was little. I think he smokes Camels now. I saw a pack of those when we broke into his place a couple of weeks ago, I guess they could have been his boyfriend's smokes ... I don't know.

He never smoked very regularly. When I was a kid, I had succeeded in making him quit with my mother's encouragement. Whenever he would come home I would go through his stuff and steal all the packs, lighters and matches I could find. I kept them locked in a toolbox with a padlock and threw them away regularly when he wouldn't see me. He quit eventually, at least for a while, frustrated by the amount of money I was making him throw straight into the trash.

The day I bought my first pack of cigarettes, I had woken up quite late. It was a particularly warm and sunny day for October. None of my flatmates were home. One of them had left me a croissant for breakfast, not the one I was in love with, the other one, my best friend.

I've always been a very touchy person, the physical contact between my love interest and me was escalating since we moved into the same room, tensions were rising. A conversation arose between the other flatmates: "What's gonna happen if they actually start dating?" We already lived in the same room, in separate beds, though. They had warned me against complicating things and making the first move.

I stood up, didn't eat the croissant and left the apartment. I slowly walked to the tobacco shop under the sun, listening to "Everything In Its Right Place" by Radiohead over and over again, a song that would follow me for quite some time after this day. That first cigarette was my breakfast.

My mom and my sister were flying in to visit. I'm taking a couple of weeks off university for this, even though I just started. I had flown in about two months earlier. This time of my life would eventually come to be the source material for my award-winning thesis in a university on the other side of the Atlantic Ocean.

I had arrived at the Charles de Gaulle airport in Paris with all of my belongings on an 11-hour flight from Mexico City. My dad was supposed to pick me up, but he wasn't there. His cellphone was off. This was very unlike him. I scanned the airport but couldn't find him. I went back to baggage claim and hopped in a taxi with a nice lady from my flight. She had offered to touch base at her place so I could contact other family members and sort out this situation.

That day I was wearing Blundstone boots, a Nine Inch Nails black T-shirt and my blue leather jacket. I'll never forget that. I didn't take the jacket off despite the intense summer heat — I needed that layer of protection.

My mom's excitement about my safe landing was immediately shut down by the tone of my voice and the content of my words. I was the first one to be aware of his disappearance and had the duty to inform everyone else. I took a cab to my aunt's place who I was not completely comfortable with and stayed with her for a couple of days until the move-in date of my shared apartment.

I knew most of my parents' history in Paris, where they had met, where they had lived, the coffee places they had frequented and the schools they had attended. I even knew the people they met in university that became their lifelong friends. My apartment was only a couple of blocks away from my dad's university, and I was currently working on my portfolio to apply to my mom's university in the same city. I was following her exact same footsteps: born in Mexico City, went to the same middle school and high school even had the same physics prof and moved to Paris to study art at the same institution.

To fully become my mother I would simply have had to meet the love of my life during first year, marry them, graduate, live the life of an emerging artist in Paris, then go back to Mexico with my spouse to start a family and repeat this cycle all over again. As if the goal was to expand the French/Mexican population of this planet.

Since our arrival, my roommates and other friends were enjoying their new-found freedom. We had all moved from Mexico to this country where public drinking was legal and boxed wine was available for 2 euros.

I did not exercise this freedom. Despite their insistence, I never went out with them at night.

I appreciated when they all came over to our place, hung out and cooked Mexican food, but I never took part in the bar hopping and night drinking by the river.

Instead, my insomniac nights for the months to come would be filled with long cigarette fuelled walks around the city.

These walks would happen as often as they needed to, regardless of weather conditions. They would usually start out of intense frustration. After a couple of hours of trying to fall asleep using different techniques with no success, I would get up, grab my cigarettes and go roam the city alone.

Hate was an overwhelming feeling during this year of my life. Hate would materialize at my jaw and neck. It would then flow down to my shoulders and arms, eventually filling the rest of my body. My solution was always to walk hate off at night, and feed it cigarettes. This was my primary solution despite it usually being almost completely unsuccessful. I would walk by the river, and stop to stare at its thick blackness. I would think about the number of bodies that may have ended up in it over the years. I would imagine this heavy liquid body vibrating and expanding, overflowing into the streets, engulfing the city and then the whole planet in its darkness.

I would wait for the parks to open and walk in to watch the sunrise from a bench, a perfectly hateful sunrise.

My second day as a smoker was the day I had scheduled my visit to the police station with my dad's boyfriend. We met in the subway and made the trip to the outskirts of the city to meet the police detective in charge of my father's missing person case. We were the only ones interested in seeing a picture of my dad's body when we were informed this was a possibility. I learned that since the boyfriend was not related to my father, he was not allowed to see the file unless accompanied by a family member. This sparked a growing rage in me towards French governmental institutions that still stands to this day. I naturally agreed to go with him.

Upon arrival, one of the only nice but condescending policewomen there confiscated the Swiss knife I had in my pocket as a keepsake taken from my father's apartment. She reassured me, as if talking to a toddler that I would get it back on my way out.

It turned out the fucking detective wasn't even there, his desk-mate had to interrupt his lunch to goofily look for my father's file and without any context present it to us.

I finally saw the picture, it was definitely him, no doubts this time. It had been 66 days since I landed in the city and for the first time I had found some certainty, hateful certainty. He did not look as bad as I was expecting. "His

Stories We Don't Tell

eyes were sewn shut as part of standard autopsy procedures," the stupid detective explained in a soft voice, as a too-late warning. I realized this was the last chronological picture of my father, and I was not allowed to keep it.

My natural reaction was to swallow my thoughts and feelings, the way I had done so far. Leaving my stone-cold face on the exterior with the persistent smile as a wall.

The boyfriend, unlike me, lost his shit.

The sight of my father's picture brought him to immediate tears, followed by rage and yelling at the surrogate detective denouncing the utter incompetence of the police department in dealing with missing person cases. My father had committed suicide a couple of hours before I landed, and they had been unable to find him or give us any information for two full months.

My third day as a smoker was the day of the wake. I couldn't really smoke, because I didn't want to let my mother know that I had started smoking. She was here now, and I was spending all day with her. I left my pack at home. A lot of people from my university came to the service, including professors despite not knowing me for that long, as well as all of my Mexican friends and a lot of extended family I had never met before. The service was way too Christian, more Christian than what was previously agreed upon. No one in my family was really down for this — my dad wouldn't have been too down for this either — but that beautiful church in the heart of the city was a good space to gather everyone on such short notice. I shook my head in protest at the hateful priest for the whole duration of his presence at the service.

We were going to bury him in the countryside, so we took a train in the evening. A more intimate crowd this time, the family, the boyfriend, and some of their close friends.

This felt better, and we buried him the next day. I had

nothing to say during the burial, but I was expected to say something as his first-born, so I read a poem suggested to me that seemed completely meaningless. We had other meaningful moments.

When I returned to the city, I was still sleepless and hateful, but I really wanted to see my friends and roommates. My stone-faced smile worked with them too. They had been partying all weekend, which I expected. The wake had coincided with the birthday of one of them. However, I encountered a couple of unexpected situations.

My roommate — the one I was in love with — had slept with and started dating this other friend from our group. She had feelings towards both of us back in Mexico, things had changed now. They were not the only ones who scored; my flatmate, the best friend, managed to sleep with my childhood best friend. They had met at the wake, I introduced them.

Feeling more disconnected from them, I took a long hate-walk and then went home by myself instead of bonding with them. When I finally got home, I went straight for my pack of cigarettes only to find it completely empty. My friends had smoked them all in my absence, and there was absolutely no way I could buy any more until the next day.

Chapter 29: Jonathan Finn

"Are you into kink?" she asks, staring across the table from me.

"Well, I've had partners that have wanted me to take on dominant roles," I reply, "I've tied people up before."

"What about Shibari Japanese rope tying?"

I think for a second. "I don't think I can do that," I say, "because I have no idea what it is."

She takes out her phone and starts flipping through it. She shows me the screen. It's pictures of her hanging, in her underwear, tied in various elaborate rope configurations.

I look at her. "I don't think I can do this for three reasons. First, I don't have the facilities. Second, I don't have the equipment, and third, I don't have the skill."

I would say that this date had taken a turn, but I can't say that all of this completely came out of the blue. I had been talking to Joanne (not her real name) on Tinder for just less than a week. I sensed an impatience in her immediately. She had been looking for women to date, she had started out telling me, but was getting bored with chasing them around. There was an aggressiveness to her candour. I got the sense that she wanted me to arrange something immediately. Moreover, her profile specified that she was into kink. I had jokingly suggested that my only kink was something called "bronzing," a practice that involved covering other people in bronzer. I told her that I was part of an elite society of men into bronzing called the "Bronze Boys." She replied that she hoped that wasn't my only fetish.

Yet, though I can't claim that what was happening had completely taken me by surprise, the entire evening had an unshakeable air of implausibility, an unbelievable quality that I was choosing to roll with. To begin with, she was really good looking. And by that, I mean that she was too good looking. She was suspiciously good looking. So good looking that I assumed that my role tonight would be as some kind of dating secretary and that I would be escorting her to her real date soon. Then there was the fact that her online candour translated into a slightly awkward, in-person frankness. She made it clear that she was only interested in pursuing casual relationships. Her impatience also found its real-life counterpart — I could tell that my insistence that we talk for a bit first before engaging in potentially risky activities was not, in her mind, ideal. But there is something oddly liberating about a date seeming unreal because suddenly everything seems possible and if everything is possible, why worry about anything?

While Joanne may have been disappointed at my lack of rope skills, she didn't show it. And can you really turn up and demand that your date participate in a highly skilled form of Japanese rope bondage?

She looks at me again with the same slight impatience, perhaps irritation, "do you want to go and have sex?"

"Alright," I reply, and we sit at the bar for another ten minutes finishing our drinks before heading back to my apartment. We walk up the stairs, say a brief hello to one of my housemates and head up the further set of stairs to my room. At this stage, I should add, absolutely nothing physical has happened. We haven't even brushed arms. So it comes as a surprise that as soon as we get to my room, Joanne starts taking off her clothes.

I want to make her kink, being dominated, a believable reality for her. After all, I think this is what Dan Savage has been telling me that I should be doing. I take off my clothes also. Of course, the irony here is that she's got the upper hand, and in doing so seems better suited to the role of aggressor than I am.

Now, I'm not God. I can't claim to know what kinds of experiences you've had, so I don't know if you've had a sexual experience where both people have taken on the dominant role, especially when dominance appears to come much more naturally and easily to one of you. It's like trying to complete a jigsaw puzzle by getting drunk, nailing the board to the wall, covering the pieces in glue and then hurling them at it. It's a super fun way to do the puzzle, but inevitably things get lost, bits break and fall off, nothing quite fits together properly. You just can't complete the puzzle like that. There's a reason why we rarely hear people talk about dom-dom relationships.

Nonetheless, and against some fairly decent odds, we're having sex. And then she asks me to bite her.

I'm not going to lie, I've definitely bitten people before, but it's been the kind of gentle, not too aggressive biting that is relatively playful in nature. So I start to bite her, pretty lightly on the neck.

"No. Bite my breast."

Now, I'm not God, and I don't know how that rumour got started.

I don't know how many of you have bitten a breast before but, to these teeth, it doesn't feel like something that should be bitten. It's soft and, if nothing else, super difficult to get a good grip on. Moreover, it just feels like something that will break if bitten too hard.

I can tell that she can feel my accommodating reluctance because her next instruction is for me to move on to biting her stomach. Her stomach is a bit better for biting because it's firm and I feel like I can bite it without the same risk as her breast. Clearly, however, my biting isn't adequate.

"Harder!" she instructs.
I bite harder.
"Harder!" she instructs.
I bite harder still.
"Harder!" she commands.

I'm biting her stomach really hard now, in a way that has gone beyond feeling uncomfortable to me into a territory that I am totally unfamiliar with. This is something she's requested, it's something that she enjoys, it's something that is clearly important to her. Yet, at the same time, I'm biting a human being. I'm stuck momentarily between those places, between the part of me that wants to accommodate and satisfy, without judgment and in loving reciprocity, this naked human person, and the part of me that knows that I'm biting someone. The only things I bite in my life are edible, and human beings may fit this rather loose category, but I don't think that I want to eat one. I worry. I worry about eroticizing violence, and I worry that this worry disqualifies me from the spirit of the act.

And if I'm honest, It's not a turn on for me, but it's not not a turn on, either. Maybe this is what I'm into? Maybe I actually really want to bite this person. Maybe I want to bite everyone.

I'm thrown into the future and, like every anxious person, it's a future where everything is going tremendously wrong, where I'm confessing to a new partner that all I want to do is bite them hard and they're staring at me in absolute disgust. "Come back," I say, but I'm alone now, satiating myself by chewing on bags of toffee. The police arrive. "Time to arrest you on suspicion of biting, Mr. Finn." "That's not a real charge," I say, but it's too late.

"Stop," Joanne says, and she lies back, seemingly satisfied by my good-natured albeit sexually confused cannibalism.

There are teeth marks on her stomach, actual, real teeth marks — my teeth marks. She'll tell me in a text a few days later that a bruise formed.

Without a pause, and I really mean that, she immediately begins putting on her clothes again, as though nothing has happened. Puzzled, I reach up and put my hand on her arm. She takes this as a cue because she suddenly takes off her clothes again, and the whole thing that has just happened ten seconds ago happens again.

When she starts to immediately put on her clothes for the second time, I don't reach up because really, I genuinely don't think I could do that again. I begin putting on my clothes and she looks at me, puzzled. "You don't need to see me out," she says with that same mixture of confusion and slight irritation as before. I wonder if the whole concept of niceties, of politeness, of civility, whether genuine or not, is itself an insult to her. She certainly doesn't find it sexy. But I am if nothing else, in my own way, aimlessly, awkwardly polite, in part a product of the uncompromising, somewhat fanatical moralizing of my idealistic (definitely not pragmatic) family. "Well, I'd kind of like to, you know, just walk you generally to the door ..." She acquiesces. I walk her to the door.

I head back up to my room, the same room I was in just minutes ago. I climb into bed, and as I fall asleep, I realize that I don't think I'll ever get very far with Shibari Japanese rope tying.

Chapter 30: Luke Anderson

This feels cozy in here. Warmth and togetherness. I'm excited to share a story about my most embarrassing moment. It's early September 1999, and I'm a university student, second year in the engineering program at Waterloo, and it's a co-op. A co-op program at Waterloo lets you go and work in the industry for four months and then go to school for four months.

This September, I'm working in a placement that allows me to go into the field and survey construction sites. The company that I'm working for is in charge of making sure that the construction site is all ready to go for the developer to come in and build the building. My job is to go and measure sewer systems and water mains and road works. I have to make sure that all this stuff is good to go for the handover to the developer.

I'm about a week in, and my supervisor tells me that I'm to go and meet up with a co-worker named Tom, whom I've yet to meet. It'll be our first meeting the next day at 6:30 in the morning. That morning I pack up my stuff and rush out of the house. And I'm really keen on going for a bike ride later that evening, so I throw all my bike gear in my car, and I meet Tom at the construction site.

Tom's already there, and we get started on our work together. He's a great guy. He notices that I have my bike on the roof of my car, and that kicks off a great conversation about mountain biking. Tom also loves to mountain bike, so we hit it off. We're both hungry, as we haven't had breakfast yet because it was super early when we started. Tom told me that a food truck comes around to some of the construction sites and delivers breakfast to the construction workers that are on these sites.

A couple hours later, the food truck comes, and we put our tools down, and we make our way to the food truck at the front of the construction site. Tom orders a big coffee and two Egg McMuffins. I follow his lead and order a coffee and two Egg McMuffins. We're so hungry we wolf them down and carry on with our work.

We're working away, and we're talking about mountain biking again and how it would be great if we met up at the end of the workday and went for a ride together. We make plans to do that, and while we're setting things up, I get this really awful feeling in my stomach. My stomach is just turning, and there's a real rumble down below, and it's not good. I try to work through it and I just can't. After 15 minutes or so, I tell Tom that I've got to use the washroom and to give me a few minutes. I race to the porta-potty that's at the entrance to the site, and I just make it in there. I just get my pants down and unleash a fury. I'm unleashing a fury for a good 15 minutes.

I reach a place of relative comfort with the situation before I go back out, and I meet Tom, who's waiting patiently to continue working. We get back out there, and we're working away for another 10 or 15 minutes, and I have to tell Tom that I've got to go back and use the washroom. Another 10 minutes go by in there, and I'm just not feeling great. I'm in and out of this washroom a good six times.

Things start to get a little bit better, and Tom tells me that he's got to go back to the office to look after some office work, and I'm going to finish my day on the site by myself. We make plans to meet up at the trailhead after work, and we set it all up so that we know what the plan is. I finish my job, and I pack up my stuff. I'm feeling a little bit better at this point, and I feel confident that I can hop on my bike and

Stories We Don't Tell

enjoy a ride at the end of the day.

I meet Tom at the trailhead. He's got his bike all set up, his helmet on and ready to rock and roll. I pull up in my car, open the trunk, and I'm getting all my gear ready, lace up my shoes, and I've got my bike shorts on. The last thing I have to do is pull my bike down off the roof of the car. I open the door and step up onto the inside of the door, and I have to reach over the roof to grab the bike that's hooked up to the roof rack. It involves unlatching a clamp, and undoing a strap.

The top of the roof is sort of pushing on my stomach. I'm feeling the pressure. I've done this many times before, but while I'm reaching over, I felt what I thought was a little bit of gas. That normal feeling, you know, the little bit of gas feeling in the stomach that I made a conscious decision to release. In the split second following, I realized that it was the wrong decision to make because what I thought was gas was definitely not. It was more of the variety that I was dealing with earlier on in the day.

Now I have a situation. I'm really excited to go for a ride. Tom's a great guy. He's waiting for me. A great guy, but I really don't know him all that well. I've just met him that day. One thought comes to mind. Maybe if I could just vanish, that would be great. But that's not an option. I think a little bit harder, and I finish getting the bike off the roof, and I get it together, and I realize that I've got to tell Tom what's happened.

And Tom, the good guy that he is, has a bit of a chuckle. We're in the middle of the bush. There's nowhere to clean up. There's no outhouse. We scramble around for something to mop up with. I waddle over to my car to see if there's anything in there. There's nothing. I don't have a change of shorts. Tom goes to his truck and finds a sock.

He throws the sock to me, and I go into the bush, and I clean up as best I can, pull my bike shorts back up, and I go for a ride. Now this goes to tell you how much I loved to mountain bike at one time in my life. But that's not my most embarrassing moment.

***

It's mid-November 2015, thirteen years since needing to use a wheelchair as a result of a spinal cord injury. I'm approaching a big, red ramp. A big, bright, red ramp that has "StopGap" written on the side of it. This big red ramp has been custom built to suit this stage that I'm about to get up on. So I hop up on the ramp and wheel my way onto the stage. I wheel on the stage and stop, and I turn and face my audience.

The audience is made up of about 400 people in the lower level of this huge auditorium and about 150 to 200 people in the upper balcony. There's the front row, just in front of the stage. It's made up of a whole bunch of people with cameras and audio gear. There's excitement in the room. We've just listened to this amazing presentation of these two guys who perform on instruments that are from found objects, like buckets and pipes and broomsticks, kind of like a stomp type of performance. It's totally charged the room up.

I'm out there on the stage, and the energy is electric. The crowd has cheered me on. They're excited. In behind me are the words "T E D X" in big, red, illuminated letters, and they form this big, beautiful sculpture that's actually made out of small red blocks of Lego.

I've prepared for this moment for three months. Three months I practised my speech over and over and over again, in front of friends, in front of colleagues, at home in front

Stories We Don't Tell

of my refrigerator. I knew this speech like the back of my hand. I had my sights set on delivering a speech that would rival the best speeches that I had ever watched. I was about to give a TED talk.

"Hello, everyone. I've got some really exciting news for you. I'm going to be sending you all home tonight with something. It's a device. Sorry, it's not a TV or an iPhone, it's even better. With this device, I'm going to give you the ... I'm going to send you home with a ..."

I've forgotten my words. The crowd let out this huge gasp. And there I was: I was a TED speaker, and I had forgotten my words. My gut sank, this rush of anxiety and heat swelled up right through my body. I felt sweat start to bead up on my forehead, and on the top of my head and my hair. I'd forgotten the words to my TED talk.

In this panic, all I could see was bright light from the spotlight that was on me. I couldn't see faces in the crowd, I couldn't even make out the crowd in front of me. There I was, with this rush of thoughts that were going through my mind. What the heck was I going to do? I wanted to vanish. That was the first option that came to mind, but that's not an option.

And the second option was to turn and wheel off the stage, down the ramp, and make my way out of the auditorium and go home and cry. I just wanted to go home and cry. In this rush of emotions and angst and anxiety and panic, I thought that was my best option. So I wheeled off the stage, down the ramp, and I made it about six feet beyond the ramp, and I couldn't go any further. I was stuck.

I couldn't get out of the auditorium because of all the audio equipment and the crowd of people blocking my way. I was stuck, and it's not like I was behind a curtain or backstage. Six hundred people were watching my every move. I wanted to disappear. I just wanted to go home and cry. But neither of those options were options.

So again in a state of panic, I thought there's only one way to go, and that's back on the stage. So I did. I spun around, and went back up that ramp. I wheeled onto the stage and made it halfway to the middle of the stage. I turned, faced my audience, and they were all clapping. They were all clapping for me. And you know, I picked up where I left off. I presented my speech. I gave a TED talk.

A lot of time has passed since then, and I've had time to reflect on what happened that day. I have to say that in that moment, I was able to feel one of life's purest forms. Life's most raw and pure forms. And that is my most embarrassing moment, and I'm so glad that I didn't shit my pants.

Chapter 31: David Hostetter

Note: this story was performed with saxophone accompaniment from Rhys Morgan.

My friend said that the best way to do LSD is to blindfold yourself and listen to music through headphones. He said it was called 'sonic driving'. Then I read an article about new research being done on the mental health effects of psilocybin on the terminally ill. This psychedelic therapy was being done in exactly the same way that my friend had described. Doctors were sonically driving cancer patients to durable contentment and even joy. So if we write these experiences off as a kind of escapist self-indulgent disconnection from reality, we're ignoring a whole territory of potentially life-altering human experience.

Now around that same time I was rooting through a bag of curry spices and happened to find some LSD I thought I'd lost. So what was there to do except to make an eight-hour playlist? Of course it would be fine. It was the most clear-headed I'd ever felt.

So on a lazy Tuesday morning I purchased a cantaloupe, cut it into cubes, put some almonds in a bowl, and filled a water bottle. I borrowed a pair of noise-cancelling headphones from my roommate Dave, said good day, and locked my bedroom door.

I took four and a half tabs of LSD and tried to meditate for half an hour as they took effect, but it was happening too quickly so I just lay back on my futon beside the window, tied a scarf around my eyes, put the headphones on, flicked the noise-cancelling switch, and pressed play on the iPod.

... ... There was singing: *Out past beyond the field beside the birches, under rising steam ... ...* Soft voices undulated: *Mind like a flower, a flower falling ... nothing is real ... but there is a spring inside. Waves breaking still reflect the moon. I erase myself and songs echo. Mind is an ocean.*

It was completely cliché: I was carried out of the window on a cloud. The sky was fresh and blue and welcoming and clean and pure, but I thought: My roommates will wonder where I went, will I come back? ... Who can say, who can care? Is there not joy ineffable in this aimless winging? More singing: *Nothing is impermeable ... I leap beyond all this into the water at night. The spring keeps opening wide.* Aha! Indeed!

But — but — but — I was fragile ... ... The music changed — the music became the entire experience: it was the texture as well as the scent as well as the vision as well as the taste. It was determining everything and it was cascading, dissonant, and crashing. Nowhere at all. Nothing at all. I haven't said goodbye. I haven't said goodbye. Plunging, plunging. I haven't said goodbye. Nobody at all. Nobody at all. It's not that I feel nothing or see nothing, but I am nothing, there is nothing. No — I am something! I will be something! I strung this frail structure together with these gritty yellow rods, one by one. I didn't know what it was, but I knew that I was making it, I was recreating, with yellow rods, obscured a little by the devastation, but still there, still there! I clung to my anxiety, I clung to my need for definitive being ... ...

But — Oh, I was glad to remain in the sensual realm. The music changed again, and I was washed up onto a mountain summit. I was pristine and surrounded by clouds where mist sweat from the rocks and two naked girls played together in a warm spring. I pranced around playing with them as in some Blakean fable. Oh — those heavenly rocks, warm and serene, water flowing.

Stories We Don't Tell

But Glenn Gould started fingering the keys. Auch! No foreplay whatsoever. He just a-sashays on in, prodding me with his transdimensional hands. His left: the salesman engaging me in hypnotic conversation. His right: the stealthy associate sneaking in the back to steal my priceless jewels! Fondling my brain with these clusters of notes, his left teased me from above while his right defiled me from below! So noble, so adroit, so implacably assured! I beheld a core figure that was trying on an infinite array of forms. Each was extremely intense in its detail, but appeared and vanished as quickly as each piano key was struck. As quickly as each key! Do you know how fast this man's hands move? I was a king covered in brilliant fabrics, a jack of hearts, a Grecian god, a Gundam Wing battlesuit, each coalescing for a minimum of time into impossibly precise detail and immediately disappearing, like this fluid symbol were infinite in its possibility! It was so beautiful — I just needed somebody to hold — ah — my friends, my friends! All I wanted was to hold one of them close to me, to be with me, comfort and love me. Oh how I love you all! If only, if only one of you were here — and then! That passionate need congealed into a single brightly pulsing female form curled up, and I heard her voice: Oh David I'm so sorr-y I am! ... And I thought: You're sorr-y! No, it's me who should be sorry — I tell you I am! My spine was pulsing with a neon light, pulsing with a neon, with a neon ... ...

The music changed again. A desolate melancholia developed. A nostalgic story of love unfolded. I had become a middle-aged punk rock couple, high school sweethearts still together after all these years. We held each other, and our sweetness and our sadness were one single alienating emotion. Our love was a slowly decaying cycle of memory and desperation, on and on through the arid mediocrity.

Stories We Don't Tell

We kept trying to force each other back into that teenaged feeling, so far gone ... and with each renewal of the cycle, something of that original candle dissolved ... ... Together, side by side, on and on through our bleak, suburban, proudly childless years, we held on.

Then a tiger entered me. It didn't seem connected with any music. I was energized. I looked around the room. I was gone, and in my body was this ancient, virile entity (hahaha). I remembered who I'd been so long ago — a Thai warrior, genius of those fighting techniques, finally manifest in a form again! How strong I was, filled with the vigour of the knowledge of myself as this fighter. Fire seemed to burst from my palms.

But things kept changing. There was Tibetan chanting. I was underground surrounded by monks and my inert body was being placed on the surface of an unadorned sarcophagus. I was a grub eating dirt in the blackness, the scruffy decay, blind and gnawing, pulsing and pulsating ... ...

The music was over. I opened my eyes. The room was silent and absurd. I tried and failed to bring myself out through meditation. The experience revived and subsided and so on and I just wanted — I mean I just didn't understand how it could still be happening or when it would ever end. I was frightened ... ... Proust writes, "When we find ourselves on the verge of despair and it seems as though God has forsaken us, we no longer hesitate to expect a miracle from him." And indeed, I was so godless that I was ready to accept any God. Any God. I chanted aloud, over and over: "I declare this place a holy place I declare this place a holy place I declare this place a holy place." Yes — my latent, atrophied Christianity — I felt it again, like a kid in church staring up at the ceiling ready to be filled with infinity. I said to myself: Thank you God, thank you Jesus, thank you, I can do nothing without you, I am nothing. I felt him. And I knew that he could never go away. The holy trinity. I sang aloud through my indefinite vigil: "Holy holy holy lord, god of power and light, heaven and hell are full of your glory, hosanna in the highest." The line is: "Heaven and Earth are full of your glory," but no, I thought — heaven and hell are full of your glory. I savoured the word, hell. Heaven and hell are full of your glory. The sanest, it was the sanest I'd ever felt. The sanest ...

The order of music listened to (the artist is listed first, then the name of the song, or the album, if more than one song was included, followed by the length of time the music played): Mount Eerie (Sauna) 32 min, Oren Ambarchi & Jim O'Rourke (Behold) 42 min, Andrew Bird (Echolocations: Canyon) 51 min, Mormon Tabernacle Choir (Then Sings My Soul) 11 min, Philip Glass (Turkish March) 3 min, Floating Points (Nuits Sonores / Nectarines) 18 min, Dan Deacon (Steely Blues) 7 min, Glenn Gould (Goldberg Variations 1955 & 1981 in an alternating sequence) 90 min, The Gyuto Monks (Ghuyasamaja Tantra, Chapter II) 23 min, Philip Glass (Metamorphosis 1-5) 31 min, Glenn Gould (Prelude, Fughettas and Fugues) 18 min, Glenn Gould (The Art of the Fugue) 70 min, Various Artists (Tibetan Buddhism: Tantras of Gyuto – Sangwa Dupa) 42 min, Logos & Mumdance (Border Drone) 7 min.

Chapter 32: Nicholas Dawkins

I've been called beautiful a few times in my life. However, it was more often regarding my fighting style than my physical appearance. And that works for me because ever since I was tiny, I wanted to be a martial artist. Shaolin monk, ninja turtle, power ranger, whatever. I wanted to be one of them.

It was a chilly afternoon in December 2013. I had finished work and classes for the day and somehow found myself at the campus bar, enjoying a pint and discussing life with a new acquaintance named Benjamin. As the conversation turned towards diet, fitness, and the fight game, I let it slip that I hadn't had a good spar in years.

"Aww man, me neither," he replied.

"... Do you wanna maybe spar sometime?"

"Yeah man, I have the keys to the old training room."

"That's sick! Are you free next week? How about we link up Sunday afternoon?"

"Sounds like a plan!"

I almost danced all the way home. I was brimming with excitement and not a little trepidation. This dude had the keys to the training gym...what did I just get myself into?

The next week passed without incident, during which I prepared myself in the usual way. Constant shadowboxing accompanied by an inner monologue that was about 50% drill sergeant and 50% understanding therapist. That weekend, I made my way to the campus gym, trying to calm myself down by constantly checking my gear. Gloves? Check. Shin pads? Check. Headgear? Check. Shorts and mouthguard? Check. Everything colour coordinated? Check! Upon reaching the doors of the training room, I flung them open with more confidence than I felt and was greeted by the sight of Benjamin already there, shadowboxing himself. Blue and black trunks, thin black shin guards, dark red gloves darting to and fro, skin already slightly flushed and his shaggy hair, unencumbered by headgear.

"Hey Nick, glad you could make it," he said, punctuating his sentence with a snap kick.

"Hey Ben, thanks for taking me up on my offer... No headgear for you?"

"Nah," he shrugged. "Headgear limits my vision, and I can usually dodge better without it."

This dude thought he was fast enough to never get hit? Who did he think he was messing with?

Then I remembered who had the keys to the place and almost asked myself the same question.

"Alrighty, lemme just stretch and warm-up, and we'll get to it then?" I said.

"Sounds good to me, three 5-minute rounds?" Ben asked, producing a round timer from a pocket.

"Perfect," I said, silently remarking that that was longer than I'd ever fought before.

Warm-ups completed, we squared off on the mats that Ben laid out on the floor. The timer beeped its shrill tone, and we started circling each other, eyes forward, chins down and steps small. We both sent out a few probing jabs, testing defences and finding range. After about a minute or so my opponent got tired of playing patty cake and quickly closed in with a flurry of jabs, which bounced off my forearms as I blocked them. I replied with a quick three-punch combo, but he wasn't kidding earlier. My fists whiffed by him each time, and he replied with his own. I took a strike to the shoulder and served up a roundhouse kick, which was rejected immediately by my opponent's raised shin. We withdrew

Stories We Don't Tell

and went back to circling. No probing jabs this time. This guy was fast. Faster than me for sure, and I'm known as the fast guy on the block. This wasn't going my way at all, and I was determined to change that so I rushed in with two snap kicks, ducked my head to set up an uppercut... and felt a hand at the back of my head preventing me from rising.

"Oh shi-" I grunted as time seemed to slow down and I was treated to a deluxe, sub-sized, knuckle sandwich. I couldn't even be angry; I walked right into that set-up. Stunned, I put up my arms in reflex and was treated to several punches to my ribs. I recoiled, threw any kind of plan out the door, and rushed in to get him in a bear hug and hopefully throw him to the ground, but the man was psychic or something because right after I got him he had me in a headlock, and his forearm was already cutting into my neck. We fell to the ground, and he was tenacious. I held on as long as I could, abandoning hope of fighting back. Breathing became my one aim in life, and somehow I held on until that buzzer rang. We rolled away from each other for the minute's reprieve, and I knew that I was utterly outclassed.

Round 2 was different. I felt strangely loose and relaxed. Some of my combos came back to me, and I let them fly. Jab, jab cross. Kick jab cross. Now we were talking. I noticed he caught my punch pattern and always leaned away from it in the same direction. "So set a trap," my inner voice said, and I happily obliged. I sent two lefts his way and feinted a third strike prompting him to slip to the right again, except this time my swinging right fist was rushing to meet the spot just forward of his temple. "Yes!" I silently screamed as it connected. "I finally hit him, I think he stumbled, good job. Yo watch out!" My elation was cut short as he quickly recovered and countered with a barrage of strikes that I only just managed to block or avoid. I kept him at bay with my own kicks and showcased my own evasion skills. "That's right! Show him he's not the only one who can dodge." My mental cheerleader bolstered my resolve, and I pressed forward with renewed wind. I launched another flurry of punches which bounced off of his closed guard. Seeing an opportunity, I ducked for an uppercut and aimed directly for his chin ... and felt a familiar hand on the back of my head. "Fuck, Again!" was all I had time to think before a crimson cannonball crashed into my cheek. Dazed and angry, I abandoned my attack at once and made a new plan. No attacks, no fancy shit, just survive. And somehow I did until the buzzer rang signalling the end of the round.

In Round 3, my inner voice was working overtime. "Is this all you got? What was the point of all your training if it's gonna end like this? Fight back!" and I did. *Fight Club* had it right. Hit rock bottom and you'll either die or find your freedom. So I let myself out, kicks and punches flew like water, and I set up a few more traps that my opponent obligingly fell into. Fake left then bash him with a kick from my right leg. Shrug off the reply and close in quick for some dirty boxing. I moved in and out of his range weaving like a cobra evading a mongoose's relentless pursuit. Then turning the tables and making him back up for a change. "From now on, this is how you fight!" I told myself. But my opponent had plenty of fight left in him, however, and wasn't about to quit. He pressured me with more punches, and I was forced to clam up in my guard. Then suddenly, the strikes abated. I was about to breathe a sigh of relief until my spidey sense roared "No Look Motherfucker Look!" Through my arms, I saw him draw his foot back for another swing kick but determined not to get caught slipping I braced myself and blocked his kick with my shin. Which was exactly what he was waiting for and had his arms around me in a second.

His chest pressed into my left shoulder as he tried to swing me over his hip to the floor. As I struggled to regain balance, my imaginary co-pilot egged me on again: "Fight back," it said, "FIGHT BACK!" Suddenly I was furious, enraged with myself and my crappy performance. So I planted my left leg, gathered all my fury and rage and pain and launched a desperate sidekick into my opponent's mid-section while he coolly switched tactics and fed me an iron knee to the chest...We rocked back. Each of us propelled away from the other by our attacks. Our eyes met across our raised fists, and I knew at that moment, I had earned his respect. As if synchronized, we began circling again. Faster now, no time for stratagems remained. We quickly closed distance and threw with earnest, fists, feet, knees, elbows. It was a good old slugfest, and I loved it! I lost track of how many times I got hit or hit him. All that mattered was the strike, the block, the decision not to stop. Suddenly the buzzer rang its final note, and I was somewhere between relieved and annoyed, but it was over. Exhausted, we high fived and hugged each other in the post-combat embrace that only fighters can share. Drained and bruised, we held each other as we caught our breath, then let each other go as we took stock of ourselves and each other. I hadn't felt that alive in a long time.

After cleaning up the training room, Benjamin and I walked to the nearest pub open on a Sunday and promptly got pints and steaks.

"Holy damn you're fast," I remarked between bites.

"Yeah, I figure the best defence is to not get hit in the first place. Still my coach always said that someday someone's gonna catch you ...You've got heavy hands man."

"Likewise," I said. Infinitely thankful for my inability to blush.

"Next time try not to telegraph your moves so much. You've got power and skill, but your technique needs polishing."

"Tru dat," I replied. "But I got you with that kick at the end though ..."

"Yeah, that was kind of epic. Like Goku and Vegeta in Dragonball Z or something."

"Yes, it was," I said simply. My smile said the rest.

Later, when I arrived at my aunt's place for Sunday dinner, my family had a few choice observations:

My dad looked at my swollen face, grunted, and went back to the game.

"Pickney! A wah di rass ya deal wid? How unu face so bruk-up-bruk-up? You mash up unu self again wid unu parkour foolishness?"

"No aunty. It was a sparring match. Completely different type of foolishness."

My sister simply said, "You need a girlfriend, Nick."

"It's not like that would stop me," I replied honestly, because despite the pain, the strained muscles, the defeat, and the small victories, the rewards were bigger, and the experience ... was beautiful. But this was just another step in the journey to become the best power ranger, ninja turtle, martial artist I could be.

Chapter 33: Rhys Morgan

One early February morning, in 2010, I stepped off a Greyhound in Port Authority and started a trip that shaped who I am today. I had been asleep when the bus pulled in, so I didn't get a glimpse of New York until I left the subway station. Heavy chunks of snow were floating idly onto deserted Manhattan streets. I walked into the middle of an empty road and felt wonderfully alone. This was the independence I had wanted. Here I was, thousands of miles from everyone I knew, totally isolated in the city that never sleeps, starting a journey that would not go to plan.

I use plan in a very loose sense of the word. I had no idea where I would go or for how long, but I had bought a magical bus ticket that got me onto any Greyhound in North America. I was going to travel the states for three months, then settle somewhere in Canada and work for a year. That is what I told my friends and family to convince them that this was a good thing, that I was fine, that they shouldn't worry. In my own mind, I never planned on getting out of the U.S. alive.

I wandered through predawn New York, enjoying how alien it all felt. I checked into a hostel on Broad Street in the centre of Manhattan and took a breath. It didn't really fit with my idea of what a hostel was, it was more like a bargain bin hotel, with the cheapest rooms crammed into the basement. I had planned for months and travelled halfway across the world, and here I was, sitting in a dripping, damp smelling basement, with four bunk beds packed into a room smaller than this one. My roommates were either never there, or not receptive to conversation at all. I stayed one week, hiding in my room, pretending to be asleep, or wandering the streets of Manhattan at night, oblivious to where I was and how much I looked like a naive vulnerable tourist.

I began self-harming when I was 13. It started in a relatively tame way, scratching and bruising and punching walls, and over the following six years progressed into a compulsion or a habit or a release. I would collect pieces of broken glass, choosing only the prettiest shards to scar myself with. I convinced myself it was practice for something bigger, like a fire drill. Whenever I needed to exit the building, I would know what to do and how it would feel. Leaving home, travelling around a new continent, this was my final fire drill, preparing to self immolate.

After a week in Manhattan, I moved to a hostel in Brooklyn, hoping for a different flavour of New York. This place conformed to my idea of hostel travelling much better. The rooms were expansive lofts with 20 odd beds, each dorm had a celebrity painted on the door and walls. I was in the Morrissey room, which I felt was appropriately morose. This hostel felt alive, people introducing themselves and forming instant fleeting friendships, saying goodbye as they go back to old lives, or forward to new ones. A community building itself and breaking down day after day. After my week in Manhattan, not speaking to anyone except the doorman, open conversation was refreshing and terrifying. I had come all this way to get away from friends who would miss me, and here I was making new friends. This was not part of the plan. Some of the people I met in that hostel changed my life. I made friends with a Canadian girl who smoked cigarettes and might have been a lesbian, things that a sheltered 18-year-old me found deeply attractive. We hung out a lot, going to the MoMA and Williamsburg, drinking coffee and playing in the snow in Central Park. When she left to go back to Montreal, she told me to visit, and that sounded nice, but my intended future did not extend that far.

For the longest time, I didn't acknowledge that I was depressed. I looked at the world around me and at people who had harder lives than I could begin to imagine. I looked at my own life, full of privilege and positivity, and I couldn't allow myself to be sad. It didn't make any sense that I could be this unhappy, so I told myself it was just pretend, I convinced myself that it wasn't real depression, I was just being lazy and weak and self-indulgent. I couldn't abide being that person, inflicting my shittiness on the world, and I didn't believe that I could ever change.

After New York, I headed south to Miami. I met someone on the Greyhound who gave me my first little baggy of weed. I had no clue what to do with it, so ended up sitting on the beach with whole buds and stems rolled up crudely in a receipt. I was too nervous to buy papers. Unsurprisingly nothing happened. Miami was where I turned 19. I spent my birthday in bed, reminding myself of the promise I had made, to not survive to see 20. A day later, two Australian guys moved into my dorm, and we made fast friends. They demanded that they get me drunk and we spent the day drinking margaritas by a pool filled with spring breakers playing beer pong.

In my last few years of school, I thought about suicide every day. I imagined fading away slowly, my breath getting shallower each second, tumbling gently into nonexistence. I thought of an abrupt stop, every time a bus passed by on the street, or I accidentally on purpose wandered to the highest point without fences, and looked down daring myself to take another step and hating myself for not being brave or strong enough to do it.

Sometimes I thought about it in an abstract third-person

way, looking at how my death would affect my friends and family. Subconsciously I tried to diminish how much people cared about me, I told myself that my friends wouldn't really care, and my family would get over it eventually. I reasoned that I was going to hit the fire alarm and run out on my life at some point, and the sooner I do it, the better. The longer I was a son and a brother and a friend, the more it would hurt them to see me go. These lies I told myself, so selfish and neglectful to the people I love the most. I couldn't deal with the image of my parents or sister finding my body, or having to go to the little village police station built into a church to identify me. Thoughts like that were too real, so I ran from them. I had to get away, to be free to pursue my end without them worrying about me.

 After Miami, I headed to Chicago. You may have noticed a complete lack of sense in the route I was taking, and it only gets more erratic from here. I enjoyed the long stretches of time I spent on the Greyhounds. It was an easy choice if I felt stagnant in one place. Just get on a bus, any bus, find a seat and settle in for the ride. I read a lot and listened to the same few albums over and over, but mostly I stared out the window and watched a land I had never seen before pass by. All that time on the road made me realize how little I had seen of the world, and how little I really knew.

 At the end of high school, things came to a head. All of my friends were making plans for university, and I was floundering and gasping for air. I couldn't even consider such a big decision as choosing a uni course as I had entirely given up on my ability to learn new things or change in any way. The only way I imagined my future was as a disappointment to the people who believed in me. I couldn't stand the thought of being such an overt failure, I couldn't abide any pity or sorrow from other people. So the only

Stories We Don't Tell

option I saw was to get off the ride early, to wilfully fail before anyone could expect failure from me.

I got to Chicago and found a place to stay. It was an old Edwardian looking building on the outside, but every room inside was a blank white cube. I lucked out and got a room with four beds and a bathroom, all to myself. This was a sign, I told myself. There was absolutely nothing between me and my end. This was my chance. I ran a hot bath and ran a shitty blunt Bic razor down my forearms. But despite my years of practice cutting, it didn't take. Eventually, the bath was a cold faintly diluted pink and I was still alive. My arms looked like a cat scratching post but nothing deep enough to scar. I had failed, proving myself right, that I really was just a weakling and a coward. Over the next week, I left my room only to make ramen or failing that, spaghetti and soy sauce.

Eventually, other people came to stay in my room. My space was not sacred anymore, suddenly my isolation was tarnished. One morning I woke to one of my new roommates stroking my crotch through the sheets. As I started awake, he rushed to his bed on the other side of the room. He asked if I'd ever been blown by a guy before. I said no, asked what time it was, noted that I had probably missed the free breakfast. By that evening I was on another Greyhound, half a country away.

I arrived in Austin and felt revived. Every time I stepped off a bus into a new place, I felt a rush of freedom and opportunity. After wallowing in self-pity and isolation in Chicago for two weeks, I found myself actually wanting to do things. I went to see some bands, I made friends in the hostel, I got a new exciting tattoo. There was a part of me that still planned to die, asap, but that voice was getting quieter. I chalked it up to being too weak and scared to do it, but really, I was enjoying myself. I wouldn't admit that, but

I was. I was excited to keep travelling, and the idea of living past the next month was like an enticing taboo. I assured myself that it wouldn't happen, obviously, but just imagine.

I headed to San Diego for a few days, where my resolve reclaimed my mood. The voice started yelling again. I would not make it to Canada. I would not see 20. There was no other option. I did not have a choice. I told myself this all the time, not giving any other ideas space to develop. I wandered numb and aimless around the city, passing by other tourists and attractions, seeing nothing but the paths in my head I'd trod so many times before. I spoke to a friend on Skype, and for the first time, I admitted to someone what my plan was. It was the first time I remember it switching from future to past tense. Instead of it being something would happen, it was something that didn't happen.

I had managed to get a ticket to Coachella and met some people on the bus there that made me excited to be alive again. There was a girl and lots of dancing and music and lots of drugs I'd never taken before. I was amazed to find that my instinct to make other people happy need not be at the expense of my own happiness and in fact, that shared joy could reflect off itself and build and build. It was also the first time I felt the acute euphoria of dancing without a care, flailing sweaty limbs, completely engulfed by the mood of the crowd. It was the most I had spoken to people or laughed or enjoyed myself in the three months I'd been in the U.S. I came away from there with a glow deeper than just sunburn. It might have been the after-effects of some substance, but I like to think it was the first time I had hope for the future in a long long time.

I gathered myself in San Francisco, trying to make that afterglow last, and before long, I was on another painfully long bus ride to New York. One of my friends from England

Stories We Don't Tell

was going to be in New York for a film festival, and I was going to surprise him. This had been an idea in the back of my head for a while, but I never expected to make it to that point. That bus trip was perhaps the most meditative of all the Greyhounds I'd taken. I took a step back and admitted that I obviously didn't have the stomach for suicide, or the strength of will. So I had to make a new plan. One that extended further than wherever the next Greyhound took me. Reconnecting to my friends reminded me that people at home cared about me, and missed me.

New York was a different city this time, full of friends and opportunity. I wasn't overwhelmed by the future, but excited to see what would happen. The thought of suicide didn't go away completely, but it was lit a different way, like a strange selfish fantasy that would never be fulfilled. I was excited to see if I could actually live on my own, actually have friends and be a human and live a real life.

I left New York, and headed to Montreal, to start living with intention.

Chapter 34: Vivek Jain

I fucking hate TTC! Unfortunately, I have to commute by TTC daily. However, there is always a silver lining — the only good part of taking public transit in Toronto is that people never cease to surprise you in this city of wonders. I get to meet new people regularly and believe it or not — we talk!

During one such TTC journey, there was a girl who sat next to me, and out of nowhere she said — so tell me about your hand. Yes, just like that — no hesitation, no apologies. I was surprised. Many have asked me about my burns when meeting me for the first time but never so casually. One look in her eyes and I knew she was genuinely interested and that she wanted every detail.

Hence began my story, and we went back in time — back to the 23rd of August, 1998. Imagine you are in rural India. There is nothing as far as your eyes can see. A few cars speed past on the highway every now and then to break the silence. Out there in the middle of nowhere is a magnificent temple campus with a few kids playing outside.

Howzzat! The kids shout with great merriment on successfully getting a wicket in the most celebrated game of India, cricket! Another prospective batsman makes his way to the pitch, and yet another ball is lost in the overgrown brush surrounding the pitch. I was a young boy standing at the edge of the field of play, doing my best to stop the balls from disappearing into the brush. Soon, however, the group was out of balls as each ball eventually ended up in the farthest corner of the overgrowth or onto the roof of the temple complex.

At the very moment when we needed a saviour, Aman came with a pack of new balls. My dad came out of the temple and insisted that I take off my silk shirt to allow my body, which was drenched in sweat, to breathe. He accompanied Aman's parents into the temple as they explained their delay and the reason they had been unable to join the rest of the group on the bus to the temple. The parents went inside and were busy offering their prayers to the Gods. Little did they know that it would not be just another ordinary day.

Aman briefly became a hero to the cricket players, but, in a jiffy, all the new balls also found their way to the dense brush. The game stopped again, needing another messiah. Now it was my turn to outshine the others and step up to fetch some balls from out of bounds. I was accompanied by a few other kids as we set out to seek the balls that had landed on the roof of a building.

The building was not much more than a room with a roof but without a stairway to reach the top. Even the absence of a normal way to reach the roof could not turn me away from my glorious quest. With the help of a human ladder, I reached the rooftop, ignorant of what was waiting.

As I retrieved the balls, I noticed an electric wire nearby. I was cautious not to touch it, but a few seconds later, I was hit by an invisible force and remembered nothing more. I was unconscious.

According to eyewitness accounts, there were heavy sparks as I flew high in the air and landed at the edge of the roof. My friends panicked. It was much later that everyone learned I had been thrown by several thousand volts of electric current.

The peculiar thing about electric shock is that it burns you from the inside out. The current penetrated all seven layers of my skin, and my bones were visible amid chunks of skin. One look was enough to cause fever, nausea, and vomiting among the people so "unlucky" as to witness the accident.

After 20 minutes, I regained my consciousness momentarily when I was in a car and began hitting my thighs like a maniac before passing out again. My dad checked my pockets and found coins that had been burning inside my pocket the whole time. He stripped off my remaining clothes to ensure nothing else would hurt his son.

After three days I woke up and learned that I'd had surgery on the night I was taken to hospital. Initially, I was not expected to live, and the doctors had warned my parents that even if I survived, several of my limbs would have to be amputated. "Lucky" is a word that seems inappropriate in my case, but yes, eventually I was discharged suffering only a severed forefinger and charred skin over much of my body.

My stay in the hospital lasted two months and included two more major surgeries. The environment in a Burn Unit is a wonderful expression of human compassion and warmth. The patients not only go through extreme physical pain, but their minds are wounded by the very thought of their deformity and unnatural appearance that they will live with for the rest of their lives.

I have many scars, but I also got one injury which marked me for happier times. My facial muscles would not fully cooperate with my attempts to smile. I am now in possession of something non-trivial, melancholy yet beautiful, "a Broken Smile" as my friend named it later. It reminds me of nothing so much as the simple strength of the love and affection which helped me to stand strong.

During my stay in the hospital, my parents helped other patients and their families cope with the aftermath of their tragic experience. And I gained valuable lessons of life which many of us fail to learn. I came to understand the true meaning, the real significance of the gifts bestowed on us in this world: time, family, and, most of all, simply being human!

In the Burn Unit, I was a little chap who with his pleasing demeanour and unfathomable spirit wanted to bring smiles to a lot of faces. When the cries of other patients echoed through the room during times of regular dressings, I was the one who would sing a different song to the nurses every day. I was the one who would hold the hand of the youngest patient in the unit, Anurag, to help him walk five steps — those five steps that were our exercise as we learned to stand on our own — those five steps that usually resulted in bloodied legs and feet.

During my 58 days in the hospital, there were numerous stories of love and compassion each day. From day 1, to spare my parents, I was determined not to shed a tear despite the pain. But my tests were still not over — the heavy medication led to numerous zits on my head. To cure the problem, it was decided to shave my head, eliminating all zits in the process. That time I cried a river, and to this day I feel guilty because I was weak and I saw my parents break down and cry along with me. My father's best friend had chosen that day to visit me — what would he think and what would he say to the outside world?

***

I'd just finished my saga, and suddenly, there was the announcement — "Downsview station. This train will go out of service — please take your belongings with you." We were both brought back to the present.

"You are so lucky man — lucky to be alive," she said as she went her way, and all I could think was — am I?

Even today, it is hard to understand whether it was divine

intervention that saved me from certain death or whether God put me in that situation in the first place. Were the prayers of my parents and others in the temple at the time of my accident answered or were they ignored? Was it only a coincidence that my father asked me to take my silk shirt off? It would have stuck to my skin had I been wearing it at the time of the accident. Was it just chance that one person had been unable to catch the bus to the temple, and so drove the car which had a huge hand in saving my life?

Perhaps the electric current that passed all through my body was supposed to spare my heart and brain or any other vital organ and that it conveniently forced me to the edge of the roof where I could be retrieved and saved!

The questions are many and yet unanswered. Maybe I was the pawn in a game between God and Satan, both trying to prove their claim over me. But be that as it may, I live to tell my story. I am the "one who survived" to bring happiness into this imperfect world with my Beautiful Broken Smile.

Chapter 35: Elisa D'Arcangelo

There are two people standing here tonight.

There is person number 1: she is the one that likes to be in control and is usually the brain of any operation. Except tonight. So it's not surprising she is not on board with what is about to be said here. She would like to sit back down, not make a fuss and, you know, just get on with it.

Which would be so easy to do, if it were not for person number 2: this one is kind of a hyper-sensitive, needy, let's-talk-about-it-and-then-hug, kind of person, who rarely gets anything accomplished.

This is an attempted dialogue.

Person 2: "There is the all too familiar, uncomfortable tickle in my throat, which I have mastered to relentless perfection. My fingers, just behind the bumpy spot at the back of my tongue. I can't miss it, and I know exactly how to trigger it. When the heaving starts again, I know the uncomfortable part is almost over; the biology of the reflex will take care of the rest. So wonderfully reliable.

"After flushing down the contents of my stomach, I take meticulous care in cleaning the toilet bowl. This thing I do is my secret, and I intend to keep it that way."

Person 1: *"That's gross. Can you please be less descriptive?"*

2: "Growing up, the mother tongue is silence. Both parents consistently at the end of their tether, silence is the safest path to tread.

"Very early on as a child, I realize that it is within my power to give them happiness — raise the curtain of anxiety that pervades our lives, ever so slightly — by being good at things: I am the A+ child, the athlete, the diligent child, the hard-working only child from a lower-middle-class household. In the mind of the child that was me, this certainty is powerful.

"As a consequence, while I lay my successes at my parents' feet and bathe in the warmth of their delight, before the sky clouds over yet again, all my failures are very much private. I want to shield them from any disappointment or yet another burden for them to carry.

"All my failures are private; all my sorrows are as well."

1: *"Oh would you stop telling this sad tale. Is this even really true? I don't recall this being that bad, you're being dramatic."*

2: "The first time I become aware of eating disorders in a meaningful way is at school, of all places, and the topic is presented to me as a cautionary tale. In the book, a description of these disorders is accompanied by a sad piece about a girl and her years of struggle. This is followed by some sort of list of the many types of eating disorders. As I read them, my mind becomes entangled with the line mentioning bulimia. I immediately fall in love with the thought; I like the reversibility of events. I romanticize the immediate tangibility of the results.

"I'm barely 13 when I try it, a few days later, after school, for the first time. I lock myself in the bathroom, even though I am alone at home anyway, and timidly and awkwardly push two fingers back until the heaving starts. It hurts .... and it works — it's like sorcery."

1: *"I knew this was a bad idea, even at the time. Just sayin'."*

2: "Falling apart is not something I can allow myself to do publicly, not when home feels like it is built on quicksand, perilously swaying around me. I can never think the thought of communicating my sorrows, which I can barely put into words myself, to conclusion. It's a task too monumental. And besides — surely these do not even classify as real sorrows?

"Falling apart privately, however, is doable to the point of being convenient...

"It becomes a routine. School — home — nobody around for hours on end — eat. Then keep eating: thousands of calories every day. Then visit the bathroom. Thousands of calories flushed away.

"And it is liberating: it is all about the time between the beginning of the binge and facing the bowl. Twenty or thirty minutes of bliss, of abandonment, un-real pieces of time when I numb myself with food and television, before being able to reverse it — make it un-happen and make it invisible to anyone but me. Eat-purge. Eat-purge, on repeat."

1: *"Twenty to thirty minutes is the time I thought it takes to digest things... Which is just plain wrong, by the way; who knows where I picked up this piece of pseudo-science..."*

2: "Over time, emptying the contents of my stomach becomes, I wouldn't say an obsession, but a routine, an ever-present thought, like some sort of demanding presence, a giant in my brain that I can't ignore just by the sheer volume he occupies between my thoughts.

"Purging always feels raw, but gratifying. I am now intimately acquainted with what different types of food look like the second time around; which ones will be easy to retrieve, which ones will be dry (meaning I will have to drink extra water), which ones will burn on their way back up, which ones, like tomatoes, are prone to staining the bowl."

1: *"Again — gross...I thought we said we'd try to be less descriptive?!"*

2: "My rendezvous with the giant is not about my body.

It isn't really about the food, either. I don't think it ever is. These are just proxies for my suffocating emotional isolation."

"And so I do not think of what I am doing as being, technically, bulimia. When I read about it happening to other, unknown people, it sounds monstrous. My giant seems to be less hateful, he is almost kind. Like a friend..."

1: "... er ... I think you need better friends ..."

2: "The giant is my friend, and he is a main channel through which I express myself. I am shouting, but in the quietest way I know how. I am hurting, but in the least conspicuous way I know how.

"I think people around me are largely oblivious of my behaviour — again, I have become a master of the technique: I can do it pretty much whenever, wherever: find the bathroom, lock the door, turn on the sink tap to conceal any sounds that may escape my throat. Kneel. Moments later, wash my face, double-check my shirt, my sleeves, the bowl, the underneath of the bowl rim, the fittings of the seat and the bowl, the spot where I touched the flush, the floor, in between the tiles, etc."

1: *"I really should have gone into forensics as a profession — ..."*

2: "I also develop strange, ritualistic relationships with objects that live in the bathroom, particularly the floor tiles: small and lime green squares in the periphery of my vision when I face the bowl. White — surrounded in green. Some of them are uneven, crooked or chipped, they tarnish the overall symmetry of the view. I gladly lose sight of them, once the blood rushes to my head, and makes them turn first bright orange, then deep red, then dark purple, then black."

1: *"Who needs drugs when you've got this, am I right?!"*

2: "He is holding my hands in his, like some sort of

fidgety, knotted ball, and he is shaking them as he speaks, so as to reinforce his point: 'Promise me, you won't do it again? Promise me!'

"I'm 18 and someone knows."

1: *"OK, come on, wrap it up, you're not workshopping a novel any time soon."*

2: "My heart is pounding, I feel ashamed and ... I do promise. For a few months, this promise is louder than the giant's persuasions. But it is, right from the beginning, a lie: I know that my true loyalty — remains with the giant.

"Like sitting on a boat and knowing you're with absolute certainty headed for a waterfall. There is nothing to do, if you have no interest in paddling, but to wait for that stretch of water to run out, and then just witness the fall.

"Purging, then, feels like coming home."

1: *"... Are you done?"*

2: "The obsession changes focus over time. As the years pass, the purge itself leaves the limelight. Instead, what stays behind, is ... a special sensation, right after a purge. A sense of fragility and woundedness. Like a hurt bird. And a sense of pureness, all the dirt forcefully ripped from my body and washed away. Often I emerge from the bathroom with a light-headedness (because of the forced pressure in my head), and an aching stomach and a burning esophagus.

"This type of pain I can do something about, this type of broken can be made better with peppermint tea. This kind of hurt I can nurture into a sensation of healing."

1: *"We're done — this is the end, right?"*

2: "You probably guessed — this story has no conclusion. Rather, it fades.

"Over time, my giant has shrunk to the size and shape of an ugly gnome that lives somewhere in the meanders of my consciousness and comes out to play occasionally. Like the

most loyal of false friends, he presents himself at the worst of times."
    1: *"... There. Can this please be over now?*
"Let's please be done with this."

Chapter 36: Paul Dore

Have you heard of the *Hulk* movie? Not the crappy *Avengers* movies. And not the one with Edward Norton. The one with Eric Bana and Nick Nolte by Ang Lee. Ang Lee could be considered a director who makes art films in Hollywood, movies like *Brokeback Mountain* and *Life of Pi*. I wonder before he made this movie, did anyone tell Mr. Lee that the *Hulk* is based on a comic book about a guy who gets big and strong and turns green when someone makes him angry?

But I don't want to talk about the *Hulk* movie. And I didn't want to talk about the *Hulk* movie when I was sitting in a tow truck on the shoulder of Highway 427.

About 20 minutes earlier, at around 5am, I was merging on to the highway when a truck clipped the side of my car and sent me spinning across three lanes. When my car was spinning, the sound got turned down, and everything went silent. My car was spinning right into the path of another oncoming truck. The silence was broken by someone screaming. I realized the screaming came from me because I saw the truck coming. It hit me head-on, and the airbag punched me in the face, and I crashed into the guardrail.

I stumbled from the car, and it was smashed from the front and from the back. The first truck stopped in front of me, and the second truck stopped behind. The driver from this truck approached, looked at me, at my car and said, "I saw what happened: you hit that other guy." And he ran back to his truck and drove away.

John the tow truck driver arrived, followed by the police, followed by an ambulance. The ambulance slowed down, a paramedic poked his head out the window and said,

"Everyone looks okay here!" And they drove away.

John suggested I get in his tow truck to keep warm. He offered me a cigarette, which was difficult to light with my shaky hands. He asked what I did for a living. I told him I work in film and television. And he asked, "Have you seen the *Hulk* movie?" He didn't mean the crappy *Avengers* movies and not the one with Edward Norton, but the one starring Eric Bana and Nick Nolte directed by Hollywood art filmmaker Ang Lee. I took a drag of my cigarette and said, "Yeah."

"I filled in for a driver when they were shooting the *Hulk* movie here," he said. "They paid me really good." I understand that John was trying to fill the air with small talk, but the last thing I wanted to do at that particular moment was discuss the *Hulk* movie. "Are you married?" John asked. I told him no, and he said, "It's probably for the best."

The police officer appeared by the passenger side window and said there were marks along the side of my car that didn't match the one truck that was still there. I told him about the truck driver that took off. He grunted and said, "Do you know what he looks like or what kind of truck he was driving?" I tried to remember, but I couldn't. The officer nodded, "He was probably making sure that you didn't have a dashcam and that you weren't dead. We're not going to find him. And this happens much more than you'd like to imagine."

John towed my car off the highway and to his garage. I just wanted to go home, but John had arranged through my insurance company for me to get a rental car. I took the opportunity to call my parents. As soon as I heard my mother's voice, I lost my shit. I started sobbing uncontrollably and couldn't get any words out. I managed to assure her that

Stories We Don't Tell

I was okay and I'd call her when I got home.

I texted a friend of mine that I knew would be up at this time. I wrote that I got into an accident, answered a few questions about the details. Then she wrote, "Do you want me to tell you what I have to do today?" Yes, please, I needed something to hold on to, some foothold, until I managed to get home. I needed someone to keep me going. I needed help.

John appeared and handed me some items from my car: a bent licence plate and two CDs from the glove compartment. I was too exhausted to explain why the only CDs in my car were TLC's Crazy Sexy Cool and Destiny's Child ironically titled album, Survivor. The rental car came, and it was the biggest and most ridiculous jeep I'd ever seen. John gave me the keys and said, "Alright, see you later!" I climbed up into the jeep and somehow drove myself home.

I dropped my bags and coat right inside my door. Made the mandatory calls to my insurance company. "Are you married?" They asked me. "Do you have any dependents?" I decided I really needed to see a doctor and walked to a clinic down the street from me. A physiotherapist saw me first, we went through the details of the accident, why I wasn't at the hospital. "Are you married?" She asked. "Do you have any dependents? Do you live alone? Do you usually present yourself in this way?" Besides feeling tired and some bumps and bruises, I felt okay. "Well," she said. "You're stuttering, sound confused, and you're searching for words." Next, the doctor came in, asked me if I was married, did I have any dependants, did I live alone?

The doctor told me not to use my brain — no screens, no television, no reading. Basically, sit in a darkened room and try not to think. There was a lot of Netflix over the next few weeks. During this time, my friends came to visit. We didn't do anything, didn't have to do anything. We just watched TV and ordered pizza and talked and went out for walks. Two weeks after the accident, I went on a business trip and then went to Ottawa for the holidays.

From the outside, I looked fine. But my brain was injured. Usually, your brain parses out the thousands of bits of information constantly coming at you, keeps the important parts and discards the rest. My brain couldn't absorb too much information, it was forced to separate things out slowly and on an individual basis. If I ventured out, I had about an hour or two before I just became too overwhelmed and exhausted and needed to go home.

I felt it the day I returned to Toronto, that I was holding things together for work and for the holidays. My body and my mind were finally giving in, finally falling apart. I was very familiar with this feeling.

I've always been susceptible to depression, have gone in and out of various degrees over the years. A while back, it was the worst it had ever been. At the time, I decided to quit everything, gave up on the work I was doing, gave up on the relationship I was in, gave up on almost everything. I barely had enough energy to keep going. It was a dark time — I was lost and lonely and really didn't know which way to turn or who to turn to. I eventually pulled myself out of it, went back out into the world, and since then have only had minor relapses.

But.

It's a scary thought when you know what's coming, and that there's no way out of it. It was like I was heading back to that time, when I was afraid to leave my house, lying on my floor on the carpet wondering how to snap myself out of it. I didn't want to go back there. I knew intellectually that it was probably the concussion that was playing tricks on me, causing my brain to be foggy, having old thoughts of not wanting to leave my house, that no one wanted me around, but it didn't matter. And so, I slipped into a state of depression that I hadn't felt for years.

Something was different this time. John the tow truck driver and the people from the insurance company and the doctors kept asking me the same questions: Was I married? Did I have any dependants? Did I live alone? How could I explain to them that although I was not married or had no dependants or might not have had a partner, but I had an extended and informal family of four, five, ten people around me to check in on me? A patchwork of people in their twenties all the way up to as old as 75.

So, I reached out to these friends, to this untraditional family, and said I needed help and they simply responded by saying, *Tell us what we can do*. Just keep talking to me, just keep writing, just keep letting me know that you are out there. They saved my life.

I haven't made radical life-changing decisions since the accident a few months ago. It's been subtle changes, a series of small revelations that made me see the people around me clearly. Who I don't want in my life, who I do want to pull closer into my life. Maybe not the substance of high drama, but I'm sure Ang Lee could make a great movie about it.

Chapter 37: Monica Hamburg

When I was about 24, the internet as it exists now was new, email was new, and groups, although then they were mostly Yahoo ones, were gaining popularity as a way to connect.

I feel that explanation might be most appropriate engraved on my senior's Medic-Alert bracelet.

I was part of a group for amateur Models and Photographers. I'm 4 foot 10, so any modelling I'd be doing would have to be amateur.

Still, it was fun to have photos taken of me, to experiment with posing, to see tangible representations of how I looked.

Sometimes, I'd look really soft and pretty. And since I was an actor who was largely not getting cast, in part because I was not attractive in a way that the industry classified as appealing, it was flattering to "model."

And refreshing to see myself — to get confirmation that I was not, in fact, so undesirable or freakish.

I had befriended the group's informal leader/moderator, Carl, who would occasionally post and organize workshops. I would meet photographers posting on the board and shoot with them.

Most often, the shoots would happen within a formal structure — a group of photographers and models. I was a number of months in when a fellow named Ed contacted me. He was a man in his late twenties, who had some decent photographs.

We spoke on the phone.

He told me he took the pictures in his apartment.

This is what we, in the business, call a fucking red flag.

You don't do that. You don't go to a stranger's house.

Stories We Don't Tell

Unless you know a lot about the photographer or you have endorsements from other models.

"No, thanks" is probably the best answer to that. But that's a hard thing to say.

My parents, when I was a pre-teen, had a guy who often did repairs around the house. He would leer at me and comment about my breasts and how well I was developing.

I told my parents, who responded: "Well, he's the best workman we've found."

My solution was then to ignore him, even when he spoke to me.

And my parents said: "He thinks you're very rude."

He thinks I'm very rude?! The guy making sexual remarks to a 12-year-old? I'll try to get over the stigma.

But it gets exhausting putting your foot down. When you're female, it too often comes across as rude, as bitchy. It feels like the basic rules should be so much more clear.

In general, I had a lot of anxiety, similar to my folks, constant fear that anything could go wrong. Escalating "What ifs" occupied my brain more than any other activity.

When I felt fear, I had to wonder if it was based on anything real.

So I'd have to bite back my fear and plunge forward if I wanted anything better for my life. Because most of the time, what I was scared about had no basis in reality.

And I know this was stupid. To be paranoid. To not take risks.

So when this guy, Ed, told me his apartment was where he shot the pictures, instead of saying, "that does not sound good," I employed what I felt was a fool-proof method of rape and murder prevention.

I said, "OK, I trust you."

Fool-proof.

Stories We Don't Tell

It's odd that it's not taught in any self-defence course.

I somehow viewed this statement as a type of Kryptonite against evildoing.

Like someone with bad intentions would think twice. "Oh, I was planning to hurt her. But ... damn, she gave me her trust."

The shoot with Ed turned out to be pretty standard. We shot some pictures. And he told me a bit too much about his life and problems.

The amateur photographers I worked with did this often. I'd hear about divorces, girlfriend drama, their general issues.

Somehow, a scantily clad girl serves as a type of truth-serum. Why this isn't used more at police interrogations, I'll never know.

At one point, Ed said, "let's take a break." And we sat on the couch. He asked me some questions. And began massaging my shoulders.

This also happens a lot. I've had anyone from guys on dates to bosses at workplaces do it.

If you're female, the best way to get a massage is to not want one.

For clarity, no guy randomly massages a woman out of kindness. No one thinks, "This woman looks tense, let me use my considerable lack of massage training and help her unwind."

I think it's a Foot-in-the-Door Technique. Something they hope will be a step towards the Cock-in-the-Cooch.

"If I touch her, if I push this boundary and she doesn't stop me, I can move forward. Maybe she won't say 'No' at all."

It wouldn't be until over a decade later, in my mid-thirties, that I would stop someone when they pulled this move. That

215

would be at a lunch after a small technology conference. I knew most of the people at the table of about eight casually and fondly — except one man who was friends with a few of the others.

He sat next to me, and at one point put his hand on my shoulders and started the unsolicited massage.

I found myself tensing up. The antithesis of a massage's purpose.

"I hate this," I thought. "I want this to stop."

But if I say anything I will make him uncomfortable... Make everyone at the table uncomfortable.

And then it occurred to me, what absolute bullshit this was. And how bizarrely ingrained: not making someone feel uncomfortable for something inappropriate they were knowingly doing ...

I thought, "Yeah, this is part of why these guys get away with it" because we're always looking for a way to not make them feel bad ...

Enough.

I put my hand on the massager's hand. Took it off me, and without a word, placed it back on him.

But a decade before, it mattered more to me to protect someone else from discomfort. So, I didn't do or say anything when Ed, the photographer, massaged my shoulders.

And then, when he went into the kitchen and made a drink that used a blender and handed it to me, I thought, "I never asked for this drink."

But I didn't know how to say that.

So I sipped at the Piña Colada-like concoction. Drank a minuscule amount.

And then, a little while later, told him I had to leave.

I'd like to say, I felt a huge overwhelming suspicion. "I KNEW something was wrong," is what's usually said in

Stories We Don't Tell

these kinds of stories.

But I didn't.

I felt uncomfortable, in part, because of some of the things he was doing. But that was only a fraction of why I felt weird and of why I left.

It was largely that I was generally awkward. That I sometimes felt really trapped around people I didn't know well. And I didn't like to drink around them and get falsely comfortable. And wake up feeling gross.

And the other fraction was that, as had happened many, many times (many, many, many times), I was in a dysfunctional pseudo-relationship with a guy who was becoming more and more distant once I'd fallen for him — and once again, it was depressing the fuck out of me and all I really wanted to do was be home and cry.

So I left, to go home and continue being depressed on my own.

And the next morning, I was at my office, alone, checking my email when I saw a message, sent by Carl, the informal leader, to all the members of the Modelling and Photography group.

It read:

"A model in this group was raped yesterday. She woke up in the morning in the photographer's apartment and knew something was very wrong. He had apparently slipped a drug like Rohypnol into her drink. She went to the hospital for tests and is very shaken up. The photographer's name was —"

And then, my stomach plummeted, and my body went cold.

There was Ed's name.

That night I was there, yesterday, was the night of the day the other girl had left.

The same day.

I'll give this guy this much: As a rapist, he was trying to be really productive — especially for a Sunday.

I eventually got out of my catatonic state.

I called Carl, told him the story. I gave him my number if the girl wanted to get in touch with me. In case I could do anything, knew anything, that could help her case.

Her father called me. A gentle and kind man. She had called him to pick her up. He was the one who drove her to the hospital. He was so grateful to me for getting in touch, and I cringed at the pain in his voice.

I never spoke to her. But I did speak to the police.

And I told my story to a female detective who called.

And I think I said, about every one of my actions, "And I know this was stupid."

Chapter 38: Elisa Watson-Smith

Dear Mama,
I can't believe how time has flown by. October will mark five years since you've been gone. Since your passing, a lot has changed. Your untimely death sparked a series of small changes that led to a shift in how I live my life.

I got the news about Uncle Freddie's accident when I was with my friend Gowri at Nuit Blanche, a city-wide art exhibition from 7 pm to 7 am, on the Saturday before Thanksgiving weekend.

We were at the Art Gallery of Ontario watching a performance installation by Heather Goodchild called "Made it Then, Make it Again." It was about the idea of employment being fulfilling work that contributes to personal and social well being. The performance was questioning ideas about how we engage in labour and created space for the audience to imagine change for the future.

The performance invited the audience to think about:

Working with others towards a common purpose
Knowing that your skilled work is useful to your community
Taking pride in buying locally made products
Celebrating goods for their quality and craftsmanship

The workers moved and harmonized in unison to music while making uniforms, chairs, posters and coffee mugs. They sang beautifully together — just like a choir would at church. I wish you could have been there. I think you would have loved it.

There was an assembly line printing posters that read:

Stories We Don't Tell

"I'd rather be working." Gowri and I lined up to get them. That's when I got the phone call from Mom about Uncle Fred. She told me he was in a coma and things didn't look good. He would wake up from surgery a human vegetable or ... he would die. I silently held her words not knowing what to do.

It crossed my mind that I would never see my uncle again, and I burst into tears. I shook so much I could barely hold onto the phone. Gowri wrapped her arms around me, shushed me still and told me to cry as much as I needed to. I sobbed, "But what about your coat? It's white. And cashmere. I don't want to ruin it." She squeezed me tight and said, "Are you kidding me? Don't worry about your make-up. Cry as much mascara and lipstick off as you need to — I can always get it dry cleaned. I still love her to this day for that. We live in Toronto. Dry cleaning here costs a small fortune!

Gowri took me home and offered to stay, but I needed time alone. I managed to cry myself to sleep, but I woke around 3 am. I was overwhelmed with grief and became stir crazy. Nuit Blanche was still happening, so I decided to go back to the AGO to get a poster. I picked up two. One for me and one for Gowri. As I moved through the AGO to look at other exhibits I started to feel calm. It was a good distraction that helped me to keep my spirits up about my uncle.

It was so hard to lose him the following day. I heard he died just before you got to the hospital. Mom told me how hard it was to say goodbye to you at the airport before you left. It broke my heart to know that you were five hours away in a different country and we couldn't be there in person to offer support.

I was desperate to see you again. I never told anyone this, but I felt in my heart that you were going to die soon. I

Stories We Don't Tell

thought the sadness of losing your last child, the sweet baby of your life, would kill you. The last time we spoke it was Mother's Day, and Mom was throwing you a special party. I didn't come because I was too tired from work. My banking job was taking its toll, and all I could think about was getting some rest. Even though we spoke on the phone and I told you I loved you — I didn't get to see you. As soon as Uncle Fred died, all I could think about was seeing you one more time to say thank you. Thank you for being the strongest woman I've ever known. Thank you for taking care of our little squad of a family. Thank you for all the Grandma letters you sent in the mail stuffed with five and ten dollar bills. I wanted to thank you for everything you did. For all of us.

But you didn't die of sadness. The morning we were on our way to the airport to fly home for Uncle Freddie's funeral, a mere four days after his death, you were beaten and stabbed to death by an intruder who broke into your home to rob you after your trip to the bank. We found out about your murder at the airport after we landed. After the shock set in, everything happened quickly. We did what we had to do, laid you both to rest, and after a week of sadness, we flew back home to our lives.

That's when things started to change. After your death, things got worse before they got better. In addition to extreme sadness, I experienced feelings of anger and resentment. I couldn't see it at the time, but I was stuck in a dead-end job with no opportunities for growth. The job I had just started and thought I loved so much wasn't fun anymore. I was working on a sales team with a bunch of male assholes and wanted all of them to die. I didn't understand how some people who could be so awful got to keep living while you, my grandma with a heart of gold lay six feet in the ground. I would have done anything if it meant I could get you back for five more minutes. I know you knew that I loved you — but I didn't know if you knew I was grateful. It was hard for me to deal with the reality that I would never get to thank you for being one of the most wonderful women in my life.

The rage I felt when you died scared me. I went to bereavement counselling to get through what I knew would be a very difficult time. On top of it all, around the same time, my living situation became unstable. I was dealing with what turned out to be a not-so-nice landlord who was using illegal tactics to bully me and my roommate out onto the street over something so silly you'll die of laughter when I tell you in the afterlife. Even though I can look back and laugh now, at the time it wasn't so funny. Grieving, hating my job, and feeling like I was about to lose the roof over my head was a bad combination. My anxiety went into overdrive — I realized how much of my life I was wasting.

Death makes you realize how little time we have and made me feel guilty about all the things I hadn't done. I always thought you'd be there to take me through the special moments in my life. I expected to have you for another 20 years. You were supposed to die of old age. It never crossed my mind that another human would end your existence. I felt guilty about not being married. I felt guilty about not giving you a grandchild. I felt guilty that you never got to see me accomplish something more than working at a job I hated.

I hit rock bottom and was almost ready to give up. One night things got so bad I wanted to commit suicide. I desperately needed someone to tell me that everything was going to be ok. I went through my phone and called all of my close friends. I dialled and dialled and dialled. No one was picking up. I knew in that moment if I didn't hear from someone I was going to do it. I kept calling until luckily one of my female colleagues picked up. She and I weren't even friends — she was one of those annoying coworkers I wanted to kill, but she had lost her father to cancer and understood my grief. She spent two hours "talking me off the ledge." By the end of our conversation, I was calm again and able to think more clearly. That's when I decided bereavement counselling wasn't enough and began seeing a psychologist as well. Through an interesting series of events, I had the opportunity to connect with four shrinks. Each of them contributed in their special way to the beautiful change that I couldn't see coming. It took a bit of time, but I accomplished a few things:

I moved into my own apartment. No more sharing.

I quit my bank job.

I went back to school, graduated from two more programs.

I stopped worrying about things I couldn't control.

I started making jewellery again.

I got a new boyfriend (we're not together anymore, but I'll tell you about that later).

I replaced toxic friends with loving ones, and I started working at a place where I get to be myself and do the things that I love while surrounded by some pretty amazing people.

And most of all, I found my way back to my life's purpose. It's funny how it all worked out. I was supposed to go to art school, but I chose business school instead (which for the record was a really smart move), and now 10 years later I've managed to find my way back to the art world to do the things I love. I'm right where I'm supposed to be.

I often look at the poster from the AGO exhibition and think of you. In times of stress and uncertainty, it reminds me that I'd rather be working. Working on the things that I am passionate about with people who are kind, respectful and have meaning in their lives. It's been a challenging journey, but I'm pushing my boundaries, and my wings are growing back. Soon I'll be a little bird again flying high above the clouds where I can be closer to you.

I still cry sometimes when I remember that you're gone, but my life has never been filled with more joy. I'm building a little empire in your memory and couldn't be more proud. I have so many projects to tell you about, but I'll save those for next time. Until then, I love you, Mama.

Your Grandbaby,
Elisa

Chapter 39: Pepper Strauss Dorper

I was standing still, as a whir of travellers packed into the Denver International Airport. One by one by one the airport shuttle buses passed me by as travellers rushed off to find their flights. Finally, a bus lingered at its stop. It looked like everyone had gotten off. And I was caught by the *pause* in the rhythm.

Odd. *But what was "odd" when the past 10 months had been a gush of emergencies and last-minute flights?*

But TODAY — today I had a plan. And everything was FINE.

And as I stood waiting, OUT pops this woman – swaying down the stairs, steadied by the rail she firmly grasped for, hair slightly askew, clothing a little too loose, who called out my name.

"Peggy Sue!"

Her joy was ... evident. She knew me — loved me — saw me.

But, who was she?

I was destined for Oklahoma — two weeks all expenses paid. It was going to be a timely vacation. God, did I need it. My soul was so wretched tired.

"Did you pack a Halloween Costume?? Because we're going to be there for Halloween and you HAVE to have a costume! Would you pack one for me as well?"

And so with our Halloween costumes packed, along with the materials to crochet 60 scarves to fill new pending orders for my start-up company. I waited. *Where was she?*

"Peg!"

It came at me like a dagger.

Her face was *NOT* familiar. It was sallow. Her eyes were

Stories We Don't Tell

beyond dilated. She had one of those gluey happy smiles as the lines of her muscles pulled tight across her face, a vibrant vacancy to her eyes. And her hands were so thin. Her body so fragile as a porter helped her into a wheelchair.

Mom?

Or rather a portent of my mother. A woman once over 300lbs who could hug you like a *freight train*, now enfolded me in her spindly arms and as happiness emanated from her, my reinforced façade of "fine" ... *cracked*, and my precarious balance began to falter entirely.

I hugged this stranger with everything I could. Hoping that if I cloyed harder that I might be able to bring forth more of the woman whom I knew to be my mother.

Nothing. Vacancy.

We were headed to the Cancer Treatment Center of America.

Ten months fighting Stage 3 Pancreatic Cancer.

Terminal.

Illness.

And as I pushed the wheelchair forward into the chaos of the airport, I found myself piling on more armour, while my insides were sliding out between the chinks. Tears flowing uncontrollably down my face while I barred my soul in silence, my vision collapsing as we tunnelled forward, and all I can think is

How the fuck did this happen? WHEN did this happen? She was FINE when I left just a few weeks ago. Why is she so high? What drugs is she on right now? Is she okay? Can she fly? She's so fragile. Who do I call to help me? Who knows what's happened? Where the FUCK is my mother? Who is this person?

And all the world, this onslaught of busy travellers, seeing but not understanding this wildly happy woman

Stories We Don't Tell

being pushed through the airport by a crumbling person who is silently sobbing with every step forward. I couldn't see them through my bleary vision. Could only feel the pressing and probing eyes of hurried travellers looking at this sight knowing something is deeply wrong or was it? We were invisible in a bubble of broken, and no one could help us, cared to help us.

And as I am pushing my mother forward through this tightening tunnel of eyes, I keep my voice pitched positively, the whimper out of my voice as I breathe deeply and I play along. Because she wants to be happy. She *IS* happy. We're going on an adventure! Just the two of us — escaping on a magical holiday!

We get to airport security — and I am shocked back into reality.

"ID and ticket please?"

Right. Airport security. They need those items to allow you on board.

Allow you......on board.

And all I can think is:

Can't you see this woman is not well? Can't you see she is moments away from DYING? You want our FUCKING ID? Just let us onto the damned plane. She may not even make it to the gate, let alone through a flight. Holy shit — would they even let us onto the plane like this? But we HAVE to get on that plane — I HAVE to get her to this Cancer Treatment Center. The people here are USELESS. Do you see what they DID to her? What they let her become? How the hell did she get released from a hospital for this trip? Where is the manager of this shit show?? I need to throttle them.

And as I hand over our ID and tickets, my mother begins to tell the officer about the incredible adventure she is about ready to embark upon with her daughter! It's going to be

MAGICAL! To which the officer gives me a look of blank dismissal, doesn't even look at my mother and I smile wide through my river of tears and say — yes! We're going on a trip to the Cancer Treatment Center of America — a mother, daughter adventure! And I look at them pleading that they play along. Please, pretend that I am fine, that this is fine. Help me keep her happy.

And as my mom begins to take note of the officer's cold, bewildered facial reaction and turn towards me, I push us into the line for metal detection, avoiding her glance with the forward motion.

And my cracked façade begins to fail entirely. *Shit. I'm losing it.* Shoes off. *Quivering voice.* Belt. Laptop. *Whimpering sobs.* Meds out. *Does she have meds in her carry on?* Liquids out. *I can't see anything anymore.* Okay — it's all on the belt.

And as I turn her chair to the detector, the officer doesn't even look at my mother, even *acknowledge* her presence, that she is *still alive*, just shifts their head up to mine, over my seated mother, gives me an oblique look and states, "Ma'am, she has to get out of the chair and walk through the detector." And in that moment of brash humanity, I lose it.

I quietly respond through clenched teeth, "She has to get out of the chair?" And all I can think is, "SHE CAN'T GET OUT OF THE CHAIR! SHE CAN'T WALK THROUGH THE DETECTOR. WHY DO YOU THINK WE HAVE THIS THING?? SHE'S DYING YOU ASSHOLE! LET US ON THE GOD DAMN PLANE!"

And as I inhale, ready to verbally skive the flesh off of this shitty human being, to release the flooding tides of vitriol, hate and loathing of the pitiless world and how unfair it is, my mother turns to me and sees my broken face for the first time and touches it with a thin finger. What's wrong Peg?

Don't be sad. Everything is fine. I can walk through.

And somehow her words of assurance cut deeper into me. And I think, *No mom — you're not okay. Everything is NOT fine. It is wrong. This is WRONG. We shouldn't be leaving home. We should stay. We should hide away from everything.*

And as people behind us in line are jumping past us to go through the detector, this fragile woman tethered together by sheer will and delusional happiness pushes out of this chair. And slowly as I hold her up and begin to walk her towards the detector, I position my body against the line of rushing travellers to protect this beautiful creature as she precariously totters through the detector.

And as I follow behind her, I walk slowly through, looking back at the selfishly unaware travellers, forward to the stone-faced officer and I think to myself: *Bring it the fuck on you shitty world. This is my mother. She is MY Mother. And WE are on a fucking ADVENTURE. And everything will be FINE.*

Chapter 40: Jennifer McKinley

I was a missing child. For two and a half hours on a Monday evening in April. But I didn't really go missing. I knew exactly where I was. Safe and sound at the Annette library followed by the convenience store two blocks away at Keele Street.

Ten years old and too old for daycare, I developed my own routine on Dad days, Mondays, Thursdays and every other Friday after school. Dad lived too far from school for me to walk, so I hung out at the library or the rec centre until he picked me up after work.

Dad had a routine. He finished work at five o'clock, went to the bank, grocery store, liquor store before he picked me up by bus. We usually got home at 6:15. The day I went missing, I got tired of waiting at the library and came up with the genius idea of meeting him at the corner where he transferred buses. This will save him some time and trouble, I thought. No transfer necessary. We can take the bus home directly from the stop he gets off to pick me up.

It was still cold outside, so I slipped into the convenience store at Keele and Annette and bought a small bag of salted corn nuts. I leaned on the metal bar on the locked door of the two-door entrance and crunched my corn nuts, close to the corner and out of the way.

5:30. I watched passengers file in and out of buses, purses, backpacks, shopping bags, stroller. No Dad.

5:45. He should have been here by now. Maybe he missed the bus because he had to buy cigarettes at the cheap cigarette store. Maybe there was a longer line than usual at Food City. I licked my finger and jammed it into the corners of the corn nut bag, brought the salty debris to my mouth.

I crumpled the bag and tossed it into the small garbage bin by the lottery station. The curious store clerk stared at me.

"Are you all right?"

"Yeah. I'm waiting for my dad. He should be here any minute."

6:00. No Dad. Did I miss him getting off the bus? I studied every single passenger, on the lookout for his unmistakable hairstyle, slick at the sides, pompadour in front, like Elvis. Nothing but a trickle of sad, flat 'dos. It's so late. Maybe someone from work was driving him to get me. No such luck.

6:15. One hour spent waiting. Every time a customer walked in the sharp door chime taunted me like a recess bully. I had nowhere to go. The library closed at six. The rec centre was not where I was supposed to be, and I didn't want to walk away from home. I thought about what I did on Mom days, Tuesdays, Wednesdays and every other Friday: go to Auntie Doris's house where I wait for Mom to pick me up after work. I couldn't go there. Not this day.

A familiar car pulled up to the red light across the street. A green Chevy Impala with my stepfather, John, behind the wheel, on his way home from work. My throat closed, and I ducked. I would not be rescued like this.

My stressful, complicated family situation: Dad and John were first cousins. Auntie Doris, the woman whose house I went to after school on Mom days, was John's mother. She was also my little brother's grandmother and my grandmother's sister. Very confusing stuff. And I knew what people thought when I told them this story — incest. But it wasn't incest. It just meant that my little brother was also my second cousin. I didn't like to think about that.

If I went to Auntie Doris's house on a day that wasn't Mom's day, I would fuel the fire Mom and John kept stoked about Dad's irresponsible parenting.

"I can only imagine what goes on at your father's house." It was one of the few things Mom and John agreed on.

If I went to Auntie Doris's house, I would be saying, "You're right, Mom and John. Dad is so irresponsible he lost me." But that wasn't true. He didn't lose me. I lost him. And we would fix this ourselves. I didn't want to lose Dad time at Dad's house, the little freedom I had away from John's endless harassment.

6:15 turned into 7:15. When the sun set, I wondered if I'd ever get home. I knew the way. I had a bus ticket but no house key. My best strategy: stay put. The store smelled like kimchi and Jamaican patties. I didn't like either, but the warm smells kept me safe. Monday was chicken leg night in our house. I was so hungry.

Somebody find me, please!

"I'm worried about you."

"I'm fine."

"I called the police. They'll be here soon."

Oh my god!

7:45. In the back of a police car.

"What's your name? Where do you live? Who are your parents? Where are you supposed to be?"

"Jennifer. Cayuga Avenue. Al and Cathy. Home."

The police officers drove me to the rec centre, where I definitely was not supposed to be. Dad and John were waiting. Dad and John, in the same place at the same time. My heart skipped a beat. I didn't know how to behave.

I called Mom at Auntie Doris's house to tell her I was safe. John drove Dad and me home. Friendly conversation, so weird to me, the first time they'd spoken with each other in a long time.

Dad made chicken legs for late dinner. We always ate

late. I watched the last ten minutes of my favourite Monday night show, The Wonder Years. Winnie Cooper got into a car accident, and Kevin stood outside her window to whisper, "I love you."

My mother still talks about the time I aged her twenty years in two hours.

"Oh my god! You have no idea what you put me through. You think the worst. Every imaginable thing races through your mind."

Dad gave me a house key shortly after. I wore it with pride on a string necklace. I found freedom on my afternoons at home and entertained myself with movies. I learned a lot. Johnny Depp taught me how to French kiss. John Waters's Cry-Baby, a classic after-school special.

I took care of myself. I was good at it. I hadn't gone missing. I knew exactly where I was. And I was safe. I was a young white girl in a relatively safe neighbourhood with middle-class parents who loved me. The police listened to them and took them seriously. Even my stepfather, who treated me like garbage, took responsibility, one of the few times in his life. Not all children are so lucky.

Chapter 41: Erin Kang

"So."

Sammy looks at me kindly from her swivel chair and sips her coffee from a dark blue mug.

"But why do you think you feel guilty all the time?"

I stare down at the pastel teal lid of my own coffee.

It's only my third or fourth session with her, but it was tremendously helpful to even hear from another human being that the things I experienced in my childhood were not actually normal. After every session, I come to some realization that I knew but didn't know or knew but didn't believe and wonder to myself what I possibly would have to talk about with her the next time I come in.

Usually, my realizations are about how my current depression or insecurity is actually rooted in some past depression or insecurity, namely those caused by my dad. It was significant enough for me to even have the space to realize that I was not okay and needed support.

I look back up to Sammy's patient face.

"Well I guess it's like I said before, I feel like it was my responsibility to hold my family together and I failed. So I feel like I let everyone down. Plus I feel like since he's my dad, I should be there for him instead of cutting him out of my life. I know I shouldn't, but ... I dunno."

She nods, tells me it's good that I know I shouldn't. She doesn't ask me if I really believe that or not, because she knows as well as I do that I don't. She also doesn't call out my mindreading or my hyperbolic statements. She knows I know.

My past birthday was what they call your champagne birthday. I turned 27 on the 27th of March. At 8:50 pm, my dad texted me for the first time in years, and the last time I saw him was sometime in my third year of university. It was not a fun time.

The message was pretty casual for something that was breaking a multi-year silence.

"Hope u had nice day. Happy birthday number 1. Gonna talk to 2 u soon. Love u always. Daddy."

When he left, I was in grade 10. Sixteen. Another pretty big year, as they say. Dad did always have a penchant for drama.

I got the text when I was on my couch watching TV. I turned my phone face-down immediately and tried to will myself to forget what I had just read. I picked at the frayed leather around a burn-mark on the middle-cushion of the couch, one that Dad made with a cigarette one time. I can still feel how I felt. How I feel anytime I accidentally stumble across an old photo with his face in it, laughing up at me, oblivious to what his future, non-photographic self ended up doing to us. To me.

When I casually mention the message Dad sent me, Sammy pulls out a purple sheet of paper. It might sound super dorky but I actually really like the worksheets she gives me. It makes me feel like an 8-year-old again, but discussing really deep-rooted trauma rather than Reading & Comprehension. She looks at me, pen poised over the sheet.

"So. You said you ended up responding, right? Tell me about that."

I stay silent while I think. I didn't respond to the message right away because I wanted to talk to my mom and sister first. On top of that, it honestly just made me feel like a pre-teen again. Hearing from him transformed me from a 27-year-old boss bitch to a 13-year-old who was just learning what crack cocaine was and was in charge of keeping it away

Stories We Don't Tell

from my father.

He had actually sent me a second message a couple days after, saying how he was going to visit Grandpa — his father — before it was too late, and wanted to visit us after. As far as I know, he lives in Alberta. When he left, he wasn't exactly forthcoming. In fact, I found out when the police called me with a Missing Persons Report filed for him.

My family and I discussed things at length. My mom, ever the pacifist and perpetually selfless, urged me and my sister to consider seeing him one last time.

"He's your father," she told us.

But the more my sister and I talked about it, the more cemented our decision was to protect ourselves from him. I told my sister how I'd come to realize that even if I could bring myself to forgive myself for everything he's done to me, I would never be able to forgive him for what he's done to her and to our mom. She told me she felt the same way. I told her how I felt guilty, how it felt like I was denying my duty as a daughter, as a human being, to be there for him and help him. But she reminded me that we had tried multiple times before, only to be hurt and let down over and over again.

Writing our response back to him took us a few days. Drugs have changed him, and we can never predict how he'll react to anything. He even still believes that the reason we don't speak to him is because Mom is coercing us into silence. He can't fathom that we don't speak to him because he ripped us all apart. Sure, it made us Strong As Fuck, but does that make it better?

We made roadmaps of possible scenarios together. Our names aren't that common. He could easily find out where we work. Does your work have security? Okay good. No, mine doesn't, but my boss is usually around. What if he finds where Mom works? We should warn her. Do you think he'd try to hurt himself again? Do you think he'll be really mad? Do you think he'll blame Mom?

Finally, we ended up with a single sentence. "We talked about it and we would really like it if you didn't contact us again." We sent the message together, standing in our kitchen. As the message flew away, we were silent. Everything had already been spoken before.

Sammy clears her throat, and I realize I've just been picking at my coffee cup lid for the past few minutes. I pick at things when I feel stressed.

Before I can stop myself, I've taken a deep breath and started speaking.

"Well, I feel really bad about it, but ..."

And she begins to write on the purple paper.

Chapter 42: Andrew Cheung

I stood in the centre of Time Square at midnight. It was packed with people, but it was completely silent. It was so quiet that when a biker rode by, the noise from his bike filled the whole place. On one of the screens, it read November 8th, 2016.

Let's rewind to a few months earlier. I joked with my friend Lucas in the summer about going to New York City on election day. Nothing really came out of it but then after a few more months we decided, what the heck, let's go.

So Garbo, Lucas, and I bought our tickets to NYC. We would hit a few bars that had election parties, and when Hillary won, we would go to Time Square and high five as many drunk Americans as we could.

So fast forward to the trip. On Saturday, we decided to either go shopping or check out the High Line. We decided on the High Line. There were two subway lines we could use: North or East. We went East. We started walking, and at one point, we realized we had walked too far. So we turned around and walked through an alley to get to the station. When we came out of the alley, we saw a line-up that stretched over two to three city blocks. We walked past it, but then I was curious about what they're lining up for so I turned around to ask.

They said this was the line to get tickets to attend Hillary Clinton's election night party, where she would make her speech. EXCITED, I started freaking out. I had to get into this event. I had to be in the same room as Hillary on election night.

I asked them who was eligible to attend this event, and one person said that you could get a free ticket if you are a registered volunteer. We immediately lined up and registered by phone to be volunteers.

After 30 minutes in the line-up, all the while freaking out from too many emotions to describe, we got close to the front. We were now inside Hillary's Manhattan campaign office.

Now the second hurdle had presented itself. In front of me, people were taking out their IDs ... their American IDs.

We realized that we had two options. We could present our Canadian ID, or we could say we forgot to bring our IDs. We went back and forth on this and finally decided to be honest. After all, it's what Bernie would've done.

As I get to the front, the person asked me for my ID, so I gave him my driver's licence without saying a word. He looked at me, looked at the ID, looked down, and typed on his laptop. He gave me my ID ... and a ticket.

We had just received tickets to be in the same room as Hillary Clinton on election night. We had not expected this at all. We were originally going to spend election night at a bar.

Had we gone shopping instead of taking the High Line, had we walked North instead of East, had we not gotten lost and walked through an alley, and had we walked past the line-up without asking them what the line-up was about ... had any one of these things happened, we would not have stumbled upon these tickets.

This was all a bit too much, so we sat down to take it all in.

I have to be honest. I started tearing up.

I was going to be standing face to face in front of Hillary Clinton when she was crowned America's first-ever female president.

This was a symbolic victory not just for women, but for

Stories We Don't Tell

people in general all over the world.

Before coming to New York, I had drafted all these snappy one-liners to post on Facebook the moment Hillary won, but the best one I had was "It's a great day for empathy." For me, Trump and his supporters stood for all that was wrong in the world. They were not empathetic, and were not supportive of our liberal ideas and progressive values.

The next few days, you could feel the election magic in the air. Both Trump and Hillary would be in NYC on election night for their election parties. On Tuesday, the entire world would have their eyes on America, and America would have its eyes on New York City.

So now it's election day. I remember waking up to clear skies and a bright sun, feeling super excited and very hopeful about the future of America.

We got to the arena at 1 pm to line up in what looked like a massive airplane hangar, and within a few hours, there was half a hockey game's worth of people lined up.

Here's the thing about Americans. They have this great sense of community. At one point, the organizers at the front used a large microphone to communicate with us, but since the hangar was so big, anyone in the middle and back could not hear them. So the people in front started chanting the message to the people in the middle, and people in the middle started chanting the message to the people in the back. It was basically the largest telephone game I've ever been a part of.

At one point, the organizers told us we couldn't bring in outside food, so everyone started offering each other their food. People would shout "who wants my chips?" or "who wants cookies?" One guy held up his half-eaten sandwich and said: "who wants my sandwich?"

After being packed like sardines with thousands of

Stories We Don't Tell

strangers for six hours, we finally got inside the Javitz Center. This is it! I'm going to see Hillary Clinton tonight! I was super excited, and I could no longer contain myself.

The arena was packed with people, with vendors serving food, and people talking on stage. We were watching a special broadcast, so when the news went to commercials, they played Hillary advertisements for the crowd.

As I look up at the screen for the first time, I realize Trump was leading Florida with 93% of the vote tallied. That was a typo, right? Anyway, Florida always goes back and forth, so I didn't pay too much attention to it.

As we waited in line for food, I spoke to one American who told me that there were going to be fireworks later tonight and Katy Perry would perform.

After we got our food and continued watching the latest results, the announcer onscreen said that this was no longer going to be a blow-out Clinton victory, and that Trump was doing better than most people expected. That's okay, not every election can be Bush and Dukakis. A win is still a win.

10 pm. Hillary takes Virginia. A large cheer erupted in the arena. Javitz Center was picked as the venue because its ceiling is made of glass, and, of course, Hillary was going to shatter it.

10:28. CNN and Fox call Ohio for Trump ... the first major swing state goes to Trump ... That's okay though, you can't depend on Ohio in your calculations.

At the very centre of the arena, there was a stage where people gave speeches. People who spoke were the mayor, the governor of New York, Khizr Khan, the father of the Muslim soldier who died fighting in Iraq, and Katy Perry.

10:53. Trump has now taken Florida. The TV analyst said that Hillary is no longer the favourite and it's now literally a coin toss between the two. But I mean, there's no reason to be upset, right? After all, Obama carried the Midwestern states against Romney, and that was the difference for him winning. Surely Hillary would do that again.

I talked to a cop and asked him where the fireworks would be, and he said the fireworks were cancelled and Katy Perry was no longer performing. Okay, so maybe it was going to rain or something. That MUST why.

11:14. North Carolina goes to Trump. He now has more paths to get to 270 votes and Hillary is on the defensive. She needs Pennsylvania, Michigan, Wisconsin, all of which are either in a virtual tie or led by Trump. Meanwhile, the Canadian Citizenship and Immigration website has crashed.

Then all the sudden, I look around me, and I see a few people crying. I also distinctly remember seeing three Latino teenagers sitting on the ground in a circle, holding hands, and praying.

I don't get why these guys are so sad. She can still pull this off. We still have the western states to work with, so there may be a surprise from Colorado and Nevada.

So what she'll do is win the swing states in the Midwest, and then she'll take the West. She'll do this. I KNOW it. She HAS to. I mean, this guy can't win, right? There's no way. In no universe would a man like that be president. I mean, this can't—

NO MORE EXCITEMENT.

... Midnight. Fox News calls Wisconsin for Trump.

As the news went to commercials, they cut to a Hillary advertisement that I'll never forget. In the ad, an elderly woman said she was born during the women's suffragette movement, and she is thankful that by the end of her lifetime, we will finally have a female president. When that ad ended, my stomach turned.

Immediately after, I overhear a lead organizer saying that

Stories We Don't Tell

Hillary will not come to the arena tonight.

***

1:30 am. The Keystone State of Pennsylvania goes to Donald J. Trump. We decide it is time for us to leave and go to Time Square. As we walk towards the exit, I look at the stage one more time, realizing that I was THIS close from seeing Hillary on it.

***

I stood in the centre of Time Square. It was packed with people, but it was completely silent. It was so quiet that when a biker rode by, the noise from his bike filled the whole place. The biker was riding around while looking up at the election results. He was riding in circles, like an American Eagle circling above to catch its prey. And as the biker rode off into the distance and disappeared, so too did Hillary's chances of living in the White House for the next four years.

And at this moment I realized that I was wrong. I had been blaming Trump and his supporters for not having empathy, and yet it was ME who was guilty of that. This entire time I took it for granted that Hillary would win. I carried myself as if the battle were already won, and that coming to NYC was just to march in the parade. It wasn't until election day that I realized how big America was, and how much of Middle America was suffering. In essence, it was me who was not empathetic towards Trump's supporters. I recall my Facebook post: "it's a great day for empathy." Well, that turned out to be a true statement, it WAS a great day for empathy. But it wasn't a lesson in empathy for Trump and his supporters, rather it was a lesson for me.

Chapter 43: Joey Brooke Jakob

I was sitting on the couch with a new lover. We were smack-dab in new relationship energy: heart flutters, eyes dashing quickly toward each other's then quickly away, coy smiles, warm feelings all over. I have no idea what we were really talking about; the subtext was lust and infatuation. There's about half a foot of space between our bodies, and Monkey, the cat, manages to squeeze her way in. She purrs at an audible level I'd never heard before, vibrating against us with her own pleasure. She'd never seemed to take notice of me or anyone for that matter. I liked her at this moment; I'd never liked her before.

Journal entry August 13, 2011: Nearing the end of my first year in a PhD. What a shitty decision. I've moved to a new province, had to make new friends (again), and for what? The noble pursuit of overthinking about one goddamn thing. In other news, Monkey is such a distracting little stinker. She makes the best sounds. The minute I get home, she runs to the door and demands butt pats. And then when I stop, makes a noise that seems impossible to write phonetically, maybe it's "unnnhhh." "Unnnhhh" is now our official greeting.

PART 1: Shit
Three years into a PhD and two years into a relationship with that lover, the three of us packed up and moved to a small American college town: my lover to begin a PhD, me to write my dissertation and Monkey to just be a cat. But Monkey became more than merely a cat: I relied on her for comfort and affection when my lover stopped being

attentive. Three months in, he asked me to altogether refrain from speaking to him in the mornings; I was too distracting to his work. Six months in, he permanently slept in the spare room; I was keeping him awake with my breathing. Eighteen months in, we had had sex three times; he also insisted on refraining from changing in front of me, to keep nudity special, ostensibly for the sex, which never seemed to happen. My heart hurt; I ached for connection to others; the kind of hurt where you wake up feeling sad but can't remember exactly why for a moment or two, and then it floods back. I had only one friend in town and spent hours each day on the phone with friends and family afar. When no human connection could be found, I relied on Monkey. Our "thing" comprised of me picking her up dozens of times each day, putting her over my shoulder so that her front legs would dangle downward, and she'd purr and purr and purr. This routinely defiant cat would ultimately give in to my affection, making me feel less like a pariah in my own home, and more like a necessary and even loved component.

 I ended the relationship. Monkey and I headed back to Toronto after a year and a half. My whole life packed up in a cube van, both of us vocalizing on the route: she made intense and unsettling cat noises, while I often pulled over to cry and dry heave. At a truck stop somewhere between Washington and Pittsburgh, I smelled a concerning smell: shit. Knowing that I had not shit myself, though given the stressful circumstances I was momentarily concerned, I realized that it could only be one thing: cat shit. There's something very special about getting out of a van that houses your entire life knowing that it's all been permeated with this particular scent. I can still hear and feel the weight of the sliding door opening on the van. Pulling her carrier out, it was increasingly clear that we had a huge problem. I

Stories We Don't Tell

don't remember walking through the convenience store, but I do know what happened when I made it to the washroom. Pulling down as many paper towels as I could (this was not a time to be conservative and concerned about environment costs), I cleaned her shit-covered carrier and her shit-covered body. The sink filled up with water that looked like diluted coffee, as I tried to hold Monkey long enough to get all that shit out of her fur; the shit had made its way all along her inner and outer back legs and up the length of her stomach. Ever good timing, a totally weirded-out woman looked at me from the unlocked doorway of the public toilet, the sight she saw: me wearing rubber gloves, pants, rubber boots, and just a bra on top — Monkey had managed to get shit all over my shirt, and I had declared it too far gone for recovery. Me, chasing a shit-smeared cat around the bathroom, ducking under and around the stall doors that did not quite reach the floor, Monkey leaving shit smeary paw prints in her wake. Me, calling after her by her given name, "Monkey" — not a reference to her species, which might have seemed an odd word to utter, and in the presence of a stranger who already thinks I've gone mad. I politely suggested to the woman that she come back another time.

That shitty experience affirmed my unending love for Monkey. She came with the baggage of problematic bodily functions, but I didn't care; it was true love. When she became really sick, it was an obvious choice to take care of her, whatever she needed. I'd had many animals all my life, and being an introverted only child, these creatures were my focal points. My touchstones. So when her once a year urinary tract infections became twice a year, then three times, then every month, I hung in there, cleaning up her bloody urine, and nursing her back to health.

Late October 2015, nearly five years into our relationship,

to the day, she hid. She had never done that before. Whenever she was in discomfort, she'd find me, and radiate her troubles outward, often in the form of a puddle of bloody piss. When I pulled her out from her hiding spot, clots of blood accompanied her normal bloody urine. I packed her up, and we went to the vet. I assumed, as with other times, that it was a UTI. I didn't know then that this was the beginning of the end.

PART 2: Vodka

Journal entry December 14, 2015: I'm just trying to be okay with everything not being okay. I'm going to be okay even if everything is not okay.

She stayed at the vet for three days. The day Monkey came home, my roommate greeted me with dinner and a bottle of my favourite potato vodka. We barely ate, watching Monkey sleep for what we thought would be the last few weeks of her life. She had lost nearly four pounds and was quite drugged to relieve her pain. When she opened her glassy eyes, she'd look about until she saw me, then look at her own body, seemingly horrified, and I'd clean her since she could no longer do it herself; she smelled of the same smell that hospitals sometimes have, of decaying bodies and rubbing alcohol. My roommate and I drank vodka; we talked for hours and hours and cried together over the sleeping pile of fur before us. Monkey had no energy. I longed to hear her "unnnhhh."

For four months, I did almost nothing but nurse her. Friends became concerned, not only for my mental health but also for my pocketbook. I had unflinchingly borrowed $2000 at that point, and I had already spent over $3000 on a graduate student's salary. I wasn't handed a large bill on a single day; these debts would come slowly over the four months; I don't know what I would have done if the bill had all come at once.

Much time was now spent calibrating to unexpected palliative care. Monkey was vomiting multiple times each day, and I was sleeping like the parent of a newborn, in hourly increments. Weekly, if not daily, vet visits occurred. The people who worked at the vet knew that I was broke, and also that I was capable of doing some of the easier, though sometimes squeamish, daily tasks. One of the things they trained me to administer was subcutaneous fluids: wrap Monkey in a blanket so she cannot squirm away, pinch the excess flesh at the back of her neck, and inject a needle containing saline until a pocket of this hydrating fluid-filled to the size of half my fist. It took about three minutes each time, and I'd hold her, talking to her in the soft voice she liked.

Journal Entry December 20, 2015: I think I'm afraid to not complete the dissertation. What if I can't? What if I've gone dumb? I haven't written anything in months.

I could have looked after her forever, except for the pocketbook situation. Even though things had been tough, I truly believed that she was content in my presence, as I was with hers; that she also wanted whatever time we had left together. This was what the vet had me believe, until her tune so wholly changed, complicating my life more than I thought possible. Up until this point, I had been led to believe that Monkey was nearing the end. I was preparing for this; I was prepared for this. Then one day the vet informed me that there were still a few things we could try, but they'll take more money: try this other food, try these

Stories We Don't Tell

other medications, what about surgery? I was dubious and said as much; it had already been four months. It was at this point I realized that the vet was pro-life, even if it meant drastic procedures and heartache. The vet was adamant, and she no longer supported the path we had been on. The vet suggested that a pet medical professional could give Monkey what she needed, with expertise, drugs, and around-the-clock care, but that I could, clearly not, provide for Monkey anymore.

I'm not exactly sure what I regret, but there's something here that resonates with that idea. The next day, the vet told me that she knew someone who could give Monkey what she needed, and suggested that I give her up: a "medical surrender." I went home and cried on the bathroom floor, without Monkey, who was staying with the vet because I could no longer afford to pay the bills. Did you know, they hold your animal hostage if it comes to this, all the while providing care, for which you are to pay if the animal ever goes home with you again.

I decided that even though I could no longer afford to care for her, if the vet truly believed there was hope, I wanted to give Monkey that chance. She had seen me through so much; she was a love of my life. On January 11th, 2016, I went to the vet to sign the surrender document. The form instructed me that from the moment I signed, I was no longer the guardian of Monkey; I would permanently forgo any knowledge of her whereabouts or health. Not one person at the vet made eye contact with me that day as I sobbed in this public space, first in the observation room with all stainless steel, the sanitized room oddly juxtaposed to the infected, deep pain that welled in my chest, and second in the waiting area, where everyone tried not to stare. I seemed contagious; people with their pets were trying not to catch whatever I had.

PART 3: Surrender

Journal entry January 12, 2016: This is the hardest thing I've ever had to write: yesterday I surrendered Monkey at the vet. I am horrified, lonely, sad, angry, frantic, calm, overwhelmed, heartbroken, and uncomfortably, freed.

Chapter 44: Jesse David

The beginning of 2008 was a pivotal year for me. I entered third-year university and I was convinced that I was going to change the world, or at least be a better version of myself. I was going to join all the clubs — I didn't know which ones but I was determined to get involved.

Then I started school, and I felt overwhelmed. I felt overwhelmed, and I felt confused. I didn't know which clubs to join, and I didn't know how to execute my very grand plan for my life, and I felt deflated.

I've always understood that a university degree alone wasn't necessarily going to get me anywhere, so I spoke to my dad about dropping out and enrolling in college, and he trusted me to make the right decision.

Meanwhile, since the semester had already begun, I decided to look for a job. It didn't happen as quickly as I wanted, or at all in the first two or three weeks that I started to look for a position. I was already feeling deflated, and it just added to my feelings of incompetence.

Going from those moments of feeling on top of the world to feeling unable to move or accomplish any task felt that much worse. You know what they say, the higher you climb, the harder you fall. The best way I can think to describe it is if you put your hand under hot water and then you immediately put your hand under cold water, you can feel the difference that much more, and for me, that was really jarring.

So I had all this time on my hands and started observing and understanding what it meant to be an adult — to pay bills, to go grocery shopping, to maintain a household. I know that most people go through this realization at some point — they realize that being an adult is hard. But when I looked at all there was to do, for me, it felt impossible. I was convinced that because I couldn't get a job in those few short weeks of trying, the future I had imagined for myself would never become a reality. It felt soul-crushing.

I was on this downward spiral, where it felt as if everything was out of my reach. I remember at one point I was watching TV, and I could feel myself getting worse and worse, and I remember thinking, God, if you're there, please don't leave me. The days kept going, and in the next few months, I felt worse and worse, and my thoughts were racing. I felt anxious and sad as if there was a weight on my heart, and I didn't know how to make it stop.

Because my thoughts were dark and everything in my head was dark, I wanted to be surrounded by darkness. I felt the light was mocking me, like haha, you can't feel this. I would nap and sleep a lot because it was the only way I could escape my actual reality. I remember one time I had gone to our basement. It was dark, about 7:00 at night. I fell asleep and when I woke up, for a split second I thought that it was all a dream. I thought that what I was experiencing, what I was feeling, my current situation, that it wasn't reality — that it wasn't true. The moment that I realized that, oh wait no, this is my reality, was so heartbreaking — I think one of the most crushing feelings I've ever felt.

I thought at that point I can't keep going on like this. I have to make a plan. I have to do something. Okay, what can I do? I didn't feel like there were any other options. I ... I have to kill myself. And when I decided that, I felt peace. I felt relief. That crushing feeling was almost gone. The thoughts stopped because I felt there's a way that this can get better.

Eight months went by, and the best way I can describe

those months is like this. I remember being at Bayview and Sheppard, waiting to take my aunt to the hospital. It was a beautiful sunny day. Blue skies, not a cloud in the sky, sun shining down. Usually, when you're in the sun, you feel good, you feel happy, like yes, this is amazing. And I kept trying to feel the sun, but every time I moved to feel the sun on my skin, there was this rain cloud. Every time I moved, this cloud moved with me. I kept trying, but I could never get there. I could see that other people could feel the sun, but I kept trying, and I couldn't get there.

Eight months went by like this and I thought, I'm just procrastinating, this is ridiculous. So I went to my garage, grabbed a plastic bag, saw some rope and a little stool, put the rope and the stool in the bag, and I went out the door. There's a park close by, and I walked down the pathway to the trail. I turned right and climbed a hill looking for a spot where no one would see me.

Not satisfied, I went back down, went the other way around and up the hill, and found a secluded place. I tried to hang the rope but didn't really know how to do it. I don't know, I didn't look it up on YouTube beforehand. It wasn't 'successful'. The best way I can describe it is that your head just feels heavier and heavier, like a bowling ball. I was hoping that I would go to unconsciousness and that it would be fine, but the body has a very strong will to survive, and I knew this wasn't going to work.

Finally, I went back down and as soon as I hit the bottom of the hill, and mind you I really hadn't seen anyone for the past year, a church member was walking along the same path. He called out "Jesseee!!!"

"Hey Frank, how's it goin?" As cheerfully as I could manage.

"How's it going?"

"Great!"

"What's in the bag?"

"My suicide kit" I mean, I didn't actually say that, but I could have. He gave me a hug, and he has a big belly, so it was this big bear hug.

"I'll see you later Frank, byeeee."

I went back home, and my mom started yelling at me about not having signed up for school, and that I needed to do it right away. I wanted to say to her, "if you knew what I just did, you wouldn't be yelling at me." But I didn't. Instead, I got on the bus, and there I saw Frank's son, Dave. And for me, that felt like a sign, like maybe there's hope.

I wasn't okay, I definitely wasn't okay, so I ordered cyanide. But in the time before it came, I got a call from a friend that I had not heard from for the past year. She said, "Jess, it's been a long time, but I want you to come to my birthday." She had been my best friend since grade three, and at that moment I thought, you know what, if after this long, somebody still cares about me, then maybe there's a way to get better and keep moving.

I kept the cyanide for quite a while after as a reminder that each day that I wake up, I'm actually choosing to be alive and choosing to live and move forward.

Chapter 45: Mello Ayo

Like Redding, I was sitting on the dock of the bay, a stale cigar perched between my lips and oblivion as I watched the smoke spiralling out above the undulating waves of my aimless life; my dull life, the blue waves and grey smoke drifting together in the same general direction away from me. To take a day and make it what you want; to wrap it this way and that way and bend it to suit your taste; not to be daunted by it or get sucked into its vortex — now, this is a day worth living. But this was not the day I was having. Instead, I was having a day not worth even living once when suddenly, suddenly out of the midst of nowhere appeared this figure of a man, an old man who hobbled over and without prompting drew himself near to me.

And the man opened his mouth and spoke:

"I am an avid beachcomber and on early mornings and during sunset afternoons I would do my daily rounds along the sand and pebble shore looking for something more. I would see beauty and peace in the brightly coloured, smooth and uniquely shaped stones that greeted me and adorned my path. Time and tempest had taken them in hand, threw them and hewed them, polished them, then placed them here for me to see. Awash by waves, the stones would appear and disappear with each receding and forward roll of the frothy sea. I would dash ahead to retrieve a particularly stunning one from its snug and sandy place only to lose it as the foamy wave rushed forward to hide it from my view. But alas, the wave would soon retreat revealing yet other stones that were exceedingly more exquisite than the ones before. And I would be thankful, relieved of my sorrow from losing the first."

And so it unfolded, this oceanic ritual between seeker and truth, repeated with efficacy each morning and dusky afternoon until I almost became inured, only to stumble upon the biggest, most magnificent gem I'd ever seen. Then it hit me like a rock to the head, the significance of my daily stroll. I fell upon the sand kneeling in prayer, knowing now more than I ever did before ... *Life loves me so much it will deny me that which I love for that which is even more lovable. Wait upon Life and Life will renew your strength. They that wait will mount up with wings like eagles. No good thing will life withhold from them that seek diligently* ... I wallowed in the sand in a gyration of joy immersing myself in the meaning of this discerning moment only to be hit by yet another jewel ... *You see ... human that I am, I miss deeply the things I have lost and miss even more the things I never had. You see I had failed to appreciate the treasures that I do have here and now this very moment. I'd forgotten how to be grateful* ... My gyration stopped, I rolled over and sobbed in the shore, adding tears of thankfulness to the other nuggets of truth that lay strewn all around me.

It was here that my cigar fell from my lips, and self-pity, like chains, fell off into the depths of the waters beneath me, waters that were no longer rabid with fear but rife with possibilities. Rising from his knees with eager anticipation, raising his eyes toward the sky, the old man held on to an outstretched hand that came seemingly from nowhere. He lifted himself from his erudition and resumed his walk. As I watched him leave, I rose from my knees. With nervous anxiety, I raised my eyes toward the same sky and reached out for the outstretched hand. Lifting myself from my stupor, I tried to walk again in search of my own stones.

Stories We Don't Tell

For many days and evenings I returned to meet the old man by the sea. We would talk for hours about his life and mine and the stones we each had found. Our conversations were long and lucid, vivid and vivacious, full of a rich intense feeling of oneness. Once I told him I felt trapped by my past; that even though I had tried to shed the manacles, they seemed inescapable. He said:

"Should we follow the dictates of our past we would be damned to live in defeat and despair all our lives. If you can turn and move against the forces of your past, then by all means, you must. Reject the destructive tendencies of your miserable inheritance. Say NO to their efforts to destroy you. Instead, destroy the ugly edifices they have constructed in your life and reconstruct a new milieu with different drives, new direction and meaning and with a new power source. You can and you must turn the tide around."

He spoke with a firm assurance as if there was no doubting or reservation, as if he knew the absolute truth in his words. His confidence invaded my qualms and swallowed them. I felt brave to face a new world but did not know quite how to, so I asked him. How can I turn back this mighty tide that threatens to overwhelm me? He looked at me knowingly and said:

"I think for someone, anyone, to do something there must first be a mental resolution and having made this mental commitment you need to work like hell to bring it to fruition. Anything less is an exercise in fantasy, a dream, a hope that something will happen without any effort on your part. You are already equipped to meet the demands of your existence. You can feel, think, visualize, analyze, theorize, synthesize, plan, project and work. Use these skills. Don't let complacency and strife rob you of your innate gifts. They are the answers to your prayers."

One night, he spoke lovingly and memorably to me. I felt his kindness piercing my vulnerability, paring it down to the point where I could trust more of myself to him. I felt one with him. I shared my fears, hopes and dreams and told him how much I have always wanted to lift my life to heights hitherto unattained by me or anyone else in my generation. He never laughed or questioned my audacity. I told him I was never able to find the right wind to take me higher, never been able to hold my own at those levels of turbulence without getting flustered, never able to sustain my grace of flight for any length of time except short. He never ridiculed, judged or belittled me. He listened earnestly. And when I told him how I had failed wretchedly in the pursuit of my own purpose, I saw in his eyes compassion and understanding. And then he said:

"Be gentle with yourself. The wind you need is beneath and behind you, ready to sustain you. Each day, be thankful. Recommit yourself afresh to the endeavour of soaring beyond. Let your thinking, speech, attitude, style, relationships, and your entire being, reflect something of that commitment to rise above the ordinary. One day, you will rise above your limitations, and your second best will be yesterday's accomplishment. Events may erode and undermine your efforts but you do not have to let them conquer or subdue you. You can rise and persevere in goodness. Circumstances do not have to have the final say. With humour and with mastery and creative excellence, it is possible to overcome. Chaos can be conquered. Life can

Stories We Don't Tell

be celebrated. With a life-affirming attitude, difficulties can be faced squarely; through improvisation, innovation, the challenge of living can be met with equanimity. Life can be a low-down dirty shame but it does not have to rob you of your humour, charming elegance and ability to persevere. Do not let circumstances overwhelm you or frighten you into doing things you don't wish to. Do not be afraid to be different, to excel. Believe in yourself without fear or shame. You are beautiful and you are ugly. Don't be afraid to be either. Don't be afraid to be humble. Build yourself as strong as you know how. Learn to stand and be free in who you are."

His words of encouragement were like food to me. No one had ever spoken with me like this before. I cried at each utterance. I felt weightless as if a load had been raised from my sagging zeal.

For the first time, I felt loved and loving in the company of an older male. I had been such a dismal failure at loving that I had grown to distrust my own sense of love. I wanted to tell him how much I loved him but I did not. Instead I told him I was grateful for his entrance into my life and how much stronger I had become as a result. I promised him I would restore wholeness and integrity to my living; that I would replace deceit with truth, weakness with strength, fear with boldness, ugliness with beauty and wayward conduct with a sense of purpose. And then he said:

"My son, the fact that you are here today suggests that you did not give up; that your flame still burns. That of itself confers upon you the right to be here. You have earned it or else you wouldn't be. What is it that you have? What is it that you bring? What is it that you have collected in your soul on your torturous and glorious journey — hate, anger, despair, resentment, and disenchantment, or is it love, compassion, insight and hope? Whatever it is, it does not matter. It is all right. It is all a part of your material. It is not where you have been that counts. It is where you are going. It is not what you bring to the here and now that defines you, it is how you use what you have that will determine where you go from here. My son, the basic essential requirement is not that you should discover love but rather that you become love. Allow love to find you. Walk on, and remember — you can never walk alone. I wish you peace, my son."

It was the last time I ever saw him, this old man by the sea. He asked nothing of me except my best and my attentiveness. I remember his words as if they were mine and as if they were spoken, not yesterday, but now.

***

The next day I woke up with my own father on my mind. I don't know why exactly. He wasn't dead but he may well have been for I had not seen or spoken with him for years. This was nothing new. It had always been like that. Ours was not the relationship where we covered each other's back. I would have liked that, but it just never happened that way between us and there was no hope that it would. With my father, it was touch and go. Actually, it was more go than touch. We rarely made contact. And yet, something deep inside me wished it wasn't so. I longed for him and wanted to love and admire him even as he would love and admire me.

If he only knew.

I regret not having my father around at those important moments: my first day at school, my first suspension from school; my first school play, my first graduation; my first track race, my first student elected leadership position; my first girlfriend, that first kiss, first heartbreak; my first fistfight or major setback; my first major achievement; first anything. His presence, companionship and advice were never available and life, my life, went on without him, and his without me.

In my father's absence, my mother fathered me and made me as well as I could be before she left. Last Mother's Day night, I imagined her all around me. She was in the stars that shone gloriously above, her light illuminating the way for lonely people. She was in the ocean that spread all the way beyond where I was standing, her love washing the shores of many troubled places. She was in the sands on the shore, each grain too numerous to count as they spread for miles further than the eyes could see. I imagined her enfolding me with her compassion, her presence, a presence that never diminished with time but got even stronger with its passing.

Yes, I had awoken with my father on my mind but it was the presence of my mother that overwhelmed me that morning.

I opened the card that rested with me that night and read it again as I had so many times the day previous:

Happy Father's Day Dad, it said.
I love you and miss you and wish you were here.
Your only and loving daughter ...

It was in that moment of epiphany that it occurred to me. The old man by the sea was my mother, reappearing posthumously to prepare me for this day. In her disguise, she had become the person I wished for the most, my father.

It was Father's Day today, my seventh. Without hesitation I called my daughter up and knew that from then on, my life would never be the same.

Chapter 46: Stefan Hostetter

The donkey showed up overnight.

We didn't know from where it had come. But I vaguely remembered hearing the sound of an engine and slamming doors through the thin polyester tent, and for a flash, the pitch-black was briefly pierced by two cylindrical beams, so I had a guess.

I don't do well with uncertainty.

Uncertainty leads to concern. Concern to anxiety. Anxiety that I feel deep within my bones; anxiety that I feel circling high above my head. Anxiety that is invasive, a vulture pecking at you before you're dead. Interrupting your life like-

Squawk

That person didn't get the joke you were making, now they'll always think you're a weirdo.

No, they got the joke, but it wasn't funny.

*You aren't funny. *Squawk**

You'll never find love.

No, you'll find love but never be exactly certain and then, slowly, over years, fall out of love until one day you'll have to ruin the life of your best friend.

Squawk

Could you stop for just 7 minutes? I'm trying to tell a story.

It's this voice that I ran from. I banished myself to the desert with three friends, a guide, and now, apparently, a donkey.

Marzuke, which we'd soon learn was his name, lounged underneath the only tree in sight. Last night we'd finished our first day of the five-day hike through the Jordanian desert

Stories We Don't Tell

on a long wide open plain that sat at the foot of a mountain. Small brush grew up around a thin winding river, but he took up the only true shade. Already packed with bags, and a throw saddle that reminded me of my grandmother's floor rugs I always thought were too fancy to step on.

Vultures soar above our heads, circling slowly, and we break camp. The path ascends into the mountains. As we walk, our guide explains to us that Marzuke is actually a legal requirement. To pass through the mountains, one has to be accompanied by a donkey. On the off chance that someone injures themselves or simply becomes too exhausted to continue, he was there to carry us.

Marzuke, the safety donkey.

A physical symbol of peace of mind.

As the slope increases, the communal chatter of the hike slows and then stops. Leaving me alone with my thoughts.

Squawk *Have you considered that every positive thing you put into this world is just to prove to yourself you're a good person?*

Of course he hasn't; he's probably hurting people all the time, but people just don't tell him. *Squawk*

You're inadequate.

No, you're actually uniquely talented, and so your consistent mediocrity is proof of your deeper failing as a human.

Squawk

The path ahead becomes all but invisible, the ground made up of uneven rocks, slants upwards, constantly slipping beneath our feet. Each step feels like two and gets you half as far as you expect. Somehow Marzuke seems to understand the way, and our guide lets him lead.

After an hour or so of hiking, we reach a bend and stop for a second to look out across a deep and wide valley. Below

Stories We Don't Tell

us the dirty green sea of what passes for a tree canopy is visible, in front of us the mountains rise to pierce the clear blue sky. Our guide stretches out his arm and points to the top of the mountain.

"That is where we are going."

"Around it, you mean?" We ask with the uptick in voice that betrays our fear.

"No, up."

Squawk *You're not going to make it.*

*You should have known this was a bad idea. *Squawk**

Your life is a house of cards, and a breeze is coming.

No, your life is already locked in, you're too afraid of change, and so you're trapped.

Squawk

Ugh, sorry.

We enter mid-morning, and the sun begins to come into play. No amount of expensive, ugly MEC equipment can stave it off, though I am grateful that at least the no-blister socks seem to be working.

We curl around the valley, working our way towards what appears to be a sheer cliff. The heat, gradually becoming unbearable. But really, what is there to do? Turn back? Not exactly an option. Marzuke carries forward, and so do we. It doesn't take long for the path to finish its wind around the valley and begin to slope upward once again. But this ascent is different, far more sharp than we've experienced so far on the trip, and laid out in a zigzag, so you never know what might lie beyond the next turn.

Squawk *It's your death.*

*Wouldn't that be terrible? I mean, what would you have to show for your life? *Squawk**

You've wasted it working countless hours of overtime.

No, at least at work you're helping others. You're

Stories We Don't Tell

accomplishing something. It's the downtime that's wasted. You need to work more, work harder. What are you, lazy?
Squawk
Tick.
Tick.
Tick.
Squawk
The landscape is overwhelmingly monochrome. A sun-parched brown, perhaps taking the form of rocks, or sand, peaks or cliffs, but all the same. My legs begin to ache, with each new step upwards my quads burn with effort, my pack, despite being relatively light, begins to pull down on my shoulders. The sun rises ever higher. Each corner offers the promise of relief, the illusion that we are nearly there. Each turn proves us hopelessly wrong. Morale drops as precipitously as the cliffs we edge beside. The views from whence we came our only reward.
Squawk Give up. You'll never do it.
You'll never be happy, you'll never be satisfied. Day by day, friend by friend, your life will pass you by. And then ...*Squawk*
You're attracted exclusively to people who don't like you. Why is that? Do you want to die alone?
Of course he does! He's hiking up a mountain at noon in the Jordanian desert.
Tick.
Tick.
Tick.
Squawk
After what feels like days but are told was only hours, we see the first splotch of colour. Poking out of the rocks is a thin green stalk, holding up five red petals that match Marzuke's pack. The flower offers hope of a refuge, nature's

Stories We Don't Tell

joke it seems as it sits at the base of the steepest incline yet. Probably close to 60 degrees and well over a hundred metres, the pack weighs heavier and legs weaken at the sight. We ask our guide for a break, and he reluctantly agrees.

"5 minutes."

We nod.

Squawk

Tick.

Tick.

Tick.

The view is incredible. We can't see our campsite anymore, but the desert extends to the horizon. Small rectangles just at the edges of our vision indicate what we presume are farms, the closest civilization we can see.

At this moment, I realize we are truly alone. The five of us, and our donkey, are hours of hiking away from another living soul.

Squawk

The vultures circle the crest of the mountain. As if daring us to try.

"Let's go." Our guide takes one last sip of water and starts up the mountain, now having to lead Marzuke to ensure he can make it up.

We start, being as careful as we can. Understanding that each step is treacherous, the rocks beneath our feet still sliding as we push ourselves upwards. After ten metres, we're scrambling on our hands and knees. After thirty, our guide and donkey have left us well behind. After sixty, the four of us have become stretched out, no longer able to really speak, I lead the pack, willing myself forward. Step by step.

Squawk *You've wasted your life.* *Squawk* *Not to mention you're messing up this story.*

No. I haven't. Not yet!

Squawk Yes, you have.
He really has hasn't he, lost the whole audience and everything.
No.
Squawk Stop trying so hard. Just lie down. You will die out here in the desert.
No.
Squawk
I slip, land on my knee and slide ten feet down the mountain. The small rocks tumble beneath me, and I catch myself just ever so slightly on the branch of a protruding shrub.
Squawk Give up.
A blue salamander darts out from behind the rock I've held onto and slips back out of sight.
I look up and see Marzuke, watching from above. The vultures still circling, but he pays them no mind.
I pull myself up and carry on.
Squawk
Stop it.
Stop climbing.
It's useless, it won't make you feel better.
It won't help,
you will keep failing,
you can't get away from us ...
The crest of the mountain brings a sight for sore eyes. Grass, a small patch, resting beneath the shade of a boulder. The boulder provides refuge from the sun, exhaustion provides refuge from the vultures. Our guide pulls tea from Marzuke's pack. We sip, staring out over the serene landscape, and for a few, precious minutes, my mind finds peace.

Chapter 47: Alice Walker

She was young, out dancing with her friends. She always felt a bit foreign in the club scene of Toronto but found it easy to have a good time. She wanted to be adventurous, and she wanted to feel attractive, something she hadn't felt since her crush left town, and even then, only sometimes.

So she danced.

Late in the night, a group of guys swarmed the dance floor. There were four or five of them, yelling her name, cheering drunkenly. They seemed taller, and they were in t-shirts and jeans instead of their usual suits, but she still recognized them from work.

When the club was closing, they were all going to a party back at his condo. She happily accepted the invitation to continue her night out. She didn't know them well, but she saw them every day, and she felt safe.

The living room of the apartment was bursting with noise. People were playing drinking games she'd never heard of. They were a bunch of young professionals, just older enough to make her feel unsophisticated. She was just their barista!

She took a deep breath and got a drink. She found a couple of guys talking about the upcoming election, and they looked at her doubtfully when she introduced herself. She said she didn't agree that the opposition had the best policies, but it didn't really matter, given our broken electoral system.

They looked at her less doubtfully. Her tension started to melt away, they chatted and debated, and she was having a great time.

He came over and asked if she wanted another drink. She said his friends were a lot of fun. He snorted, yeah, they're all on MDMA. She didn't actually know that's what he said, she had no idea about drugs, and it took her years to piece this acronym together.

He took her to his room, and they started making out. It was nice. She was thinking about the time she made sure she was the one to take his order when she saw him line up for coffee.

She wanted to set the boundaries right away, so she could relax.

"Hey, this is great, but I'm not going to sleep with you."

He didn't agree.

***

I don't hear from her for five years. Not because of him — sadly, his actions are too common in this world.

It's her I've been afraid of.

It's like she suddenly turns into someone else, and I can no longer account for her actions. Looking back, even with the gift of hindsight, especially with the gift of hindsight, I can't understand.

And for a long time, I don't want to understand.

Or maybe I'm afraid that I'll understand too well.

So what is it about me, now, that allows me to look back? Is it that now I have no problem using words like feminism, patriarchy? I've taken courses on criminal law? I post articles on facebook about issues that survivors face in the justice system?

I can hear a lesson repeated a thousand times, but it doesn't sink in until its time has come. And I can't bear to understand her until the lesson sinks in.

It's never ok.

***

Stories We Don't Tell

Her fight instinct has left her breathless.

She listens. There is no way she could have won this struggle. He's much stronger than her, a hockey player, or something, but he's passed out.

She listens. He was so drunk. She tries to move, and he's so much heavier than her. The shock is weighing her down, tearing at everything she thought she knew about the world, and leaving her bare.

It's a frigid January night. The party outside his room is louder than ever, and somewhere out there, through another door, or a closet? She can't remember where her coat is.

And he's passed out! She never thought she'd be grateful for alcohol.

She looks around the room, dark and mostly empty, except for the twinkling glass buildings outside his floor to ceiling windows. She tries to take stock of her jeans, her little black purse, but can't see them. One of her socks is missing.

The living room outside erupts in a cheer — someone must have won a drinking contest.

She looks at his silhouette, passed out in the dark. She starts to fill in the blanks that the reflection of the Financial District lights doesn't show. His blond curls. "Large coffee, black. To go." "That will be $2.10, please. Can I have your name for the order?"

So what the hell happened!?

She looks out onto the stark night, the condos like tips of glassy icebergs bobbing in the dark.

She doesn't understand, so she stays.

This simple action, or rather, a lack of decisive action, haunts me for years.

She had said it, she had said no, how much more clearly can the line be drawn? He stepped right over it, and what does she do??

Stories We Don't Tell

She re-writes the story as if it never happened!!

She stays there, watching the room slowly regain texture. She dreams up excuses for his aggression.

When I think about it now, the right thing to do seems so simple. He's the one who ignored my boundaries. I can't then pretend I never set them up. Of course, I would walk out into the crowded living room, tell everyone that their host is an entitled jerk. I would find my coat and leave!

Because where else can I draw strength from, if not from staying true to myself?

But this was years ago.

The whole world was turned upside down, and so I do the only thing I know to somehow erase the violence of the previous night. I tell myself a story that can make it seem ok.

The sky turns to lighter grey, and a pink reflection of the dawn slowly lights up the glass towers.

That morning, he walked me to his apartment door.

I turned to him and said, "call me."

Chapter 48: Joshua Stribbell

Alone he stood among the silence and the cold, wind whispering thoughts in his ear, the Inuk pilgrim facing off against the arctic tree line battalion. Long had he journeyed to reach this place, and he wondered if he could leave it all behind and wander bravely into the dark. The only footprints in the snow were the elliptical tracks of his snowshoes pressing clumsily off into the distance. It was not strange for him to feel alone in this desolate wilderness, where forest met tundra.

The wind began to pick up, its icy breath kissing his skin through caribou fur as the traveller lost himself in reckless contemplation. Two worlds lay on either side of him. The weight of each had pressured him into this lonely purgatory, leaving him unsure of which way to go. He had a southern heart that betrayed his northern face. However, to his kin in the south, he felt like another disappointing commodity in their fast-paced consumerism who failed to offer everything that was advertised. The wanderer had not found himself in the place of his birth, and so he entertained the idea that he might find it in the place of his dreams. Perhaps now he could share in how wild the spirit becomes north of the short, white spruce.

A crippling fear lay north that paralyzed the traveller. He had never experienced the arctic beyond echoes overheard by others who had, and although one of these echoes had said it was customary in northern culture to enter someone's home without knocking, who was he to show up unannounced claiming to be their brother? He knew well that he was Inuk, but did that make him Inuit? Was it blood that made him a part of the people? He once learned that to his ancestors names and souls were synonymous, that in them the spirit of the ancestors continued to live on. What would they call him? Frobisher? Hudson? It was this fear that they would not see their reflection in his eyes that stopped his tracks in the snow at the same line as the trees. Amidst this fear was a hope that he would arrive among them as an old relative who had left on an adventure, returning as someone they used to know with a thousand stories to tell and eager to hear what had happened while he was gone.

The pilgrim passed his hours in lonely meditation, unaware until now that the shivering had begun. He had been standing still for far too long. He could almost feel his veins constricting with every tighter breath. He needed to start moving, but where? The wind rose now from a whisper to a howl, picking up the snow until it was swirling like ghosts all around him. The homesick wanderer sought shelter in the comfort of the trees. Panicked, the thoughts in his mind froze and all he could hear was the sound of the two worlds' howling ghosts screaming as they entered his ears. The small amount of exposed skin on his face seemed to split apart. The warrior was being devoured by these ghosts, eaten alive at the valley between their kingdoms. The worlds themselves became mountains with insurmountable peaks. He wished he had never come to this place. Staring into the eyes of his demons, he longed instead for the neon-glow of the city.

The demons screamed "Fall! Lay down your life and fall!" as he almost lay fetal in the snow. The south had pushed him here, yes, it was they who had brought him to this desolate wasteland, and it was the north that held him back. It would not allow him to move forward. The demons continued to scream "Fall! Lay down your life and fall!" So many times that the traveller fell victim to their rhythm. Embracing the ground that would soon become his tomb, tears freezing on his face, the traveller found a moment of clarity in the storm. The south didn't push him here. He had brought himself. It wasn't the north holding him back. He was holding himself back. The ghosts weren't demons at all. In fact, they were the opposite. They were angels. Angels who were telling him to keep going. He heard their voices now, so loud, so melodic it was like a song moving through his weak and shivering body giving him strength. They sang, "Get up! Get up and rise!" As he had lain in the snow, wishing there was a bridge between worlds, he realized he was already on the bridge. His trajectory bore testimony to that fact. He wasn't just walking on the bridge, he was the bridge! At this time he realized he wasn't the only one. People had been engineering these bridges for thousands of years. It is our lives themselves that allow us to travel to other worlds.

His muses continued to sing, "Get up and rise!" The song played so powerfully that he could no longer ignore it. The warrior let out a thunderous roar that swelled like the howl of a wolf above the storm. He tore himself from the comfort of the trees and charged into the fray. His soul would walk tall, far taller than the short white spruce as he dared to travel where they were afraid to go. His soul would walk taller than the summit of the mountains of the two worlds. The clumsy tracks of his snowshoes became completely straight, graceful in their strides like a rabbit through the snow. The traveller returned home to a world he had never known to reunite with family he had never met.

The arctic showed no sympathy for his sudden transformation. The spirit of the north would continue to test his strength and endurance. A gust of wind broke the warrior from his charge. He fell hard onto the snow and ice, the air being knocked out of his lungs. As he struggled to reclaim his breath, he once again received the gift that creates all champions of faith: doubt. He wondered if the silence and the cold had helped him find his blood by spilling it. The snow began to cover his body until he was being buried alive. It seemed the only thing he had found on this quest was his grave. But was this any grave for a southern man? Was this any grave for a northern man? No. It was a grave for a weak one, or an unlucky one. The warrior did not believe in chance, so if he could find one more ounce of his strength in his failing body, then he could deny the cold his soul once more.

    The storm reached its peak and the muses sang louder than they had before. "Get up and rise!" His eyes obeyed, looking up towards the top of the world. In the distance was a colourful glow, beckoning him in the sea of ice like a siren. His hands were the next to listen clawing the ground and pulling him forward as the snow began to fall off his back. His legs would follow, inching forward until he looked like a frog crawling on the landscape. He was surrounded by the spirits of the north, his angels, his demons, and the ancestors of both worlds who had long passed, all watching him decide what kind of person he would choose to be. "Get up and rise!" he yelled, his spirit now obeying the call. His muscles struggled to find their proper footing as the swirling ghosts danced around him. "Get up and rise!" he yelled once more, and as suddenly as a bolt of lightning scorches the hard earth, and as slowly as thunder rumbles through the night sky, so too did the storm begin to stop. The ghosts had finished their ballet, the muses their symphony, and the arctic spirit relented its ruthlessness. They all seemed to retreat into the colourful display of lights that painted the northern sky.

    The Inuk pilgrim rose now so that he stood alone among

the silence and the cold, facing forward like a general with the arctic tree line battalion behind him. Long had he journeyed to reach this place, and he was ready to leave it all behind and wander bravely into the light.

Chapter 49: Adrianna Prosser

I'm standing beside Andrew on the subway platform on the Bloor West line around 6:13 pm. I know it's not HIM, I mean, my brother died over a month ago, but it looks eerily like him. Looks just like him — so tall, glasses, but short hair like he's trying to go business. He thinks I'm looking past him to the TV screen arrival times. I'm looking at him and his nose, which is Andrew's. The subway arrives; he lets me on before him. I like "Subway Andrew." He has a gym bag — Andrew was working out and trying to live a healthy life just before ... He took up running. I almost ask this guy for a hug at one stop before mine. That way, I can squeeze him and then run out at my stop. I play with the idea of riding the train until he gets off. But that's insane. Right? What if I just stand here and have some tie with my "brother." At what point did this turn insane? The part where I fantasized the hug? Or where I stalk him ...? Get off the subway. Get off the subway! Get off before you live too Dangerously ...

I get home, and I need to unwind after all that, so I take a long shower, and that was when the heaviness took over me. It felt so good to sit. To let the floor take all the weight I was holding. Then I heard the front door to the apartment open, then the bathroom door open.

My soon-to-be-ex-but-he's-kinda-not because we still have to live together until the lease is up, comes back to our non-home and says, "How long have you been showering?" I dunno — I got home. Got in.

"You have been showering since you got home? That was like an hour ago ..."

He sat me down on the bathroom floor. He wouldn't even hold me. He could barely look at me. Days until moving trucks and stale goodbyes. But he was still a knight in shining-leather-jacket to me. So we sat. I couldn't even speak. What was there to say?

My phone rings, I have to answer it, it's my friend, Christa. Hello?

"Oh ... I don't know if I should be telling you this!"

Just tell me — my brother died by suicide so it can't get worse than it is!

"Okay. Well. I had a dream, well more like a daydream, but anyway, a dream about your brother.

"He had this wild hair everywhere and glasses and a cheesy 70's jacket with a fur collar on. It was clearly not real leather, and he seemed pleased about how ratty it was. Thing is he was putting his hand in one of the pockets and showing me that his hand could pull through — like it was ripped? Ya, a rip in the lining. That something is caught in the lining. You have to find that jacket and see what's in the lining of his jacket — he wants you to have it."

I proceed to ask if she is tripping balls. She isn't, she says, she is really certain in fact. She also apologizes over and over that this may be too hard to hear and that she doesn't know why he came to her and not me directly. Thanks Hun, I'll talk to you soon, okay?

What are you supposed to do with that information? I call my Dad ...

Hi Dad, it's me. I need to know about Andrew's pleather jacket? Ya. I know weird. Do u still have his pleather jacket? I think I want it ...

You gave it to Goodwill?!

Crapnut. How do I ask about getting the jacket back without sounding bat-shit crazy? Okay, ya, let me know if you find it. I hang up.

Dad gets the jacket back from Goodwill for a few bucks

and turns it inside out. Nothing. There is a rip though ...

He checks the laundry for me (because they washed all his stuff before they donated it!). And he finds something — a wet card — a family photo laminated with our birthdays printed on the back. We were all smiling. Except, the only place the laundry machine-washed away the image, is where Andrew's face should have been. Andrew was erased. Like in Back to the Future with Michael J. Fox. The lead character Marty McFly has this photo of his brother and sister, and they are fading out of existence as he tries to correct the past into his future. My brother was faded too, but there is no fucking time machine for me to hop into to go back and save him. And I don't think that's fair.

Chapter 50: Adam Zawalich

I wasn't familiar with the San Francisco airport parking garage.

No matter how close you park to the terminal, you still have to trudge up this long sloping hallway that seems to go on forever. She was groaning every step of the way. Last time we visited my parents, we borrowed a cane from my mother who was recovering from knee surgery. It was one of those extendable aluminum ones that snap into place with the little button on the side that fits into a series of holes. It rattled in her hand as we inched our way to the terminal.

I always stress about time at airports. I could hear the stress in my voice as I tried to sound encouraging, to keep us moving forward. My shoulder was throbbing as I pulled the lopsided suitcase at such a slow pace. There was a forty-pound portable recumbent bike sitting on top that bounced into my knuckles with every step. We got the bike during the month we were living at the residence inn. Since she could barely walk most of the time and hadn't been able to for months, a few minutes of moving her feet on the pedals every other day felt like a big improvement.

These painful steps up this slight incline were going to be the last we saw of each other for three weeks. I was putting her on a plane to go across the country to my parents' house while I stayed behind to pack up our home. We had driven out to San Francisco from Boston a little more than a year before. I don't remember what our original aspirations were, but I know they weren't this.

I booked a wheelchair days in advance. We didn't want to risk her collapsing while she tried to walk through the security line. Apparently at the San Francisco airport even if you book a wheelchair in advance, you have to wait. I left her by the wheelchair stand while I went to check her bags in. When I came back, I couldn't find her. All the seats had been taken over by a large family of elderly Indian women. They looked miserable and pissed that they had to wait too.

I found her on the floor behind them. Curled up between a trash can and a fake plant. It looked fake, at least. We spent the next forty minutes waiting mostly in silence. Only speaking to complain about how shitty the customer service was or to point out when someone was heading toward us with a wheelchair only to have them turn at the last second to pick up one of the elderly women. I impatiently checked the time every few seconds. She tweeted at the airport's twitter account to no avail.

We hadn't figured out the problem until about a month before. We were in Brooklyn for a wedding, and she felt good. The first night of the weekend, she let me know that she was going to head back to the hotel room as soon as was socially acceptable. It kept getting later, and she kept saying she felt fine. By the time we stumbled back to our room at 2 am, we were certain something was different. It was the house. It had to be. We spent the next two days annoying everyone we could with our theories and anger at something that it took so long for us to see. It was the fucking house. It had to be. I told her I wasn't letting her go back there.

Luckily, my parents love the Marriot hotel rewards program. They were able to get us an extended stay with their points. The San Francisco residence inn isn't in the city. It's in an under-construction business park twenty minutes south of downtown. The only thing within walking distance is another Marriot hotel. Not that we were able to do much walking.

I'd left her at the hotel when I went back to the house to

Stories We Don't Tell

meet the landlord, Dave, and the mould inspector. We went room to room with nearly identical results: the inspector asked if there was a history of water damage, Dave said "no", the inspector pointed out a horrifying stain or a bulge in the wall, and then Dave would remember "oh yea the toilet broke and flooded three rooms one time" or "oh yea there was a hole in the roof for over a year" or "oh yea we didn't put a vapour barrier in when we did the new construction because it seemed unnecessary".

While the inspector's moisture meters flashed red and excitedly chirped out their warnings, Dave told me "of course there's moisture in the walls, houses are outside aren't they? The inside walls keep it out." While the inspectors took samples of spores from a window sill, Dave told me, "they just call it toxic mould to scare you."

With twenty minutes to spare before her flight left, an attendant finally came over to us with a wheelchair. We had a hurried goodbye, and I watched as this stranger whisked her off through the crowd. Part of me was unsure if this was the last time I would see her, and the other part of me was angry at myself for even thinking that. I don't remember the drive back to the house, but I probably shouldn't have been on the road. My hands ached from how tightly I had been gripping the wheel.

I spent the next few days in a weed and pizza induced stupor. I needed to pack, but where do you start dismantling the life you had just started to build? Do I start with the wedding gifts? Or the room full of knick-knacks and memories from our road trip out here? The new doctor said the only real solution to deal with mould is to just get rid of everything. I lay curled up on the couch staring at the pile of boxes I needed to assemble and fill. The couch that we bought together when we first moved into this house, the couch that was now probably covered in poison.

We spent most of our days side by side on that couch. When she was in too much pain to stand up, when she started to involuntarily shake, when she couldn't hold her head up to look at me. I spent the next weeks packing, and cursing Dave, and sobbing in progressively emptier rooms. I constantly checked my phone, wondering what had happened if she didn't answer my texts right away or anticipating a phone call from my parents that they'd had to take her to the hospital. I'd been her caretaker for the past year, and no one else knew how to keep her safe.

I have this fantasy. It's not sexual. Well, maybe a little bit sexual. Even though she's walking now, I still let it run through my head when I'm in a bad mood. It's a rainy Saturday morning. Dave loves waking up to the sound of rain, especially on a day when he has nothing on his schedule. It's a soothing natural alarm clock, letting him know that the day is his, take your time, relax. As he rubs the sleep from his eyes, a new noise sends him bolting upright in bed, a guttural engine roars to life much closer than it should. He slowly creeps to the window and sees me. Standing in the street in front of his house. With a brick. Standing next to an idling bulldozer. We make eye contact, and I put the brick on the gas pedal. Confusion and disbelief spread over his face as gravel incrusted treads begin to tear through the pavement of his driveway and turn his lawn to mush. Just as the blade of the machine is about to demolish his front step, I turn around and walk away. Comforted by the sweet sounds of scraping metal and cracking timbers as I walk down the street.

Chapter 51: Nicole Borthwick

I met Dan through my volunteer work with the Victoria AIDS Respite Care Society, as a respite care provider for him over the last few months, which turned into a meaningful friendship for both of us.

When the weather was a little brighter and, most times, pleasant on the south coast of B.C., Dan and I decided to get some spring bulbs to plant. Along the side boulevard was the perfect spot! After purchasing them at the nursery, we planted tulips and daffodils to bloom in the spring. Dan loved brightness and vivacious colour, so he decided to get the brightest colours possible. We brought them home and planted them in the yard with care, and he tended to them, if the rains didn't do the job for him first.

Christmas Day of the same year, Dan was feeling a little less than comfortable, and I mentioned dropping something off for him later in the day. After dinner, I made a dinner plate for him. It was raining, and I'd need a ride over to his apartment, so my mom and I got in the car, and drove across the city to drop dinner off to him. He opened the door, met my mom, and accepted the dinner with gratitude. I told her that I'd stay with him for a while. He ate some dinner, and I planned to bus my own way back home. I ended up staying with Dan while we watched. It's a Wonderful Life. (I swear, the longest movie ever made!) He fell asleep before the movie was finished, so I draped a blanket over him, turned off the television, locked up, and left. It's still a Christmas I'll never forget.

I provided respite for him for as long as I could. Maliah was born on February 22nd, 1995.

I had called the office the day after to let them know that

I'd given birth and that I wouldn't be back right away.

A week later, I got a call asking if Dan could see Maliah at six weeks. I took Maliah to see Dan for the first time, and the joy on his face when he was holding her was full of glee and excitement. I captured that moment on film and got it framed. Dan's dad decided to get a few copies made: one for him and his wife, one for the PWA office and one for me. He also gave me a large framed picture as well, that sits in my bedroom, and has gone with me on every move since.

I went to Dan's apartment one day to do the usual clean up and laundry, and found him sleeping on the couch in the living room. I called out to him to let him know I was there, and let myself in, as the door was unlocked. He woke up half asleep and exclaimed to me that he was tired of living the same way every day and not getting any relief, so he was quitting his med regime of fourteen pills a day, cold turkey! I didn't sway him, I just let it be. He explained that he quit because he was ready — no more schedules, no more after-effects of the meds, none of it. He quickly changed the subject and asked me if I would plan a party — his "living wake." He knew his time was close, and he wanted to go in style, so I accepted my mission, and, soon after, we were planning everything from a guest list, food, music, the whole shebang.

The party was planned for a week that Saturday, so I was on the phone, calling guests, inviting them to come. Right away, people said yes, knowing exactly what this party was for. I then hit up the dollar store with Dan to get party supplies, some snacks, drinks, and everything from streamers, balloons to party favours. I made him a cake.

Saturday morning, I went over to decorate and prepare. Pat also came over to give me a hand in getting everything ready. The apartment looked amazing! Music was playing,

Stories We Don't Tell

we were streaming streamers, setting up food, making sure things were set for that evening.

By about 6 pm, everyone had arrived. The music started playing, people were quick to join in the party, socializing, dancing, talking to each other about days gone by, reminiscing about days where being gay and party central of the city in the '80s was all the rage. Especially in conservative Victoria, the gay scene was underground, and not widely accepted until much later — most likely the '90s and the new generation of being out was cool because you were accepted by your peers.

The shenanigans continued until midnight when the last of the buses were running. People were well on their way home. Guests filed out one by one, thanking us for the party, and bidding adieu to Dan. This would be the last time anyone saw him as healthy and "together" as he was, considering.

I returned Sunday afternoon to clean up, letting Dan sleep as comfortably as he could, and stored some leftovers to tide him over the rest of the day.

One afternoon in May of 1995 at around 3, I got a call from Mairi, saying that Dan had gone into hospice care, and asking if I could go up to see him. He didn't have much time left.

I bussed to Victoria Hospice, went into Dan's room, where I saw a shrine of flowers, cards, and a smaller framed picture of him holding Maliah. I saw Jim and Michael alongside his bed. I sat with him to softly cry and say my goodbyes. The moment was surreal, I couldn't believe he would be gone so soon. The room itself was full of the familiar things he treasured, and pictures of his cat, Mercury, named after Freddie Mercury. I stayed to sit with them a while, to talk, to laugh quietly, and to cry.

Mairi called me a few days later; Dan had passed away in

his sleep that morning. I was preparing for a funeral.

The service was short, attended by friends from Victoria and relatives from Brandon. Later that day, Dan's ashes were scattered at Esquimalt Lagoon.

His dad had a few prints of the picture of Maliah and Dan made for both the family and myself and a smaller treasure of individuals, for the office, him, and myself. In the corner of the smaller frame, it reads:

"A new life, a passing life.
Maliah Joy Borthwick: Feb. 22, 1995. Daniel William Luckins III: Oct. 26, 1962 – May 12, 1995"

I started a quilt. Pat decided to help me with it, alongside Lisa, Michael's sister. We worked on it for a few weeks; the quilt had Dan's picture with Maliah, other photos, other aspects of his life — like music, his hobbies, his love for nature, things he treasured — his cat. The quilt hung in the PWA office for a while until Jim suggested it be taken down. We sent it to Dan's family. A week later, his mom sent a thank you letter and a photo of the quilt hanging in the family living room. I was overwhelmed with a bucket of emotions: happiness it arrived safely, sadness, loss, and hope, that these types of losses would become fewer every year with the discovery of new medications, and hope for a cure, or at least sound management.

I arrived to clean the apartment. I noticed the flowers blooming in the warm sunshine, blooms that, I believe, he saw from the heavens, where souls and spirits live free of pain and disease. Dan was finally at peace, somewhere up there, sitting at a bar, with a drink in hand, dancing to "Walk of Life" by Dire Straits, which played at his service.

Dan died at a time when AZT was the only drug available

for persons living with AIDS. He was bold to disclose his AIDS diagnosis because it was his truth and everyday reality. He was just starting the combination therapy, and back then there was a shopping list of combinations. Look how far we've come! The baby in the photo is now 23, and the pride of my life.

I miss Dan every day, and he is the reason I still do what I do, 23 years later.

Chapter 52: Jessica Singh

When Love Lived Alone
In the forlorn hours, when love lived alone,
It dreamt to be red, to be pampered and fed,
It begged to be read, to be ironed and tread,
It fought to be said, to be conquered and to conquer the head.

I wanted to be able to write and write poetically well as much as I wanted long hair and long lustrous silky hair. It did happen, long hair long before my first proper poetic prose came along. Somewhere in between the sultry school summer vacation at my mansion-like grandparent's house, the 10-year-old me was scrambling through the neglected dusty cupboards to uncover the stored and forgotten literary treasures. There were plenty, but the tiny ones stood out the most, 'Reader's Digest' from the 1970's — and I have had a grabbed collection of those since then. I also picked up a few books with deep pale whisker-thin brittle pages that I was perhaps too young to read. More than what the text said, I was experiencing books as entities and the affinity I felt to them. It was clear that my grandfather was a lot more than an avid reader. My grandfather was a poet, and it very recently became 'was'. He passed away last December — something I am still wrapping my head around. He used to write in Urdu, published a couple of books too, and would recite on the radio. My mother tells me that when she was young she witnessed a lot of artists' get-togethers in their massive living room. There were musicians, singers, writers, poets, actors, visual artists — everyone came together, a creative confluence of sorts. My mother's involvement in these was pretty much limited to serving tea but when she describes it I cannot help but imagine the energy in the room at the time. I have spent several long afternoons in the same room over at least 16 summers if not more, basking in the warmth and recreating how it would have been — like a daytime 'Midnight in Paris' with Indian artists of all ages, the imaginary visuals break in and out while a strong aspiration to recreate that in some manner becomes more focused.

    I believe that artists thrive in a very specific symphony of being alone and being in collaboration. A little more than five years back, I quit my full-time job to work as a freelance consultant and run my start-up, artySORTS, that professes 'Live Your Art'. That carved out space also enabled me to have the time to waltz in and out of events and discussions around art. It was the perfect brewing environment for some form of art to flow, I was a photographer first, I then conducted art immersion walks and workshops and after that I also became an author. On 1st October 2017, my book was launched, When Love Lived Alone — prose poems with Illustrations. And that is the key milestone the other random bits are around today.

    Just so you all know I am quite a scandal in the family, a daughter who would soon be 32 — not married and does not seem to have any plans to do so either. This has been and is a major cause of stress and worry, a concern grave enough to consult not one but several astrologers who came up with ridiculously superstitious solutions that my mother made me follow. Trust me, you do not want to know what these solutions were, but now you all know how effective they were as I stand here before you — so hot and so single. None of the astrologers could give my parents the solace of a single date, month or year in which I would get married or

Stories We Don't Tell

the description of someone whom I might end up marrying. All of them, however, did unanimously believe that it would be a man. I know I have had moments when I doubted even that. Interestingly, all of them also believed that I would write; one clearly gave the month when I would publish a book and the kind of work I would end up publishing. Commendable, isn't it?

So ... after my brave and bold move to leave a good job, I immersed myself in art and travel and the leisure of working on my own terms — the city that I grew up in afforded me the luxury to do that. During this period what I oddly and ardently followed was this phrase that stuck to me in one of my psychology classes, Carl Rogers 'Openness to Experience' to get closer to your real self as opposed to the ideal self. And I lived up to that rather recklessly. I went out of my way to be outlandish and experimental, there was no routine to my life, I took work assignments that were out of my league, I met people I had absolutely no reason to meet with, and I went on trips that I could not always afford. My Euro-solo (27 days, 7 countries, 16 cities) in the summer of '16 is definitely worthy of being chronicled as long as my immediate family never gets to it. For the record it does not start and end with kissing a stranger in Paris. My phone got stolen on a club night in Barcelona and my new phone broke down exactly a week later in Bruges as I was rushing to the train station and dramatically collided with someone — entirely his fault — and I accepted the 100 Euros he offered as compensation. It was not just my phone that was broken — or that I was crying — I had missed the last train. In that trip I risked couch surfing and beyond that I spent two nights in a stranger's house — talk about living on the edge. The rest of my trip in Europe was spent without a phone, navigating with directions on pieces of paper and at some point a kind person I met on the bus paid for my Uber ride to nowhere (I didn't have a hostel booking) because she felt that Amsterdam might not be safe that late at night. The point is that I was THAT open. I experienced so much and felt even more all through those years and a vivid patchwork of all those feelings poured out into coded prose poems. Coded, because I never could write a diary while growing up, I was too scared of the judgment and almost certainly knew someone would scan through those secrets in the sacred pages. So the coded poems were no effort; my subconscious made sure that the poems came out inexplicably and fairly unclear about the exact circumstances — which also made it poetic — a great default plus I believe. I now present a couple of codes for you to decipher.

Kaleidoscope Me
I will not end before you do – you can keep tracing. For in that, I become much more and many.
Shades and shapes and figures and figments.
Kaleidoscope me, keep doing that.

The Tamed Surrender
I would get breathless very often; not in pleasure but in some sort of anguished pain. Pain that resides, that blames, that transforms.
I breathed into myself as I exhaled in writing.

Chapter 53: Brianne Benness

As soon as I walk into the lobby, John takes the belt off from around his neck and starts whipping it haphazardly at a baseball player dressed as a cowboy who he doesn't even know. John, who I'd broken up with a week before, although I didn't have the strength to insist that he stop sleeping in my room. John, who I'd been speaking to less than an hour earlier and who'd promised me that he'd take his drunk upset self home and call me in the morning. John, who was dressed as autoerotic asphyxiation for the party.

I'd walked in with a boy dressed as Hulk Hogan, but he quickly jumps into the fray to pull a gladiator off of John. A former marine (a real one, not just for the party) soon has John in some kind of hold and now the cowboy is sitting there quietly, gingerly touching his face to see if his nose is broken.

I stand there, stunned. I'm wearing this ripped t-shirt that says "I love bad boys," and my skin is covered in fake bruises and there are leaves in my intentionally messy hair; I'm just one half of a catfight costume who was totally blindsided when a real fight broke out. I don't know what to do so I throw my wallet in the trash and hurry outside, where I sit on a low concrete wall and wait for somebody, anybody, to find me.

Eventually, somebody does find me and escorts me inside to reclaim my wallet. I find Hulk Hogan and a few other friends and we head back to a lounge to watch Aqua Teen Hunger Force; the prospect of the party in the wake of this violence is just too much. Eventually, I get a call from the local police department, and I thrust my phone at a friend to deal with it.

Hulk Hogan looks at my ripped tights and my black eye and asks what happened to me tonight. These bruises are just makeup, but everything still feels different.

***

When I first met John, my mom's cancer had just gone into remission. That spring I applied to be on student staff, and I got it. And I applied for a summer internship with NASA, and I got it. And when I found myself sitting on a hill near campus watching a thunderstorm with this strange, smart boy, I got him too.

But my friends didn't really get along with him. And we fought constantly on the phone during my summer in Los Alamos. And when he came to visit me at my parents' house that August, I discovered him secretly wearing my dirty underwear.

And then I found out my dad had been diagnosed with Alzheimer's disease, and John fell asleep that first night while I wept alone and tried to shake him awake. And then I fell off my bike and needed surgery, and John would help me eat and tuck me in and then sneak out of my room to go to parties.

So when John cornered me before the Fetish theme party, I wasn't feeling sympathetic. He was really upset but couldn't articulate why. He wanted me to leave with him, to talk with him, to soothe him.

This was my first big party since the bike accident, and we were broken up, and I didn't want to miss it because of this vague uneasiness that he couldn't even express. He agreed to go home, that we could talk about it when he was sober.

***

Stories We Don't Tell

My friend takes my phone and calls the police station while Shake yells at Meatball in the background. It turns out that John was really arrested, not just held-for-public-intox arrested. We can't pick him up tonight like he'd suggested in his message, we'll have to go to the county seat tomorrow to pick him up at the courthouse after his arraignment.

When we're alone the next day, John tells me what he can remember about the night. He remembers heading home down the covered walkway between the dorms. He remembers liberating a chair through the walkway's window. He remembers holding a can of spray paint in a back room while a girl that he used to date pleads with him not to use it. He remembers the former marine immobilizing him. He doesn't remember taking the belt off his neck. He doesn't remember me walking in. He doesn't remember attacking a virtual stranger.

He does remember talking to me before the party. He remembers feeling like he had too much testosterone coursing through his body. He remembers knowing that he had to fuck it out or fight it out. He remembers how the latter became inevitable when I declined the former.

While we were together, I didn't understand why John couldn't stay awake and hold me on the day I found out that my father as I knew him was never coming back. After we broke up, John didn't understand why I wouldn't leave a party with him so that he could fuck out his excess testosterone.

Over winter break, the administration will ask John not to come back.

At the Chains of Love matchmaking party, Hulk Hogan and I are handcuffed together. That night we spoon chastely on my loveseat, and it's not long before we're dating. Things move slowly, and we keep our clothes on until the night of Mary B. James, the annual cross-dressing party when I invite him to shower with me. So we undress, and I wash off my honey and coffee grounds beard, and I start to get nervous. Because our faces are touching and then our bodies are touching, and I get down on my knees and I ... begin to panic. My eyes start to well up so I close them but my heart is still racing. And I can't stop because what if it's the testosterone in his body that makes him want to be there with me? What if I stop and then he needs to fight it out?

And then something happens that never happened with John: he notices. Hulk Hogan sees my panic, and he gets us both dressed, and he holds me. He will be the one who holds me when I wake up at 4 am after a nightmare about John's return to campus. He will be the one who wakes up and holds me when my stepmom calls and tells me it's time to come home and say goodbye to my dad. He will be the one who stays awake and holds me nights later when my dad is really truly gone. And he will be the one who spends six years trying to keep any anger at bay so that I don't see it and wonder if it means that too much testosterone is coursing through his veins.

Chapter 54: Jon Aaron Sandler

I couldn't believe it. My first year of university, and I was assigned to live in an all-male dorm. I spent my teenage years in an all-boys high school, pushed on me by my parents, and now this.

I was cursed.

Persecuted.

Fated to never meet girls or go on a date.

My first dinner home, I couldn't stop complaining about it.

"And the only guys on campus who always have a girl around," I said to my brother. "Are the ones I see playing acoustic guitars!"

He tensed up. He could sense the question coming. I waited for dinner to end and my mother to bring out some kind of pie for dessert, and then, in the spot where I would normally ask my brother to pass me the ice cream, I said, in an offhand way, "Hey man, would you teach me how to play something on guitar?"

"Yeah. Okay," he said, his hand twisting in the air above the French vanilla. It was too late; he knew he'd been tricked fair and square.

"What song?" he managed.

"'Crash' by Dave Matthews Band?" I said.

"Okay. Fine," he said.

For a kid who loved the blues back to Robert Johnson, who worshipped Thelonius Monk and Dave Brubeck, who was playing the hillbilly runs of Leo Kotke to relax at night, The Dave Mathews Band, especially their song 'Crash', a sappy song about a wannabe peeping tom that sat, self-satisfied, on one chord, empty of harmonic or rhythmic curiosity, was a deep, deep insult to his instrument.

Half-way through my performance later that week, he reached out and muted the strings.

"Fuuuuck man." he said.

He had recently taken up the habit of swearing in casual conversation.

"Look. I know what you're up to. Annnd, this shit only works for a Third Guitarist."

"Like, in a band?" I asked, and his nostrils flared.

"No man, that's a fucking bassist," he said. "No real band has a third guitar. This is, like, a process you go through."

The First Guitarist, he went on, would be me in a week after I'd learned one or two songs.

"You'll bring your guitar to the fucking first party you can," he said, "and just around the time people are getting comfortable you'll play something, BUT:

You won't have an ear yet.

You'll only hear what's in your head.

You'll run out of songs.

And then you'll go home with just your guitar."

"And the next day the people at the party will whisper: Who was the weird guy playing terrible guitar?"

"If you keep pushing though," he went on, more to himself it seemed than me, "you'll be the Second Guitarist. Your guitar will stay in its case at the party. At first. Until people are dancing and then some hot chick will ask you to play her favourite song. But you won't know it. You'll offer her a song she doesn't know — something flashy that shows off your skills — and move to the kitchen, but you'll be so focused on your playing you won't notice when her boyfriend pulls her away."

"The next day, the party people will murmur: Who was the guy playing guitar alone in the dark kitchen corner?"

Stories We Don't Tell

"And the host will say: It's the same guy. I don't know why I keep inviting him."

I should add that my brother was not generally wise with insight. I was the one the family listened to, moved less by the content of my opinions, and more by the Golden Boy packaging bestowed on me by the Fates: the firstborn son to my parents, the first male born in all the extended family, the boy who grew taller by a foot than all the other generations. But as my brother spoke, he looked at me with the gravity of a Moses.

"Either you'll quit," he continued, "or you'll keep playing the same songs over and over, in a room where no one can hear you, which is the same fucking thing as quitting, OR you'll become a Third Guitarist. You'll develop your tastes, and play everything you can. And around two in the morning, when the party has burned down, and there's eight people left, some other First Guitarist will exhaust his one or two songs, and someone will ask if anyone else can play. And you'll say sure, what do you want to hear? And that's the guy that gets the girl."

After the lesson I immediately rented a steel-string guitar from a local shop and felt compelled to practise, playing so loudly and so poorly a visiting girlfriend of a roommate skipped her normal polite knock, burst through my door and said with a whispering hate, "I know you're trying to find yourself or whatever, but please stop doing it beside our room."

I brought that guitar to the first party I was invited to, and girls were interested in a First Guitarist, or at least I thought so, but it was only for a few days, a week at most. Eventually, you left the party alone with your guitar.

My brother and I would try to play music together whenever I came home, but the Golden Boy sheen rubbed off under the pressure of his spontaneous melodies and rhythms, his deep knowledge of different styles, and like a glamour removed by True Love, my part in the music soon shrivelled up and died.

I began to feel stuck. When I would walk to class through the student ghetto, a limbo of student rooming houses encircling the main campus, I would hear other First Guitarists calling out from the unwashed porches with the same four chords and the same tired lyrics of infatuation. If you stood still for a moment, you sometimes heard them, through clouds of marijuana smoke, speak their philosophies of spontaneity over study. They were always there; always available for a girl.

I didn't want to end up like that.

Instead, I signed on with a guitar instructor in the music faculty, a religious man who loved music from South America and Cuba. I learned notation and practice technique. I soon started to perform: first in living rooms, then small local cafes, then weddings, and eventually dedicated concerts for a hundred or so people at a time. I began to feel a new confidence in music, and asked my instructor if I had what it took to become a true professional.

"You're good," he said, "but you're a big fish in a small pond. There's a festival in Quebec where you can raise your profile. You've got to get out of here. Don't get stuck as an adjunct instructor somewhere."

He paused.

"God does not will talent lightly," he added, but he sounded unsure.

I went to the festival he suggested. The concert hall was on a hill looking out over the moment the St. Lawrence meets the ocean. The instructor was an internationally renowned Parisian guitarist, who delicately smoked a cigarette beside me on stage as I performed before an audience of fifty professional musicians from all over the world. I hit my last note, the crowd clapped enthusiastically except for the master Parisian guitarist, who said nothing. He said nothing and he did not move, except to occasionally bring the cigarette to his lips or tap it out on the new pine of the stage. I don't know how long he sat silent, unmoving but smoking — maybe five minutes, maybe an hour, but it was long enough for the crowd to grow restless. Throats cleared small birds of laughter, as I nervously sweated through the back of my shirt and searched the St. Lawrence in the window for untroubled whales.

Finally, the master Parisian guitarist took a long final drag and said: "I know what you are attempting to do, but I want to tell you: it will not work, you are too boring."

The crowd laughed, but the master Parisian guitarist brought his hand down like a guillotine.

"Chut! I am not making a joke, and I am sorry to be, uh, sévère, but I have been all over the world with these festival and I have heard the same thing too many time: a student who has good hands, but who only cares to play the note perfect, who knows nothing of the music. This music is about two people from different tribes falling in love and being ripped apart for it. This melody here, right here, it is them falling in such love they are happy to risk death. And I don't feel it when you play. Do you feel it?"

At that moment I just felt suddenly very hot.

"The rhythms are Cubano — danzon, salsa, bolero — have you ever danced them? You are what, mid-twenties? You have never been to Cuba? Not to Miami?"

I wanted to say something, but the only place I had been to was Disney World.

"You need to care about more than yourself to play this

music, you need to care about the audience, the history. Otherwise they are just notes. Boring unconnected notes. I am sorry. Right now, you are boring."

I walked stone-faced down the aisle to the exit under the silent gaze of the audience. Outside the concert hall hiccupping and wiping my cheeks, I could no longer keep my composure. I cursed and complained and hurled insults.

The truth was he was right. I was worse than a First Guitarist — at least they were excited. I was a boring Second Guitarist playing for myself in a dark kitchen.

I could no longer bear to be the centre of attention; I was done with the guitar.

Back at school, there was the quartet making a name for themselves abroad, and they needed an agent. I signed on.

I travelled and listened and enjoyed my silence.

Finally, the Fates conspired to send both my brother and me back to our parents' home.

There was still pie and ice cream, but not much to say. We were both regrouping and deciding on next moves. Music became a way for me to pass the time at first. As I played more and more, I could also hear new things in the melodies and rhythms. Soon I began to develop my own ideas, my own small innovations. This time, when the lovers fell in love, I could feel it. The melody moved slower when it needed to, faster when it wanted on its own. It seemed self-contained, satisfied.

Then one day, I heard a melody in the hallway while I was playing.

I thought my brother might be trying to drown me out, so I played louder, and he matched me. But when I played softer, he also changed his dynamic. When I slowed down, he followed. When I added an unexpected key change, he added a surprising, amused lick. There was no awkwardness, no latency between the two of us. I realized I was playing music for its own sake.

I felt then that my brother had tricked me with his story: there was no girl to get, and there was no Golden Boy sheen, no God that had willed talent, just my brother who, out of nothing, had fashioned a Third Guitarist.

Chapter 55: Mathura Mahendren

For years, I've felt older than I am. A 400-year-old living in a 25-year-old's body.

In December of last year, I listened to a recording of my astrological reading that my parents had commissioned from our family astrologer. Now before we go any further, there are a few things you should know:

1. These readings are based on a chart that's drawn up using the exact date and time of one's birth. My sister had recently asked my parents to send her reading, so my parents had emailed me mine as well.
2. I'm not particularly bought into astrology. I also don't think it ruins lives. I think humans are meaning-making machines and astrology brings our attention to a vague enough plot onto which we can project our own stories.
3. And last but not least, my family's astrologer is also our accountant. The fact that this man does our taxes makes it a little bit harder for me to dismiss what he says as entirely woo-woo.

So I'm sitting on my bed, headphones in, listening to this reading, and about halfway in, I'm pretty amused. So far, he's said that I'll have lots of success as a student, that I'll do well in my career, but that I won't stay with any one organization for too long, and has carefully outlined three optimal windows of time in which to get married (one of which has already passed). He moves on to explain that I'll live a long life, and that the latter half of my life will be dedicated to service—giving away my time, energy, and money in support of friends and strangers.

"The reason for this," he says, "is that this is her last life. This means that debtors from all of her past lives will come back to collect their debts, so that when she leaves, the balance sheet will be at zero."

And there you have it, a reading from an accountant slash astrologer.

Considering that I had never thought seriously about reincarnation or the idea of multiple lives, this last piece should have been just as amusing as the predictions before it. And yet, my body reacted.

It took my brain a few moments to catch up, to decipher my body's reaction and explain it back to me. This is my last life. Which means my soul has lived many lives. Which means it's likely very old. Which means there might be some merit to all the times I've said and felt, that I'm a 400-year-old living in a 25-year-old's body.

At least in the expert opinion of my accountant slash astrologer.

***

My 25-year-old, on her first date with her partner, sensed he might be older than her and tried to casually ask for his age. When he shared that he was 10 years older, she wondered if she needed to be concerned. Meanwhile, my 400 year old murmured, "What does it matter? You're the one whose 400. If anything, you're the senior citizen in this relationship."

My 25-year-old body is broken after an 8-hour hike in the mountains, meanwhile, my 400-year-old soul is dancing among trees that share her age, her confidence, and her calm.

My 25-year-old mind worries about money and scarcity

Stories We Don't Tell

and being in a place where she needs to depend on others to meet her basic needs. A place where she doesn't feel free. Meanwhile, my 400-year-old knows that I'll be taken care of. She just knows. She sees me not as me alone but as a part of a larger community that is basically waiting to pay me the moment I stop resisting.

My 25-year-old worries about her heart and what would happen if her and her partner ever chose to go their own ways. She worries prematurely about what it would take to put that heart back together. Meanwhile my 400-year-old knows that our partners are meant to be one of our greatest teachers and whether they're our teacher for a lifetime or a few years, they will teach us, and we will teach them what we both need to know before our time together is up. She knows that the gift is in those lessons—not in the number of years clocked.

My 25-year-old worries that her curiosity-driven approach to her career is irresponsible. Should she just pick a job and commit? Is choosing to work in the gig economy just an excuse for a fear of commitment? Meanwhile, my 400 year old Just. Wants. To. Learn. She wants to understand our deepest human motivations and bear witness to humans doing their most humanly things—loving, grieving, dying. She wants to be present with humans in these moments that transcend cultures, careers, and age. And no matter the job title on my LinkedIn profile, for her it will just be a container in which to play.

There are times when my 25-year-old gets in the way of my 400-year-old. Where it feels like the 25-year-old's anxieties and insecurities get in the way of the 400-year-old's flow. And there are times when the 25-year-old feels extremely weary and weighed down by everything that the 400-year-old represents—wisdom, autonomy, unattachment, years and years and years and years of experience.

My 25-year-old is triggered by every other thing her parents say. She wants them to trust her, and trust that she'll find her way on the road less travelled. Meanwhile, my 400-year-old doesn't even see them as parents. She sees them for their anxieties and their insecurities. She wants to comfort them.

There are times when people come to the 25-year-old with questions that are meant for the 400-year-old. And in those moments, the 25-year-old feels like a vessel through which the 400-year-old wisdom is channelled. And when people reflect that back to her—that what she has shared with them is wisdom—it doesn't feel like hers. It makes her feel like an imposter, almost as though she's taking credit for wisdom that's not hers.

The 25-year-old holds anxieties and insecurities around enough-ness. Am I doing enough? Am I trying hard enough? Am I putting in enough time, am I putting in enough energy, am I enough? She constantly contends with this idea that she's not enough. In these moments, my 400-year-old lets a laugh slip and asks, "Enough for what? What are you trying to be enough for?", leaving the 25-year-old speechless.

The 25-year-old went to The Gambia and Malawi and, working in communities there, she was acutely aware of the ways in which she held privilege and power and was always so careful about how she navigated it in the community. Meanwhile, the 400-year-old was sure that she belonged there. She felt so at home on this red soil, and was certain that it was neither the first time that she had been there nor the last time that she would be. She felt a deep-seated connection to the red soil that the 25-year-old couldn't bring herself to share out loud because she didn't want to be one of those people who came back from "Africa" and felt a connection.

My 25-year-old moves through this world like she's trying to survive, and my 400-year-old moves through the world like she's been there, done that, many times over.

***

Our accountant slash astrologer had said that this was my last life, and my body had reacted. My 25-year-old, a sucker for a great story, was enamoured by the idea of past debtors, from past lifetimes, coming back to collect their debts in various forms. Meanwhile, my 400-year-old breathed this incredibly ... deep sigh ... of relief. "Almost there," I could hear her say. "Thank goodness, I'm almost there."

And in that moment, as my 25-year-old felt my 400-year-old's relief, she broke out into the biggest grin. This was real. It all made sense. There was indeed a 400-year-old living inside of her body. And if she didn't believe it when her accountant slash astrologer told her she was living her last life, the relief that was now radiating through her body was proof enough.

Chapter 56: Kale Ridsdale

I'm cross-legged on the floor in a small room, empty of anything but a pillow, my body, and my mind. My hands are carefully placed on knees, all I hear is my breathing. When I open my eyes a crack, I see just a sliver of light coming through the crack under the door. I'm in a meditation cell, a few days into the 10-day retreat. Removed from sensory input and given tools that have worked for millennia to soothe the mind, I'm here practising maintaining equanimity while I simply observe what happens around and within me.

Here, my goal is to simply observe my mind race down a narrow path, deep into fantasy, as I imagine the woman who sits next to me in the meditation hall finding me in meditation cell #3, quietly opening the door, pushing me against the back wall of this dark closet, her hands around my waist and ...

Fuck. No. I pull my mind out of this lusty vortex. Back on track.

I observe my heavied breathing.

This is my first time at a meditation retreat. I'm here for 10 days in complete silence. No music, no reading, no talking, just me and my mind — alongside the others that are here too.

We occasionally have the opportunity to sit in a meditation cell, but for the most part we are all together in a big hall, sitting in assigned places on the floor for the duration of the retreat. I'm next to Paula — the only reason I know this is from the piece of paper on the floor indicating her seat. Nobody may speak or make eye contact. Those are the rules.

We're not talking, but I begin to notice Paula. Look how she sits. Out of the corner of my eye her arms look soft and tanned. I can hear her swallowing. She seems equal parts cool and kind. I can almost sense her sensing me in return, a kind of alertness to an outside world detectable by implicit signals, an energy with direction. Like how sometimes you can tell you're being looked at, but this time our eyes are closed.

Back on track. Calm the mind. Observe my breathing.

Days go by and I begin to understand what meditation is all about. Simply observe the stirrings of my mind and body without attachment, as a distanced observer. And yet when I'm apart from Paula in my meditation cell my mind brings me closer to her than the metre of space that separates us sitting in the hall. Is she thinking the same thing I'm thinking? What if we're thinking the exact same thing at the exact same time? Will we act on this fantasy of ours? And am I the kind of person who would break the rules

Then, on day 7 or so, I'm walking out of the women's washrooms on our 10-minute break, absorbing the last of the dampness from my hands with my pants, when I lift my eyes and lock eyes with Paula, who is sitting on a bench looking right in my direction. She tries to hold my glance. Blood rushes to my face.

Let me explain here; if anyone has ever meditated for days on end you may know how acutely you begin to feel your inner sensations. If you haven't, I'm not sure I can explain to you the intensity with which I felt every subsequent sensation generated by this brief locking of eyes. I feel hot heat run up my neck and into my cheeks, then my forehead. An electric shock runs from my chest down to my stomach, followed by a heavy thud behind my sternum. My legs feel wobbly and stop functioning properly. I see myself being seen, my eyes widen, I curl my lips and I jerk my head down to look at the beige carpet. NO EYE CONTACT PAULA!

Stories We Don't Tell

THAT'S THE RULE! In complete upheaval, I find my way back to my place on the floor, Paula joining shortly after. Just observe the sensations.

After a long evening of sitting and dharma talks, the group is dismissed back to our bunks. As we meditatively saunter through the dark, someone walking calmly in front stops and turns her head up to the sky. She's looking at something. Another person stops and turns, I join them and now there's a group of us standing in the woods on a warm fall evening staring up at this hovering greenish light in the sky. Upholding our vow of silence we stand there for minutes on end just staring, mesmerized, in awe of the beauty of this light. Maybe a sliver of the northern lights...an astrological anomaly... I'm wishing I had my phone to look this up, but here in the land of equanimity we are content in the mystery and majesty of this thing we are witnessing and sharing together.

The days finally pass and the retreat is coming to an end. On the final day we're allowed to talk to acclimatize back into the world of others. I'm sitting outside surrounded by the beautiful coloured leaves that by now have started to fall and I'm talking to the group of women that have gathered around. We talk about the green orb in the sky — what was that? Nobody knows, but we're dazzled.

I make them all laugh by telling tales of the chaos of my mind, leaving out details of Paula. "I didn't even know HAKKUNA MATTATA COULD RUN SO LONG ON REPEAT IN MY HEAD!" I'm gesticulating wildly entertaining this group, but my eyes are locked about 10 metres ahead of me where Paula sits at another picnic table, also with a group of our meditating comrades, looking straight in my direction. We hold each other's gaze for what feels like minutes. I see her seeing me, see her seeing me charismatically entertain my group, and I like how I look. Something is happening here. I turn back to my group.

I can't decide how to approach Paula. I feel so much that even thinking about walking up to her spikes my heart rate and sends prickles to the back of my neck. What would I say? What if she's straight? Unavailable? Where could this go? What if it wasn't shared? Or just not what we imagined it to be. I don't know. I'm too nervous, I feel too much, too acutely. They separate men and women but nobody thought about the queers. The best course of action is to avoid.

I return home and tell my friends about my retreat. It was so great, so centred, so equanimous, and I FELL IN LOVEEEEEEEEEEEEEE GUYS I WAS IN LOOOVEEEEE. I realize this is not equanimity more than my friends do. I try finding my girl online but don't have much to go on. Nothing. I let it go.

I return to the comforting distractions of day-to-day living, and eventually my meditation practise wanes.

Two years go by and I decide it's time to refresh my practice and I sign up for another retreat. My mind can't help but wonder — what if Paula is also registered? Will I get to do this again? Oh I can't wait to fall in love all over again.

On the first day we're sitting as a group in front of the organizer, we're going over the rules and she's telling us some updates about this place. I scan the group and don't see Paula anywhere. This is probably for the best.

"Another thing to know," the organizer explains, "is there's a club that has opened up down the way and sometimes you can hear the music at night, but don't mind, and on weekends they sometimes shine lights." "You know what's funny," she says, "when the club first opened we had a group here who thought they saw something magical in the sky, a ufo or something." And with the kind of softness of

Stories We Don't Tell

someone who has done a lot of Loving Kindness meditation, she proceeds to gently mock the "enlightened" beings that were mesmerized by the mystical club light, and I realize that was me. That was my group, clinging to the significance we imbued on a light that was merely a projection.

This is important information. Because that first retreat wasn't actually the only time I saw Paula. As luck would have it, I found myself at the house of one of the people I stayed in touch with from the retreat. I'm sitting on her plush couch and there on her coffee table I see a couple business cards, and the name Paula catches my eye. I pick it up. "Was this person at our retreat?" I asked. "Yeah, she owns this shop in the city." I've located my girl.

The next time I find myself sauntering through this neighbourhood in the chilly night air, I see the sign, and I lead my friend in. Slim chances she's actually here, I think. Yet after only a few seconds of sniffing around I spot Paula at the back, casually beginning to walk towards the door to greet her new customers. Fuckfuckfuckfuck Iwasnotpreparedforthiiiiis.

My heart rate, my face. Everything feels ...

Abort! In upheaval, I retreat towards the door.

We are once again walking down the dark street and my friend asks what the hell that was all about. With shortened and impatient breath, I explain what happened between Paula and me at the retreat, and what led me to the shop.

"So why didn't you talk to her!" she implored.

I wasn't really sure how to explain myself. I felt like a wimp. I spent the next several days playing out all the different ways the exchange could have gone down, wondering if she had seen me before I fled, and what she would have made of it, and romanticizing our connection.

Now, as I've gathered more information about the world

and the human mind, I've come to understand my behaviour differently. As I think back to everything that happened during the 10 days of my first meditation retreat, I've come to understand that sometimes the mind, in all its clinging and imbuing of significance, does not want to discover that that which dazzles is just ...
   projected.

Chapter 57: Rob Shirkey

"You need to get up. Get up, Rob. Your body can't be lying in the middle of the street like this."

It was a Tuesday afternoon last October. The sun was out. There was a light drizzle. It was a warm fall day.

And I found my body sliding down the middle of Yonge Street at around 50 kilometres per hour, my head hitting the pavement as I flew off my Yamaha. It would be my second concussion in under two years. And it happened just as I finally felt that I was over the first.

***

I grew up riding motorbikes at my grandpa's farm in Saskatchewan. I loved them. The first time I got on one, I was maybe 5 or 6. The engine was idling and, to keep me steady, my dad was on my left, and my grandpa was on my right.

"Now, gently ease the throttle, Robbie." I twisted it as far as it would go and started doing laps around the farm. They eventually gave up trying to chase after me.

When I was old enough to ride a motorbike on the road, my parents forbade me from getting my licence. In fact, my dad knew me so well that, when I moved to British Columbia for law school, he made me promise that I wouldn't get one. He even used the cancer card.

When your terminally ill father makes you commit not to get a motorbike, you choose your words carefully: "Dad, I promise I will not get a motorcycle."

A week later, I was in B.C. riding a scooter.

With the ocean or mountains in front of me, the sun

shining, I'd turn that thing full throttle and this giant smile would come across my face.

So, when I finally started to come out of my first concussion, I asked myself, what makes me happy?

Getting my motorcycle licence for Ontario was an easy decision.

***

That first concussion two years ago was tough.

I had a meeting scheduled with an MPP to lobby him on my non-profit's climate change work. It was December 2016. His office was in the east end, and I lived in the north end. With a whoosh of air, and the sound of wheels screeching on tracks, I knew the subway was pulling into my station. I started to run. As I rounded the corner to take the steps down to the platform, I slipped. The first point of impact was the left side of my head against a metal railing.

I found myself lying on my left side, dazed, and looking down the stairs as the subway doors slid open.

At the time, it looked like there might be bipartisan support behind closed doors for my bill. The meeting was important to me. It was about climate change.

So I pushed myself up off the ground and ran down the steps, taking two at a time. The doors slid shut just behind me. I made it. But when I sat down, I just felt ... weird.

Should I go to the hospital? A friend who got a concussion from a car accident earlier that year told me that he began to slur his words afterward. I covered my mouth with my hands to check.

"Hi, my name's Rob, I'm a lawyer who runs this environmental non-profit, we're asking politicians ..."

Sounded fine. I dusted off the left side of my body and

went to the meeting. When I got there, I told the MPP about my accident, told him I was feeling weird, pointed to where I hit my head, and asked him to call an ambulance if I passed out. I then launched into my pitch to secure his support for the climate bill.

After the meeting, I stopped at a nearby coffee shop to collect myself. Halfway through my coffee, I realized something was definitely wrong, and I went straight to the hospital.

What followed was this non-stop headache. Dizziness. An aversion to lights. And I constantly felt on edge. A week and a half later, I found myself in my kitchen, lights off, blinds drawn, and on my knees, both hands pressed against the sides of my head with this pain I'd never felt before. I wound up in an emergency room.

The triage nurse took my info: "My name's Rob, I hit the left side of my head a week and a half ago while running for the subway. I've been feeling headaches, dizziness ..."

He cut me off. Someone had come in who was apparently bleeding heavily. "Hold on," he said, "I'll be right back."

He returned a few minutes later. "Okay, pick up where you left off."

"My name's Rob, I hit the left side of my head a week about a half ago while running for the subway. I've been feeling ..."

"Stop. You know you just told me this, right?"

"Uhhh, no ..?"

I couldn't form short-term memory. It was Christmas Day, and I found myself lying on a cold table that was sliding my body into place for a scan of my brain.

Later that night, I wondered: I used to love being in court and cross-examining opposing counsel's witness. I always thought that if this environmental advocacy thing didn't work out, I could go back to that. But, if I'm having trouble following a conversation — if I can't form short-term memory — can I do that again?

In the months that followed, I could barely read. It required a level of focus that I just didn't have. And I didn't tell people. I was too embarrassed. The constant dizziness and headaches meant I couldn't exercise. I lost muscle. My body looked and felt different. The book I was writing was taking me forever: I just had such a hard time working on my laptop. The advocacy I'd been doing ... I couldn't do it anymore. It took a dive. I felt like I couldn't do anything. I withdrew. Was less social. Stopped dating (who would even want to date me anyway?). My confidence, my sense of self-worth, gone. And the world just felt wobbly. 24/7. All the while, I kept hearing, "but you look fine."

Studies show that the rate of suicide in people who have experienced a concussion is significantly higher than that of the general population. Some of this is, I'm sure, from the emotional fallout of it all, but some of it is just... something happens to you when you hit your head.

During sleepless nights, I would lie in bed thinking of a sharp knife that was in my kitchen drawer. For weeks, I'd have to glue my back to the wall while waiting for the subway. Standing in the middle of the platform or close to the edge... the pull was too strong.

But I hung in there. My symptoms gradually lifted.

I think that's why I was so happy that day last October. Sure, I still had the odd lingering symptom, but I had mostly recovered. I was finally feeling like myself. The advocacy I was doing had won awards, both in Canada and abroad. I had just sold my home a few days prior, and my plan was to spend the next two months before closing, looking for work in the climate field. In fact, that very day, I was riding to

Stories We Don't Tell

a library downtown to finish creating an online portfolio. I wanted a job where I felt like I would be having an impact; and I had just upped anchor, ready to move anywhere in the world to do it.

That warm fall day, riding down Yonge Street, I finally felt hopeful.

***

The last thing I remember thinking is, "Oh fuck, she's not stopping."

The following are excerpts from an email that a witness sent to the investigating police officer:

"I was travelling immediately behind the motorcycle when the accident happened. We were heading southbound on Yonge just south of Lawrence Avenue in the curb lane. As we were heading south, a car parked on the west side of Yonge pulled out unexpectedly (the female driver did not look or, if she looked, did not see the motorcycle). This forced the motorcycle to make an emergency maneuver (sharp turn to the inside lane) to avoid the car and, given it was wet, the motorcycle slid, and the rider fell off into the inside lane going southbound ... he was lucky to be alive."

For me, there were a few seconds of darkness ... quiet ... but also this feeling of a really hard thud. And then ... there I was, sliding down the street.

When my body finally came to a stop, I turned, instinctively raising my arms to protect my face from the car behind me. It braked to a stop, just a few feet away from me.

And that's how I found my body lying in the middle of Yonge Street on a warm, fall Tuesday afternoon.

***

"You need to get up, Rob. Get up. You can't be in the middle of the street like this."

My back hurt. My neck hurt. My legs hurt. And everything in the world was moving so slowly.

But I got up.

I limped to my bike that was lying on its side, engine still running, hit the ignition kill switch, hobbled over to the curb, and gently lowered myself to sit. I took off my helmet. I was breathing fast. My heart was racing. But everything around me felt so, so slow.

A woman who was walking on the sidewalk approached me. She asked, "Are you okay?"

I carefully turned my head to look up at her. Processing those words. "Are. You. Okay." I replied, "I. Don't. Know." And as I heard those words crawl out of my mouth... the pace of my speech... I just knew. I knew it instantly.

And I started to cry. All of my symptoms would come back. And I'd spend the next month with the curtains drawn shut in my now empty home.

***

That was almost five months ago and, while I've come a long way, I have this constant pressure in my head, the world still feels wobbly, and I sometimes worry if I'll ever get better. A few weeks ago, I was having lunch with a friend and her child. They were sitting on a colourful carpet with A, B, C written on it in big block letters. So I started to sing to her little boy: "A-B-C-D-E-F-G..." I stopped. I couldn't remember what came after G.

I was flooded with embarrassment. How could I not know the alphabet? I know that I know the alphabet. But what comes after G? I just started to make up words to the tune,

Stories We Don't Tell

as if what I did was intentional, hoping my friend didn't notice. All the while, I was wondering: what have I done to my brain.

***

What are you supposed to do when the things that make you "you" get stripped away? When I was an undergrad, I'd make it a game to get straight A+'s on my report card. When I was in law school, there were some courses where I'd skip every single class just to walk along the ocean and stare into tidal pools. I'd then cram the night before the hundred percent final, and still end up with a B+. Before these two concussions, I was giving talks on climate policy and lobbying governments across North America.

Could I still do that? Will I get better? And if not — if that's no longer "me" — then who am I? More practically, if I can't spend too much time on my laptop, if I have this constant pain in my head, an inability to focus, mental exhaustion ... what about work? What do I have to offer? What is my worth?

But, when I think about what I value in others, it's none of that. It's kindness. When I was sitting on that curb and started to cry, the woman who asked if I was okay took my hand and she held it. I can't describe how comforting that gesture was. She stayed with me, holding my hand until the ambulance took me away. It's qualities like compassion, empathy, thoughtfulness, and humour that matter. And I believe I have those. I have to believe that, at my core, I'm still a person with lots to offer this world.

So, while I'm not exactly sure what's next, I do have some ideas; but that's a story for another time. The one thing I do know is this: these concussions have shown me something

about myself. And it's something that gives me hope.
When I hit my head against that metal railing, I got up.
When I hit my head against that pavement, I got up.
So that is exactly what I'm going to do.

Chapter 58: Jette Stubbs

I was about 8 years old as I prepared to walk into the police station. I held my mother's hand tightly as the police officer explained, "There will be six men. If you see the man, point him out to us and tell us which number he is wearing." I pulled my mother with me as he led me to the door. "No, you have to go by yourself," he said. "You'll be alright. They can't see you. Only you can see them."

"They won't see her at all? Are you sure the mirror works? " my mother said. He nodded. Her lips shaking as tears ran down her cheeks. I released her hand and walked in.

***

I was outside my parents' house on an island in the Caribbean. It was late in the afternoon and my brother, Fritz, and I were trying to build a tent the way we saw the white people doing on TV. We had a clothing line, rocks and my mom's good sheets, but the wind kept blowing, and the tent wouldn't stay up. We were getting frustrated and started fighting. Eventually, Fritz got angry and went inside to sit on my mom's lap and play computer solitaire with her. I knew I was right about how to build a tent.

I stayed outside into the evening to finish building the tent just to spite Fritz. As it got dark, I finally stood between two sheets forming a tent's peak along the clothing line only slightly waving in the air.

I turned to the house to get Fritz when I saw two masked men walking up to the front door, dressed in black and hiding behind the banana tree near my front door. "Pull your mask down," the one with the gun whispered to his partner as they crouched beneath the tree.

I froze and took a deep breath, still hidden by the tent. If I backed away slowly without being heard, I could follow the secret path along the wall to the neighbour's window and ask them to call the police. So, I took a step back but leaves crackled under my feet.

Both men looked over at me in the dark.

"I thought you said the kids were inside," said the masked one with the gun. "And I told you to pull down your mask."

"I thought everyone was inside," the other man said as he pulled down his mask over his mustache.

As I watched them watch me, I opened my mouth to shout to my parents, but nothing came out. I opened my mouth wider. Nothing. My feet were frozen and heavy.

"Grab her and take her to the bushes until I'm done," said the man with the gun.

Every lecture my mother ever gave me about things men could do to you in bushes flashed through my mind. I knew it was time to fight. I opened my mouth wider to scream to warn my parents and barely heard my own muffled squeak, as his large hands covered my mouth. He pulled me back into his chest, silencing me.

I kicked frantically, but my feet barely brushed the top of the grass. I tried to scream again but his grip tightened over my mouth and nose. Suddenly my feet hit solid ground and I pushed back with all my might.

"She doesn't want to go to the bushes. She's fighting me," he said.

The man with the gun grunted in frustration, "Bring her inside then."

My feet hung inches above the ground as he carried me across the patio, the front door open and waiting for me.

The man with the gun walked in first and from the

far corner of the room, Daddy looked up blankly from his newspaper and cleared his throat. Fritz was still on Mommy's lap, playing solitaire at the computer, their backs to the door.

She turned around, "Holy shit."

I gripped both of my hands over his and pulled down as hard as I could. His arm didn't even budge. It was like he couldn't feel me.

The one with the gun walked toward my father. "We're here for the money. Take me to the safe."

My dad cleared his throat. I felt my eyes widen as I struggled to breathe and I kicked and pulled at the mustache man's arm. I looked at Mommy as I felt two tears run down my cheeks. She was watching the man with the gun. I kicked once to catch her eye.

"Oh my god. You're suffocating her! You're suffocating her!! Please stop! Put her down! Please," Mommy pleaded.

She looked me in the eyes, one arm clenched Fritz and the other reaching for me.

His muscles relaxed and my feet finally fully touched the floor, as he released my mouth and nose and turned my face up to the left to look at his.

I saw his eyes widen through the holes of his mask, "I'm so sorry. Are you okay?" he said as I gasped for breath. "Are you okay?"

I nodded and gasped, confused, looking at his mask. Mommy's voice shook, "Can she come and sit with me? Please give me my child."

I ran to my mother and Fritz at her desk.

My father stood up on the other side of the room.

"Don't do anything stupid," the leader said as he tapped Daddy's stomach with the gun.

Then he said to the mustache man, "Go get a knife from

333

the kitchen and stay with the wife and kids." He returned with a butcher's knife and sat next to us.

"He'll stay with them," the leader said, "while you take me to get the money. Stay calm and don't do anything stupid. We're here to deal with you." My father nodded slowly.

The room was suddenly very quiet. My mother's legs were shaking us as we sat on her lap. The leader poked Daddy's back with the gun a few times to lead him into the kitchen.

The masked man tapped the butcher knife against the wood of the desk. Taptaptaptaptap. All three of us stared down at the tile floor. My mom was trembling all over. Taptaptaptaptap. Mom pulled Fritz and me closer to her chest, one of us wrapped in each arm. Taptaptaptaptap.

She continued to look down at the floor as she nervously blurted, "I don't want to upset you, but the tapping of the knife is making me nervous. Please stop. I can't take it."

TapTapTapTapTap.

And the knife froze in the air, "I'm sorry ma'am. I didn't mean to upset you," the mustache man said, his words falling over themselves.

"Don't worry. We are not here to hurt you," he said.

She took a deep breath. "I know you say that, but it's hard to believe as you tap a knife in front of me."

The mustache man turned his chair toward us with the knife still in his gloved right hand. "Where do you go to school," he asked me. My mother shook me to not respond, but he asked again, "It's okay I won't hurt you. Do you both go to the same school?" Fritz and I nodded. "What do you want to be when you grow up?" he asked. Fritz and I looked at each other in silence, and then up at our mother's face, eyes wide.

"I don't know," I said, and we both shrugged our shoulders as our mother's lap shook beneath us. "Please don't hurt my children. Take what you want, but don't hurt my children," she said.

"No, ma'am. That's not what I came here to do. I just want the money," he said as he looked her in the eyes. She watched him rest the knife down on the desk away from us. "Are they getting good grades, miss?"

Then, he turned to us, "You two need to stay in school so you don't end up like me. I didn't pay attention in school so when I finished I didn't have any opportunities. Now, my grandmother is sick and I have to do this to afford the medication." He looked up at my mother and back at us, "Your parents are paying a lot of money for you to get an education. Education leads to opportunity. Get a good education. I don't want to see you be like me. Stay in school." Fritz and I nodded and glanced at each other from the corner of our eyes.

The man with the gun came back into the office with my father. "They didn't have it. The safe was empty." My parents ran a car and villa rental from home and apparently, a rumour had started that they kept $30,000 in the safe in the house — the truth was the safe just had old papers and a combination they frequently forgot.

"Are you sure there's nothing else, old man?" the man said as he pointed the gun to my father who had his hands in the air. His left hand was missing his gold watch and ring. The gun poked him in the back as the robber returned him to the desk. "Stay quiet and don't call the police for 10 minutes. If we hear sirens, we'll have to come back." He shook his head, "You don't want us to have to come back." The mustache man followed the man.

Daddy asked us, "Are you okay?"

The three of us nodded as my mom asked, "you?"

He nodded back, and we sat in silence for a few minutes.

Stories We Don't Tell

When we felt it was safe, my father picked up the phone and called the police. A mix of plain-clothes and uniformed officers arrived and separated us for questioning.

The robber's gun had seemed ornamental. I didn't feel like he would hurt me. These guns seemed as though they would do real harm, as though they could have already been used to kill somebody.

My mom told them I had seen one of the robbers. My dad said, "She's a talented artist" to the officer, and turned to me, "Why don't you draw him?" I felt pressured, but I eventually drew a quirky Hitler-esque drawing of a mustache that I knew was useless. The officer took it, looked at it, and said, "Good job. Thank you," a patronizing platitude. I knew it wouldn't help.

And then, the next day was school as usual.

Two weeks later, they called my mom to come in with me to the police station.

As we drove to the police station, I sat in the front seat. "I don't want you to identify the man," she said. It was the opposite of everything Daddy and Fritz said.

"While I was a teller at the bank, the bank was robbed. I saw his face, just like you, and I went into court and testified against him.

"But he saw me when I testified. At his sentencing, as the officers were taking him away, he looked me in the eyes and promised me, 'I'm going to find you, and I'm going to kill you when I get out.' My testimony put him away."

She glanced at me and said, "It feels weird saying this, but I was lucky, he died in jail after a few years. If he hadn't, I'd be living every day in fear. I don't want that for you."

"But this robber wasn't like that," I responded. "Not the one I saw. He was nice."

"If you testify, know you helped send him to jail and if he

goes to jail, even if it's for a decade, you'll only be in your teens when he gets out. I just don't want you to live your life in fear. But I need you to listen, it's important you don't tell anyone I told you this. The police would say I'm obstructing justice and I could get in trouble. But, the decision is up to you."

A few minutes later, I stood with two officers looking through a one-way mirror. On the other side stood the nice robber, clean-shaven in jeans and a shirt. "Take your time," the officers said. "Look good."

I stood in silence for a few minutes. Then, I slowly walked the length of the mirror. I figured this would be the only time I'd see this room in my life. The officers watched me, and asked, "Do you see him?"

I looked at the robber's face one more time, and then in the officer's eyes, "Nope, I don't see him."

"You have to answer yes or no. No variations on the word," he said.

"Then, no. No, I do not see him," I said.

Chapter 59: Veronica Antipolo

Dear Diary,
My mom read you. So, this will be the last time that I write in you, that I write to you, that I write. Is this wrong? Maybe. But as it turns out, writing is the synonym of what I've done wrong.

A lot of 15-year-old girls, like me, have diaries. Or, they call them journals. Journals are for serious almost adults. Diaries are for Saved By the Bell Kelly Kapowskis. I don't know what I call mine. I don't fucking care. It's a book. I have a hiding spot for "my book." I have a few hiding spots for it. I change the spot all the time because I can't have anyone find it. No one. Not ever.

I'm standing in my bedroom holding my book. I should've left already. Like, I should be, like, 20 minutes gone, but I needed to write first. My bedroom is actually a den. So, it has no closet. Instead, I have a white IKEA wardrobe and a slate-grey foam futon couch. It looks like I'm standing in the middle of a healthy, green lawn. But, it's not a lawn. It's the carpet from when I first moved with my mom, three years ago.

"Veronicaaa!"

Ugh.

Already, I want to be gone and to not interact with my mom. Fuck. She's at one of my doors.

"VeroniCA!"

She spits my name out, staccato-like. Her voice rises forcefully on the "CA." Shit. She's so irritated that she doesn't have time to say my name. What a bitch. She's the one who named me! Serves her right.

Oh my God! I have to hide my book! My door starts to

open. As naturally, but as quickly as possible, I shove my book into my open wardrobe, under my sweaters that are on the top shelf. I turn around casually, like "oh hey there," but she's there and glaring at me. Was I fast and casual enough? I close the wardrobe door, grab my purse and leave, slamming the front door so that I get the last word.

A few hours later, I walk through the front door and feel something different in the air. It's not the usual still, sterile, impartial air like when no one is there. And it's not the tired, annoyed air that feels heavy but unruly. It's just ... different.

I walk into my bedroom, and I know that something is off. My wardrobe door is open. My heart feels like a woodpecker that's pecking sharp and fast in my chest. My eyes lose focus. I feel like I'm looking through a kaleidoscope. I reach hesitantly under my sweaters and feel around for my book. It's there. I let out a long exhale. I guess I didn't shut the door.

I open my book. There are some other papers folded up in it now. Oh. My. God. Oh my God, oh my God. Oh, my fucking God. She read it. She read about the four or maybe five (I still can't exactly recall) guys who raped me. But I never wrote the word "rape," even though my cousin says that's what it really was. I wrote about fucking and being drunk and being at a party. Because what girl wants to admit that she let this happen. Didn't I let it happen? I mean, I don't know.

This is why I had to write about it. I had to see it on paper. Maybe the words I wrote could explain to me what I was feeling and explain to me what the truth was. I can't tell things apart when they're swirling around inside of me. My thoughts and my feelings are caught in whirlpools in my head and in my heart. I can't tell which whirlpool I'm in sometimes, and I can't recognize what is swirling past me.

Stories We Don't Tell

But, I can catch them with words when I write. My book gathers all my random thoughts and feelings like a net. And my pen attaches words to them. And the words stay in this net until I get to sort them out.

There's a loud, angry buzzing in my ears as I unfold the paper. It's two sheets of ruled, loose-leaf paper that you'd put in your school binder. The pages are filled mostly with my mom's small, erratically neat handwriting. But, on one of the pages, she's drawn a picture.

I can't even ... Why the hell did she even put it back under my sweaters?!

I read "The Story of Veronica's Life." It fucking has a title. She read my book! Then, she did a creative writing assignment on what my future would be like, based on details of the night of my rape. She dipped into the net of my feelings and my thoughts which weren't sorted out yet. Then, she arranged them into some Mad Lib story with misplaced nouns, adjectives, and verbs.

Her story reads:

Veronica's life consisted of a couch stained with spaghetti and meatballs because that's what trash eats. Veronica's life was spent caring for multiple, fatherless children with snotty noses, watching the Cosby show. Veronica's life would be spent on her hands and knees, constantly cleaning. But anyway, she was used to being on her hands and knees.

She ends my biography with a short note, "Keep writing. You're good at it."

This is Veronica's life. This is me. This is my future life according to my mother. The picture she drew was an accurate representation of her words. Very creative MOTHER. I. Hate. You.

I read the story over and over again. The words jump off

the page and join the already turbulent whirlpool in my head and in my heart. Every thought and every feeling is crashing violently around inside of me; though, there's no fucking way that I can ever let them end up on paper again. Ever. I'll just have to learn to move with this current. I can keep my head above it all, even while it's thrashing me around me. Right?

It feels like I've been thrashing around for the last 30 years. I never seem to make sense of what's going on, and I don't know how to. I write sometimes, but I rarely keep any of it. I tear my writing to pieces or burn them to ash. I buy a recorder that I hide in my car. Driving to work, I tell my recorder every frustration and every celebration that I encounter. I feel safe because words spoken aren't tangible. They're air.

So, now.

Now, I've started telling jokes and telling stories to you. And you can judge. But poof. It's air. I don't care. But you surprised me because you listened. You laughed. You saw. And I thought to myself, "what the fuck are they looking at?" So, I looked too. And I saw words.

Chapter 60: Paul Dore

I've gone and done something that I believe is never a good idea. Like, I have actively told other people not to do this. I was working on a story for a few months for tonight and decided at the last minute to scrap it and go with something else.

I was once in the audience at another storytelling event where a person got up on stage and said, "I was so inspired by that last story that I decided to throw away what I was going to talk about and do something completely different." And they dramatically threw their papers up and my heart sank down into my stomach, I might have even put my hand over my mouth, and said out loud — "Oh, no." But, I think my decision was right because in a moment, this new story became so much more important to me than this other story.

I want to tell you about a friend of mine that passed away last week. He's one of the major reasons why I am even here standing in front of you. Our friendship lasted for a decade, and every moment spent with him was significant. I wish I could explain the whole story, but I've limited myself to three experiences because the organizers of this event have a strict 7 to 10-minute policy. Okay, I've written four experiences, but one of them is short.

Ten years ago, I had a nice corporate job with a great salary and was on track to keep moving up the ladder. Only one problem: I hated every minute of it. So, I quit. Quitting is highly underrated. I used my last paycheck to pay for a week-long intensive course at the Humber School for Writers, where I found myself in Wayson Choy's class. Before the course, I read all of Wayson's books — *The Jade Peony*, *All that Matters*, *Paper Shadows*, and *Not Yet*.

Pretty great stuff. That week at Humber changed everything for me. I can't tell you how — because of the 7 to 10-minute policy. Just know that it was mind-altering.

At the end of the week, we walked into the last class, and there were three things spread out on the desk in front of each of our spots. Wayson said, "These three items are all you need to be a writer. First, a pencil to write with. Second, an eraser to understand your mistakes and fix them." And it's even in the shape of a butterfly. "Third, and perhaps most important, a fancy pencil to dream with." And he walked around the room, stopping at each of us. He folded a piece of origami paper into a butterfly as he told us what he learned from us. He got to me. "Paul," he said, "You have shown us a break in the clouds, now show us the entire blue sky."

After the course, we started writing letters to each other. Like, through the mail. I recommend writing people letters. When I found out Wayson passed away, I spent the afternoon reading through our correspondence, and was able to hear his voice again.

Although he was retired from teaching, he took on one or two people per year to mentor, those that he felt were committed to writing in a deeper way. A year, two years went by as we worked on my writing together. I re-wrote another draft of my first book. I met Wayson at our usual cafe, and brought him the manuscript — I was so excited — and said, "Look, I re-wrote this using all the things you taught me." I don't remember exactly what he said, but it was something like — Hmmm. For the next six months, I submitted the manuscript to pretty much every literary agency and publishing company in — like — the world probably.

After those six months back in the cafe with Wayson,

I explained how I'd gotten all these rejections and how upsetting it all was. He looked at me and said something like — Hmmm. But then he said, "I knew when you showed me that manuscript six months ago that you were only going to get rejections." I said, "Oh, yeah, you could've told me that then." — Because I can be a smartass sometimes. He continued, "I know you can write better. But you were so proud of your finished manuscript that you wouldn't have listened to me. Now I think you will listen, and I think you're ready to go deeper." I remember thinking at the time, Oh, that's some Jedi Master mind trick shit right there.

About two years after this, he decided that he couldn't teach me anything more. The power dynamic that exists in a mentorship can sometimes become unbalanced. He wasn't interested in that, and I respected and appreciated that he regarded me as an equal. We were just friends now, getting together almost every month or two. Wayson would call and dramatically announce, "Paul, we have much to discuss!" We'd usually meet at a cafe or diner and talk about life, death, faith, art, movies, and perhaps his favourite topic — gossiping about my love life.

Being the same age as my father, I often looked to him for advice or counsel. In the wake of my father's death, my mother needed a break, and I brought her here to visit me for a few days. I set up a lunch with Wayson, and the three of us spent the afternoon together. Wayson was comfortable talking about death, and my mom was able to express her pain without judgement. When she started crying, it was Wayson who reached across the table to take her hand, holding it tight, and I was grateful that he was able to comfort her in a way that I couldn't, and they could share these moments of comfortable silence between them.

"Paul, we have much to discuss!" Our lunches turned into

all-day events. We'd start at our usual cafe, and visit book stores, second-hand clothing stores, and sometimes I'd just hang around to help him grocery shop. Because, every moment with Wayson, no matter how small, was important. He taught me to pay attention to these small moments. Pay attention to the details, to the signs, pay attention to others, to the world, to your feelings, your instincts, your heart.

The last time I saw him was at a book launch a couple of months ago. I was not in a good place in my life, but was trying to get out more. I did not want to be at that book launch, but something told me to stick around for a bit more. Later in the evening, someone tapped me on the shoulder, I turned around, and there was Wayson. Noticeably weaker, but still smiling, he said, "Paul, we have much to discuss!" We made plans to get together, but it would not come to pass.

I'll end on a note he wrote to me on March 28th, 2014. This note was to me, but I switched out our names, as his words have more meaning than anything I could possibly end with: *Dear Wayson, After clinging so tightly to the self waiting inside you to skip, hop, jump, run. I hope you let go of this internal block and see yourself as others have come to see you — brilliant, attractive, and sublime in all the ways that matter. My dear friend Wayson, I'm glad to hear that the riptide of currents in life holding you back has set you free. Has set you free. With love, Paul.*

Chapter 61: Katarite san

We have been on and off for as long as I can remember, but this last stint I think we have finally decided that we will go for the long haul.

It has so far been about eight months since I sent the letter asking her out. It was a written unloading of all the things I have felt, and still feel about her.

I did not want to ask her out casually. We had too much history for me to simply look at her and say: Hey wanna go out.

I had cancelled too many times, ditched her for greener pastures too often, ignored her flat out at too many junctures.

As I mentioned we had been on and off forever and I had been responsible for the off times most of the time.

Except that last time, she had broken it off.

They say you don't come to appreciate someone until they are no longer there.

The memory of the day she left still sends shivers down my spine.

It is not like she had not warned me, she had mentioned it, started packing and stacking boxes of her things in our house in preparation.

She does not own much so her boxes had been dwarfed by my stuff.

I almost did not notice that she was packing.

But then again, I seldom noticed her much anyway.

To be frank I thought I could get away with the usual, give her a day and she would stay.

But she had been complaining of our relationship for a while, more and more each time we would get back together.

Reminding me of how long it had been since we cooked together, went dancing, saw a show, had a mani-pedi, went for an impromptu lunch together.

I mean, she still had the best collection of shoes a girl can have and I HAD BOUGHT MOST OF THOSE.

So I owed her at least a letter.

I want to tell you why I owed her a letter, well at least a letter.

What I owed her was a commitment, one in writing, one that she and I could use as a reference, almost a contract.

To tell the truth I owed her more than a letter, what I owed her was encouraging her running again, what I owed her was not ridiculing her dietary choices and her body, what I owed her was space since I had filled all of ours with my knickknacks and stuff while she the minimalist only brought the beautiful and practical.

What I owed her was better access to my friends.

What I owed her was a better relationship with my parents.

What I owed her was love.

The kind that removes judgement, the kind that believes and does not expect.

The kind that warms and does not burn.

The kind that she had always given me.

What I owed her was honouring her faith and spirituality.

What I owed her was the kind of orgasm that I so often shared and given to my other partners. Yeah, with her I just took, often imagining something else, definitely travelling to other places in my mind as we did it.

What I owed her was lovemaking.

What I owed her was quality time.

What I owed her was the time and space to read quietly together.

Stories We Don't Tell

What I owed her was the respect that is due to her writing.

So, the letter was my version of the big romantic gesture, because I know that there are few things she responds to in the way she responds to truth read in words.

The thing is, I would often call her weak whenever she was being vulnerable.
She wanted to be seen, and she had desperately been asking me to see her.
I had been too busy looking to be seen by other people, I never noticed that she was seeing me, gently and candidly, never retorting with strife when I assaulted her with judgement. Never forsaking me when I spent so much time running away from her.
Whenever I paid attention to her, it was to berate her, calling her behaviour masochistic, after all why did she stick around, why else would she let me treat her that way.
She must have wanted something, gotten something from me. Most people did, so why would she be any different.
Funny thing is I am kind to so many, capable of empathy, taking on their pain as if it were mine. Going in the trenches with them and getting them through it all.
But not her. If anything I would often drag her into the trenches and then let her figure the way back on her own.

After the letter, I made my walls bare and threw out many knickknacks. I kept throwing things out, purging, making sure that my promise to make space for her was clear.
We bought things together.
Compromised over the fact that neither one of us liked dishes, so a tabletop dishwasher was brought in.
We hired our life-saving cleaning lady.

Stories We Don't Tell

We started dating again, and as every bit of clutter was removed from our home she brought in plants, then the artwork and souvenirs she had collected from all her travels started appearing in our home.

For the last couple of weeks now we have run together almost every day. She has me on an almost completely plant-based diet. She does not really like to drink so more often we do not.

We have been spending a lot of time together, exploring tantric sex, walking around the city, hosting our friends, doing things with the family.

Little by little we are welcoming friends in our home, when there are too many of us we sit on the floor and eat with our hands.

Strange thing is I have lived in my apartment for almost 10 years, yet never felt at home and she within months has made me call it mine, ours.

I look at her now, each day. Pay attention to her. Over the years she has softened; I tell her she is beautiful now and mean it. I can't believe she is mine each time I lather body butter over every inch of her body, slowly gliding my hands over her smooth skin.

We spend every morning exchanging over three written pages going back and forth honouring our deepest fears and scariest hopes.

I brought her to therapy a few times now and she has catalyzed more than a couple breakthroughs.

Whenever I say better half, she shoots me a look of frustration even though I mean it.

She says that she cannot be my better half because each time I say that I am excluding myself from her.

She says a unit is a unit with its complexities and clarities.

She says she knows that my hurting her hurt me more,

Stories We Don't Tell

that the most painful part of our dark years was seeing me in anguish.

Now, every morning waking up with me, being aware of each other fills us with joy.

I spent so much time divorcing myself from her that it did not occur to me that not fighting might actually bring me peace.

I spent so much time silencing her that I never noticed that there are other ways to be noticed than being loud.

Because while I was loudly tap dancing, conducting my own cacophony of noises in the world, she was quietly and silently building, creating, connecting, so when I took a breath and allowed her to be seen in my life, a funny thing happened.

I learnt something about each person in my life, this whole time I have been the one in the dark, she is the one they know, the one they love, the one they have always seen ... and I am the last one to catch up.

So when I finally said I love you this time around, she did not avert her almond-shaped eyes or crinkle her nose or twist her mouth in disbelief, a few tears fell from her eyes because this time I meant it.

I had finally learnt to love all of me including the part that I had always been at odds with. The softer, quieter, vulnerable me. All of me.

Acknowledgements

Brianne Benness: This book never would have happened without Paul and Stefan. I mean this both literally, because they did the lion's share of the work on this book, and cosmically, because of everything they do to produce each event. I'm so grateful to you both for keeping this precious space alive after I left Toronto. I'm also grateful to my husband Adam, who jumped wholeheartedly into storytelling when it became such a big part of my life. And really, I would just love to thank everybody who has ever come to an event, come to a story workshop, shared their story, or listened to the podcast. Stories We Don't Tell could not have happened without your courage.

Paul Dore: I would like to thank all the incredible people that have had the courage to walk into a stranger's house and participate in this strange experiment of ours, whether it be those sharing their story or people just coming to listen. Naturally, none of this wouldn't be possible with my co-conspirators, Stefan and Brianne. Of course, I would like to thank my mother, who has been there for every step of my strange writing journey. One of the most important people to encourage both my writing and getting up in front of people to read it was Wayson Choy. I'm happy that my story about him was included in this book, and I was able to add yet more anecdotes to the mountain of evidence that attests to his brilliance and wisdom. Wayson: you are missed, but we still have much to talk about!

Stefan Hostetter: Firstly, I'd like to thank Brianne and Paul, it's hard to believe that what began as the three of us sitting around half a table at the Reference Library would become all this. I couldn't ask for better collaborators or friends. I'd also like to thank my parents, all four of them. You have been the solid rock I've built my life on. My siblings, all six of them. With special mention to Megan, the north star to whom I shall forever look ahead. And Dave, my most constant, most trusted, most cherished companion. Finally, thanks to all the living rooms and their hosts who've welcomed this show, you gave us a home and we'll never be able to repay you. Love you Mom & Dad.

We want to collectively thank Tyler Blacquiere for his amazing book cover design. Steve Hostetter (Stefan's dad) for giving his time, knowledge, and talent to edit each story. And of course, every single person that has supported Stories We Don't Tell - as storytellers, audiences, and hosts.

About Stories We Don't Tell

There are some stories that we get really good at telling, we tell them to our friends, our coworkers, and even strangers at parties. We tell them because they are a part of us, and in doing so, they build up our sense of self. There are also stories we don't tell, maybe because they're sad, or weird, or just a little too intimate. These truths are just as much a part of who we are, despite being erased from our day-to-day conversation. The Stories We Don't Tell was founded by Brianne Benness, Paul Dore, and Stefan Hostetter, and is a monthly live event, held in living rooms across Toronto, and podcast that gives you a window into experiences that are so often left unseen. Find out more: storieswedonttell.org.